Regions and Regionalism in History

16

WOMEN AT WORK, 1860–1939

HOW DIFFERENT INDUSTRIES SHAPED WOMEN'S EXPERIENCES

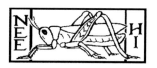

Regions and Regionalism in History

ISSN 1742–8254

This series, published in association with the AHRB Centre for North-East England History (NEEHI), aims to reflect and encourage the increasing academic and popular interest in regions and regionalism in historical perspective. It also seeks to explore the complex historical antecedents of regionalism as it appears in a wide range of international contexts.

Series Editor
Prof. Peter Rushton, Faculty of Education and Society, University of Sunderland

Editorial Board
Dr Joan Allen, School of Historical Studies, Newcastle University
Prof. (Emeritus) A. W. Purdue, School of Arts and Social Sciences, Northumbria University
Dr Christian Liddy, Department of History, University of Durham
Dr Diana Newton, School of Arts and Media, Teesside University

Proposals for future volumes may be sent to the following address:

Prof. Peter Rushton,
Department of Social Sciences,
Faculty of Education and Society,
University of Sunderland,
Priestman Building,
New Durham Road,
Sunderland,
SR1 3PZ
UK
Tel: 0191–515–2208
Fax: 0191–515–3415

peter.rushton@sunderland.ac.uk

Previously published volumes are listed at the back of this book.

WOMEN AT WORK, 1860–1939

HOW DIFFERENT INDUSTRIES SHAPED WOMEN'S EXPERIENCES

VALERIE G. HALL

THE BOYDELL PRESS

First published 2013
The Boydell Press, Woodbridge

ISBN 978–1–84383–870–8

The Boydell Press is an imprint of Boydell & Brewer Ltd
PO Box 9, Woodbridge, Suffolk IP12 3DF, UK
and of Boydell & Brewer Inc.
668 Mt Hope Avenue, Rochester, NY 14620–2731, USA
website: www.boydellandbrewer.com

The publisher has no responsibility for the continued existence or accuracy of
URLs for external or third-party internet websites referred to in this book,
and does not guarantee that any content on such websites is,
or will remain, accurate or appropriate.

A CIP record for this book is available
from the British Library

Papers used by Boydell & Brewer Ltd are natural, recyclable products
made from wood grown in sustainable forests

Printed and bound in Great Britain by
CPI Group (UK) Ltd, Croydon, CR0 4YY

I dedicate this book to my three sons,
Russell, Steven and Michael, and to my grandchildren.

Contents

Figures and Tables

Acknowledgements

Many people have helped me in the process of writing this book and I would like to take this opportunity to thank them. My friends and colleagues, Dianne Newell, Professor of History, University of British Columbia and Katrina Porteous, poet and local historian, took time off from their many duties to read my manuscript thoroughly, offering many useful suggestions which allowed me to improve my work greatly. I wish also to thank the readers for the press, especially Jane Humphries, Professor of Economics and Fellow of All Souls College, Oxford, for careful reading and thoughtful and generous comments. I also owe a debt of gratitude to my mentors Jay M. Winter, Professor of History, Yale University, and Joan W. Scott, Professor of Social Science, Institute for Advanced Study, Princeton, who have been unfailing in their support and advice over many years.

The archivists at the Northumberland Archives, in particular Keith Gilroy at Woodhorn and Linda Bankier at the Berwick-upon-Tweed office, were very helpful to me when I came to Northumberland from the United States each summer to conduct research and they deserve my gratitude.

I also want to thank William Peace University for providing funds for me to travel to Britain each summer over an extended period.

My thanks also go to Peter Sowden, my editor, for his patience and guidance through this process.

Last but not least, I want to recognize the help of my interviewees, almost all of them deceased. This book would not have been possible without them. They invited me into their homes, served me endless cups of tea and home-baked scones and cakes and told me of their lives and work, asking about my family and my work as a Scot in America and inviting me to come back to visit as often as possible. Needless to say, I became friends with many of them and grieved when they passed away.

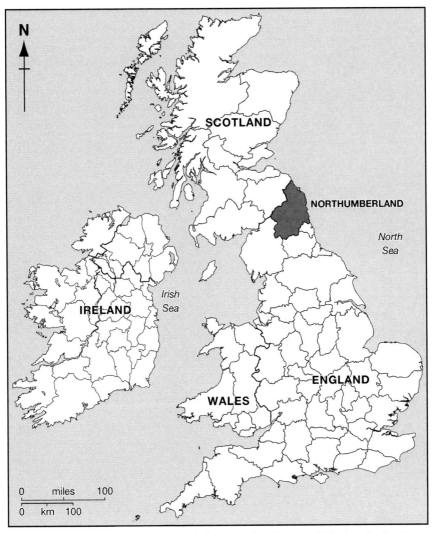

Map 1. Map of England and Wales delineating the County of Northumberland

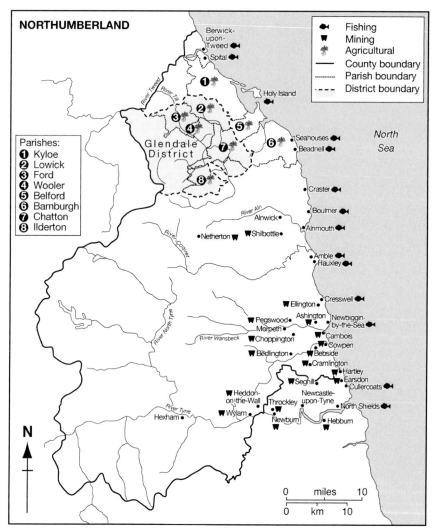

Map 2. Map of Northumberland showing selected mining and inshore fishing communities, rural districts and parishes

Introduction

In the late nineteenth and early twentieth centuries, mining, inshore fishing and agricultural labouring communities often figured in the national consciousness, people drawn by the drama and danger faced by miners and fishermen and by the picturesque qualities of all three groups. The representations of these groups were highly ambivalent. Some were positive. In the case of mining and fishing communities, we frequently read expressions of admiration for the bravery of miners and fishermen and sympathy for their losses in times of tragedy. Agricultural labourers, often called hinds, profited from the romanticisation of the countryside that had begun in the eighteenth century in, for example, the paintings of John Constable or in their role as 'quaint carriers of English folklore'.[1]

The images of the women of these communities, frequently found in literature and art, were mostly sympathetic and often dramatic. In *Germinal* by Émile Zola, we read of women huddled at the pit head waiting for news of the men and boys trapped below ground in the flooded pit. This reminds us of the horrendous Hartley Pit disaster of 1862 in Northumberland in which 262 men and boys from one village were entombed. When found, the bodies of the boys were clinging to their dead fathers, who had left hurried notes pinned to the bodies of their sons. This event garnered much sympathy, as did the tragedies which befell the fishing communities. In the late nineteenth century, colonies of artists at Cullercoats in Northumberland and Staithes in Yorkshire, and photographers such as Frank Meadow Sutcliffe in Whitby, believing that they had 're-discovered' a peasantry and particularly fascinated by the women of these communities, often depicted them in tense, even dangerous, situations. One picture, for example, shows women staring desperately out over the churning ocean to see if the boats were going to be able to make it to shore, out of danger. Another has the lifeboat women straining to pull the lifeboat back to shore through the high waves.[2] Such images were not just the product of the artists' imaginations. When a storm blew up and the boats were out at sea, the whole community would run to the shore to watch their progress. The pattern of family boats, with three men and a boy from the same family as crew, led to the frequent loss of whole families at a time. Though lacking such dramatic elements, depictions of women in

---

[1]   Karen Sayer, *Women of the Fields: Representations of Rural Women in the Nineteenth Century* (Manchester, 1995), p. 24.

[2]   For these images, see Chapter 4, pp. 108 and 110.

agricultural labouring families have also been poignant. We think of Tess in *Tess of the D'Urbervilles*, set in Dorset. Thomas Hardy describes Tess, after her fall as a result of the birth of her illegitimate child, as reduced to what he describes as degrading field work, pulling turnips from the frozen ground, her hands red and raw, her companions rough, coarse and masculinised women. If the degradation is more a literary trope than reality, women field workers in any part of the country endured hard, gruelling work in bad weather. Indeed, such labour on the part of women continued in Northumberland until after the Second World War.

Yet, reflecting the ambiguity of middle-class attitudes towards the lower classes, observers frequently depicted all three groups in negative terms: mining and fishing communities as 'races apart' from civilized society, alien and inbred; agricultural workers backward and unintelligent, referred to as 'Hodge'.[3] The women in these three communities shared in the negative assessments. The variations in their depiction, from the sympathetic to the outright negative, reflected the biases and ideologies of middle-class observers. Such observers read into women rampant sexuality, the potential danger they and their husbands posed to the social order at times of industrial strife, the social chaos arising from their supposedly disorderly homes and, in the case of the female agricultural workers and fisher girls and women, the crossing of gender lines. The result was anxiety and, at times, panic on the part of the observers. At other times, tragedies and hardships suffered by the three groups of women superseded the negative images of them. This ambiguity was most obvious in the case of fisher women whom people, at times of tragedy, regarded with great sympathy, while at other times they were viewed with suspicion and even disgust.

I will focus on these three groups of women – those in coal mining, inshore fishing and farming communities – in Northumberland, the northernmost county in England, in the period 1860 to 1939. These women lived in communities which were based on very different industries: coal mining, pursued in Northumberland since Roman times, was a heavily capitalized industry whose labour force had been proletarianized since at least the end of the eighteenth century. By 1870, it was the main non-agricultural industry in the county, employing 17,000 men and supporting a population of around 119,000, not counting those people working in the service area in the mining towns and villages. The next industry, inshore fishing – that is, fishing on a daily basis within six to seven miles of the shore (as opposed to deep-sea fishing) – was also of long vintage, having been pursued on a commercial basis since medieval times. Inshore fishermen used a coble, a small boat which was fast, capable of being sailed near the wind and ideal for launching off the beach in communities which lacked harbours.[4] The industry

3   Sayer, *Women of the Fields*, p. 23.
4   John Salmon, *The Coble: A Few Papers Written During Leisure Hours of the Winter of 1884–5* (South Shields, 1885).

had expanded in the decades around 1870. Unlike mining however it was based on small, family owned – and operated – entrepreneurial enterprises. In 1871, the number of fishermen amounted to no more than 450, resulting in a fishing population of around 3,150. Agricultural labourers were much more numerous at that date, amounting to 19,794, 14,038 of them men and 5,756 women.[5] It is impossible to estimate the size of the community because a household might include several workers. Also, most married women worked intermittently and were thus not counted in the censuses.[6]

Over the period of my study, 1860 to 1939, all three industries underwent significant change that transformed all three communities. Coal mining expanded nationwide around the turn of the twentieth century. By 1911, the numbers employed in Northumberland had reached 51,925 and the mining population approximately 311,550.[7] The numbers undoubtedly increased in the next few years, as a consequence of a great expansion of the coal industry, especially in exporting districts such as Northumberland. Unfortunately, we don't have the data to substantiate this assumption. But after World War One, coal mining in Northumberland and the nation entered a period of depression, ten years before the Great Depression, becoming the 'sick industry' of the inter-war years. The number of miners had declined by 1931 to 46,008, many of whom were on part-time work.[8] By 1939, the number in Northumberland was 40,675 and the population around 203,375.[9] The same pattern is clear in the much smaller inshore fishing industry which boomed from the mid nineteenth century up to the first years of the twentieth century as a result of copious herring stocks, but waned thereafter. By the 1930s, the number of inshore fishermen had declined to around 140, about 25 percent of what it had been. By the mid 1930s the community averaged probably no more than 3,500.[10] Agricultural communities too declined in numbers, partly because of new technologies but also due to the attraction of urban areas which drew young men and women from the isolated farms. Though it is difficult to estimate the numbers of agricultural labourers at the end of the 1930s, we can assume that it was around 17,000.

---

[5] The numbers of miners, fishermen and agricultural labourers are taken from the *Census of England and Wales, 1871, Vol. III, Ages, Civil Conditions and Birth Places of People* (London, 1873), Tables 11 and 12. The numbers of all three groups are difficult to assess and some, notably of inshore fishermen, are estimates. The figures for numbers of people in the mining and fishing communities are gained by multiplying by seven, assuming an average of five children per household. Later community sizes are gained by multiplying by six, assuming an average of four children per household.

[6] See discussion of the deficiencies of the censuses, pp. 12 and 13.

[7] *Census of England and Wales, 1911, Occupations and Industries* Part II (London, 1913), Table 24. Again, the exact numbers of miners are difficult to assess, because different censuses include different groups of workers connected to the mine.

[8] Barry Supple, *The History of the British Coal Industry, Volume 4: The Political Economy of Decline* (Oxford, 1987), Table 9.4.

[9] Jack Davison, *Northumberland Miners: 1919–1939* (Newcastle upon Tyne, 1973), p. 278.

[10] These figures are estimates. The 1931 census gives a number of 163 for fishermen but that includes river fishermen, and there was further attrition of inshore fishermen in the 1930s. *Census of England and Wales, 1931, County of Northumberland* Part II (London, 1935), Table 2.

My decision to study these three groups of women grew out of the differences I perceived in their experiences. It is well known that one cannot treat
women as an undifferentiated group. Middle-class women and working-class
women had little in common except for bearing children. But working-class
women were not a monolithic whole either, as was once thought.[11] Over the
last few decades, scholars of women's history have revealed a more complex
picture. While many have written about working-class women in general,
others have chosen to focus upon single groups of women. To list just a few:
Nicola Verdon's *Rural Women Workers in Nineteenth-Century England*[12] has
revealed the specificity of the experience of women farm workers; Eleanor
Gordon's *Women and the Labour Movement in Scotland*,[13] the industrial
actions of the jute workers of Dundee; and Jane Long, in her essay 'Women
and White Lead Work', the hardships faced by women white-lead workers in
Newcastle upon Tyne.[14] Numerous essays in collections such as *Women, Work
and Wages in England, 1600–1850,* edited by Penelope Lane, Neil Raven
and K.D.M Snell[15] and *Women's Work: The English Experience 1650–1914*,
edited by Pamela Sharpe,[16] have added greatly to our knowledge of different
types of women workers. Comparisons of the experiences of different groups
of working-class women have been rare, however. Exceptions are Carol
Morgan's *Women Workers and Gender Identities, 1835–1913: The Cotton
and Metal Industries in England*[17] and Miriam Glucksmann's *Cottons and
Casuals: The gendered organisation of labour in time and space*.[18] The latter
contrasts the experience of full-time textile workers and the casual, part-time
workers who provided services for them. It remains true however that there
is a deficit of studies which compare different types of working-class women.

I hope to help redress this omission. By examining the life and work
of mining, fishing and agricultural women living in the same county, in
reasonably close proximity, I will show how divergent the experiences of
working-class women could be and how these differences were shaped by
the dominant industries in their particular areas. Thus, I will stress that the
experiences of women varied not only between classes but within the same

---

[11] Ivy Pinchbeck was an exception to this pattern. She revealed the different work experiences of
women throughout the nation. Ivy Pinchbeck, *Women Workers and the Industrial Revolution,
1750–1850* (London, 1981; 1st edn, 1930).

[12] Nicola Verdon, *Women Rural Workers in Nineteenth-Century England: Gender, Work and Wages*
(Woodbridge, 2002).

[13] Eleanor Gordon, *Women and the Labour Movement in Scotland* (Oxford, 1991).

[14] Jane Long, '"You are forced to do something for a living": Women and White-Lead Work' in
Jane Long, *Conversations in Cold Rooms: Women, Work and Poverty in Nineteenth-Century
Northumberland* (Woodbridge, 1999), Ch. 3.

[15] Penelope Lane, Neil Raven and K.D.M. Snell, eds, *Women, Work and Wages in England, 1600–
1850* (Woodbridge, 2004).

[16] Pamela Sharpe, ed., *Women's Work: The English Experience 1650–1914* (London, 1998).

[17] Carol Morgan, *Women Workers and Gender Identities, 1835–1913: The Cotton and Metal
Industries in England* (London, 2001).

[18] Miriam Glucksmann, *Cottons and Casuals: The Gendered Organisation of Labour in Time and
Space* (Durham, 2000).

class. I will show these divergences through examining the fabric of these women's lives, employing, when possible, their own voices. At the same time, I will reveal their contribution to their families, their communities and to the economies of the industries in which they were involved.

My previous work was a catalyst for this larger endeavour. In studying women in coal mining communities in Northumberland, I found significant differences even within that one community.[19] Most of the women fell into the category I called 'domestic women' who, denied the opportunity to engage in economically productive work outside the home because of the character-istics of the coal mining industry, fulfilled an exceptionally heavy domestic and maternal role. A minority, whom I called 'political women', took on an important political role in the twentieth century, becoming the backbone of the Labour Party in their districts in the 1920s and 30s. That pattern I traced to the economic and cultural organisation of the mining communities. In a later study, I contrasted these two groups of mining women with women in inshore fishing communities, whose experiences were again different.[20] As part of family based fishing enterprises which resembled pre-industrial crafts, they performed the preparatory work at home for their fishermen husbands. Also, while women had to share the selling of fish with fish merchants by 1860, they still hawked fish in their creels and baskets around nearby towns and villages. They were as much, if not more, workers in the fishing industry as homemakers and mothers. In this new study, which aims to deal in greater depth with these two groups of women, I have added another group of women: female agricultural labourers who exhibited yet further differences. Although many of these women worked within a family unit, others were independent workers. All however performed heavy, dirty labour in fields and barns. Indeed, to be a woman in these communities was to perform work that, to many outsiders, appeared 'masculine' in nature.

Northumberland is a good choice for a local study of this kind for a number of reasons. To begin with Northumberland, set in the far northeastern corner of England, has seen little attention from historians. Further, all three industries, coal mining, inshore fishing and farming, existed alongside each other and – in a curious way – were related: as work in fishing and farming declined, many men turned to the collieries. Northumberland also had some characteristics which set it apart from other counties. Like Westmoreland and the eastern border counties of Scotland – The East and West Lothians, Roxburgh and Berwickshire – Northumberland had a unique system of female farm labour. Indeed, women were a crucial part of the farming labour force in Northumberland and remained so until after the Second World War, at least sixty years after they had disappeared from the fields of southeast England,

[19] Valerie G. Hall, 'Contrasting female identities: women in coal mining communities in Northumberland, 1900–1939', *Journal of Women's History* 2 (2001), pp. 117–31.
[20] Valerie G. Hall, 'Differing gender roles: Women in mining and fishing communities in Northumberland, 1880–1914', *Women's Studies International Forum* 27(2004), pp. 521–30.

though women labourers were to be found in southwestern England at the turn of the twentieth century.[21] Moreover, Northumberland's early adoption of advanced farming methods – in the late eighteenth and early nineteenth centuries – had made it a favourite object of study for government commissions, whose reports yield valuable information. Happily, Northumberland's mining communities were the classic type – one-industry towns – making study easier, especially when one is using census records.

A local study of this type is invaluable for several reasons. The kind of detailed examination engaged in here is impossible on the national level. Yet we can make important generalisations about patterns in the nation. For example, while coal mining co-existed with the textile industry in Lancashire and Yorkshire and with the pottery industry in the Midlands, mining communities in regions such as South Wales, in parts of Scotland and in many regions in other countries were largely one-industry towns. Thus, conclusions drawn from Northumberland have application to such areas. Also, inshore fishing communities, which dotted the entire coastline of Scotland and England, exhibit a remarkable similarity. While female farm labourers, called bondagers, have no parallel in our period in the rest of England (except Westmoreland, and the borders counties of Scotland), their uniqueness allows us to draw important conclusions about the factors affecting, for instance, the roles of women, the sexual division of labour and what it meant to be a woman. The communities chosen show, for example, how cultural and economic factors can take precedence over gender ideology, conclusions which have broad significance for the study of women.

It is important to study the lives and work of these women. Although, as we have seen, art, literature and public discourse have featured the women from the three communities, historians have paid much less attention to them than to working-class men who joined organisations such as trade unions and, at times, wrote autobiographies. As Jane Long has noted, working women have suffered from the 'double silence of both their gender and their class position'.[22] True, women's historians have been filling in this gap with considerable speed in the last few decades, but much remains to be done. For one thing, with the exception of the works of Jane Long and of Judy Gielgud,[23] who have studied Northumberland female agricultural labourers, historians have largely ignored these three groups of women which are the subject of my work. This study pieces together the particularities of their lives, revealing the considerable skills that were necessary to run a house-

---

[21] Edward Higgs, 'Occupational censuses and the agricultural workforce in Victorian England and Wales', *Economic History Review* LXVIII, 4 (1995), pp. 700–16. It was formerly thought that women agricultural labourers had disappeared from the fields in all but the northern counties in the last quarter of the nineteenth century. For a discussion of the inadequacies of the censuses as a guide to the employment of women, see pp. 12 and 13.

[22] Long, *Conversations in Cold Rooms*, p. 4.

[23] Judy Gielgud, 'Nineteenth Century Farm Women in Northumberland and Cumbria: the Neglected Workforce' (PhD thesis, University of Sussex, 1992).

hold on meagre resources, the physical and emotional burdens of constant heavy work combined with large families, the frequent pregnancies and the resulting toll of miscarriages, still births and ill health.

Another factor addressed is the important contributions made by women to the economic survival of their families. It has become clear that working-class women's participation in the world of work has been under-recorded and that census returns are an unreliable source of women's employment, as of other aspects of their social and economic position.[24] This conclusion is as true of these three groups of women as it is of other working-class women. Both fishing and farming women played an essential role in the industries in which their men were employed. In each case, the men could not have functioned in their employment without the participation of their wives and daughters. While the censuses generally recorded the work of single agricultural labouring females and sometimes that of married, female, full-time workers – though not that of the intermittent, though important, women workers – virtually none of the participation of fishing women appears in them. In the case of mining, women played no such direct economic role, yet their careful maintenance of their husbands' work clothing, boots and even bodies, their management of household resources, their taking-in of lodgers and their other small-scale entrepreneurial efforts were crucial to the well-being of their families. Such efforts of course went unrecorded.

These examinations inevitably contribute to many of the broader debates in gender history. Exploring the participation of these women in the world of work, for instance, shows that the sexual division of labour was variable and that it could change within one industry if the technology changed. This finding underscores the conclusion that other historians have drawn since the 1980s – that the sexual division of labour is a social construct.[25] Gender ideology, that is, the idea of sexual difference, defined the division of work in all three industries though tradition, technology and economics also played a role. In all three industries men monopolised machinery, as was the case in virtually all industries. Invariably, even when women were involved in the industry in which their husbands worked, and even when their labour was vital to the success of the industry, such as agriculture, the farming population regarded their work as less skillful than that of their husbands and often demeaning to men. Furthermore, if the women received payment, it was generally half as much as that given to men. This pattern was common to occupations throughout the nation and was justified by the often erroneous idea that women were not breadwinners and that their work was less skillful.

---

[24] For a discussion of the censuses, see pp. 12 and 13.
[25] See, for example, Eleanor Gordon and Esther Breitenbach, eds, *The World is Ill Divided: Women's Work in Scotland in the Nineteenth and early Twentieth Centuries* (Edinburgh, 1990), Intro.

Custom also played a role in determining a lower wage.[26] So too did the fact that women were generally less strong than men.[27]

As I have suggested, it took significant skills of varying kinds to run a home in the period under study and such skills were crucial to the survival of the family. The term 'good wife', that other historians and I, who have done oral history, have heard often articulated by men, had real meaning. A 'good wife' provided a clean, comfortable home, solid food and good care of their children, and men clearly put great store in such results. The term 'good wife' however had additional meanings in these communities we are studying.

As might be expected from my earlier discussion of the middle-class reaction to these three groups of women, my study fits into a broader debate about the clash between the ideology of working-class women and that of the middle class, and the criticisms of the working-class women which ensued. As many historians have pointed out, by the second half of the nineteenth century, the middle class had a well-defined notion of femininity and despaired at how far working-class women in general diverged from such standards.[28] The bourgeois ideology regarding women grew out of the notion of separate spheres which saw men in the public world earning the money for the family and women in the domestic sphere responsible for domestic duties and the children, maintaining the moral tone of the family and dependent on the patriarchal male head of the family.[29] Although separate-spheres ideology was not as rigid even for the middle class as researchers once thought, it was still very important.

Middle-class observers applied this ideology to both young, unmarried women and married women who worked outside the home. Although they realised the need for single working-class women to be employed, they believed that the only really acceptable forms of employment were domestic service, in which girls could be controlled, or some other employment under patriarchal control or parental supervision. They became deeply concerned over what they regarded as unsuitable employment which allowed women economic independence and the ability to mix with men to whom they were not related. The rough working clothing of such young women, their lack of corsets, their milling around in public and their loud voices made them appear to the middle class not only as unfeminine but downright immoral, almost on a par with prostitutes. Middle-class observers of working-class women expressed moral panic over their being engaged in what seemed

---

[26] Penelope Lane, 'A customary or market wage? Women and work in the East Midlands' in Penelope Lane, Neil Raven and K.D.M. Snell, eds, *Women, Work and Wages in England*, pp. 67–101; Harriet Bradley, *Men's Work, Women's Work: A Sociological History of the Sexual Division of Labour in Employment* (Minneapolis, 1989), p. 244.

[27] Joyce Burnette, *Gender, Work and Wages in Industrial Revolution Britain* (Cambridge, 2008), Ch. 2.

[28] For a good description of the moral panic regarding women's work in the fields see Sayer, *Women of the Fields*, Ch. 6.

[29] An early articulation of this ideology is C. Whitehead, *Agricultural Labourers* (London, 1870), pp. 52–3 and 73.

masculine jobs, such as the female tin workers in Cornwall,[30] those who worked at the pit head in Lancashire[31] and those who worked in Newcastle upon Tyne in white-lead work.[32] Married women who engaged in economically productive labour also failed the test of true womanhood and were crossing gender boundaries. If they worked outside the home, they ran the risk of being polluted by the outside world and being unable to teach their children moral lessons. Further, they would be unable to maintain the comfortable home that would ensure that their husbands would not stray to the public house. Another concern about married working women was the belief that they were poor housekeepers and mothers and were responsible for the high rates of infant and child mortality in the nation. Not content with mere criticism the middle classes, through official actions, intervened in several ways to correct working-class behaviour. In the late nineteenth century, local authorities appointed district nurses even in rural areas and, after the First World War, the government, on the basis of the Maternity and Child Welfare Act, authorised Maternal and Child Health clinics. As I have indicated earlier, and as I shall discuss in the forthcoming chapters, all three groups of women faced one or other of these criticisms, some several.

There is little indication that the hysterical criticism of the middle class permeated the culture of our three groups of women, or indeed that of other working-class women. They, for instance, regarded it as perfectly acceptable to do rough, even masculine work, and did not see it as demeaning or unwomanly. Indeed the women took considerable pride in their work, although most of it was regarded by men as unskilled and was poorly paid, and revelled in their physical strength. These women regarded female delicacy, so prized in the middle class, as undesirable. They therefore did not fit into the definition of femininity of the bourgeoisie. Such was the case even with mining women, most of whom remained in the domestic sphere.

Sources

The sources for this study are wide and varied. It is hard for the historian to reach working-class women. In fact Kathleen Canning has suggested that the historian has only snapshots of working women.[33] The literary and artistic images of our women, though they capture some of the essence of these women's lives, fall into that category. Women generally did not write autobiographies, although a few in mining have put pen to paper. These works

[30] Sharron P. Schwartz, '"No place for a woman": Gender at work in Cornwall's metalliferous mining industry', *Cornish Studies* 8 (2000), pp. 69–96.
[31] Angela John, *By the Sweat of Their Brow: Women workers at Victorian coal mines* (London, 1980).
[32] Long, *Conversations in Cold Rooms*, Ch. 3.
[33] Kathleen Canning, *Gender History in Practice: Historical Perspectives on Bodies, Class & Citizenship* (Ithaca, 2006).

include Mary Wade's *To the Miner Born*,[34] Adeline Hodges' 'Up the Ladder',[35] and for the mid twentieth century, Cissie Charlton's *Cissie*.[36] Another work, *A Tune for Bears to Dance to: A Childhood* by Linda McCullough-Thew,[37] though not authored by a miner's wife but by someone brought up in a mining community, offers useful insights, as does Violet Clarke's 'Tied to the Soil'[38] in the case of female agricultural labourers. Unfortunately, nothing of the sort exists for fisher women.

In common with numerous other historians, I have been able to overcome the difficulty of silence through the use of oral interviews. These, most of which I have conducted myself, span the last 30 years. The first of these focused on coal mining communities. Information from them helped inform my Master's thesis, 'The English coal mining community'[39] and my PhD thesis, 'Aspects of the political and social history of Ashington, a Northumberland coal mining community, 1870–1914'.[40] I made use of a few on mining conducted by the archivists at Northumberland Archives for the Mining Record Survey of 1976–77.

When I moved on, in the mid 1990s, to study fishing women, I was lucky to gain entry into the isolated community through an introduction by the local librarian. This led me to a number of elderly fishermen and fisher women who provided me with much valuable information on their work in the fishing industry and on their lives. One was an amateur historian of the fishing industry. I was also able to interview Katrina Porteous, a local historian and poet, who is very knowledgeable about North Northumberland fishing communities. She had conducted many interviews and included some of her findings from these in her book, *The Bonny Fisher Lad*.[41] Also helpful were the interviews done by Paul Thompson of Essex University and held at the British Library.[42] Although they deal with fishing communities in Scotland, they are entirely relevant for fishing communities in Northumberland and elsewhere in the nation. As we have noted, the fishing communities that were dotted round the entire coasts of England and Scotland were remarkably similar.[43]

---

[34] Mary Wade, *To the Miner Born* (Stocksfield, 1984).
[35] Adeline Hodges, 'Up the Ladder', Tuesday Club. Occasional Paper, No. 2, N.D.
[36] Cissie Charlton, *Cissie* (Newcastle upon Tyne, 1988).
[37] Linda McCullough-Thew, *A Tune for Bears to Dance to: A Childhood* (Newcastle upon Tyne, 2001).
[38] Violet Clarke, 'Tied to the soil' in Brian P. Martin ed., *Tales of Old Countrywomen* (Newton Abbot, 1997), pp. 135–45.
[39] Valerie G. Hall, 'The English Coal Mining Community, 1890–1914' (MA thesis, University of North Carolina, 1978).
[40] Valerie G. Hall, 'Aspects of the Political and Social History of Ashington, a Northumberland Coal Mining Community, 1870–1914' (PhD thesis, University of London, 1993).
[41] Katrina Porteous, ed., *The Bonny Fisher Lad: Memoirs of the North Northumberland Fishing Community* (Seaham, 2003).
[42] British Library, QD8/FISH/52/C773.
[43] James G. Bertram, *The Unappreciated Fisherfolk: Their Round of Life and Labour* (London, 1883).

It proved more difficult for me to find interviewees for my third subject, female agricultural labourers, because most women from the period in which I was interested had died. Although only able to find three interviewees, I gained valuable insights from them and, fortunately, I was able to make use of oral material from other sources. One of the most useful was the unpublished PhD thesis of Judy Gielgud, 'Nineteenth Century Farm Women in Northumberland and Cumbria: The Neglected Workforce', based on oral interviews of women agricultural labourers in Northumberland and Cumbria, as well as on government documents, farm records and a variety of other sources.[44] The collections of oral histories of Scottish bondagers conducted by Ian MacDougall: *'Hard Work, Ye Ken': Midlothian Women Farm Workers*[45] and *Bondagers: Personal Recollections of Eight Scottish Women Farm Workers*[46] were invaluable. While the women are Scottish and their responses frequently expressed in the Scottish dialect, their experiences replicate those of their Northumbrian counterparts. The similarities between Northumberland women farm labourers and ones in the border counties of Scotland, which have allowed me to make use of these Scottish interviews, appear in the various nineteenth-century governmental reports on agriculture – the 1843 Commission on the Employment of Women and Children in Agriculture, the Royal Commission on the Employment of Children, Young Persons and Women in Agriculture 1867, and the Royal Commission on Labour The Agricultural Labourer 1893. Contemporary accounts and, most recently, Dinah Iredale's *Bondagers: The History of Women Farmworkers in Northumberland and South-East Scotland* verify these parallels, as well as giving valuable oral information.[47] Again, several recordings of farming people made by Northumberland Archives proved useful. Fortunately, there are numerous nineteenth-century books written about farm workers and these, together with the above-mentioned government commission reports, also make up for the lack of oral evidence although, with the exception of one – the essay by Mrs Williams – they are all written by men.[48]

Another very important source for all three groups of women has been archival records. The rich collections held by Northumberland Archives have been the most significant. Its collections range over a multitude of subjects. The main ones I found useful were Urban District Council records, marriage records, Northumberland Labour Party records, Medical Officer of Health reports for the County of Northumberland and for several of the

---

[44] Judy Gielgud, 'Nineteenth Century Farm Women in Northumberland and Cumbria : the Neglected Workforce' (PhD thesis, University of Sussex, 1992).

[45] Ian MacDougall, *'Hard Work, Ye Ken': Midlothian Women Farm Workers* (East Linton, 1996).

[46] Ian MacDougall, *Bondagers: Personal Recollections of Eight Scottish Women Farm Workers* (Edinburgh, 2000).

[47] Dinah Iredale, *Bondagers: The History of Women Farmworkers in Northumberland and South-East Scotland* (Berwick-upon-Tweed, 2008) www.the bondagers.com.

[48] Mrs Williams, 'The Bondage System', in Anon., *Voices from the Plough* (Hawick, 1869).

urban districts, the records of schools, churches and chapels, the courts (both the Petty Sessions of the various townships and the Assizes and Quarterly sessions), account records of farms, the National Coal Board records, the Northumberland Coal Owners Association records and the Northumberland County Council Education records. For information about inshore fishing I found the records of the Ministry of Agriculture and Fisheries, housed at the National Archives, Kew, most useful.

In addition, local newspapers provided a wealth of evidence of every kind. In the case of mining communities the most important of these was *The Morpeth Herald*, which provided many details on every aspect of life in the mining communities of mid Northumberland for the whole period. For fishing communities *The Berwick Advertiser*, *The Blyth News*, *The Whitley Advertiser* and *The Shields Daily News* proved particularly useful, while for farming communities *The Alnwick News*, *The Hexham Courant* and *The Berwick Advertiser* were most valuable. The Newcastle upon Tyne newspapers such as *The Newcastle Journal* also provided useful information.

I have also made substantial use of official documents. The censuses which are available in individual form up to 1901 gave invaluable information about family structure, migration patterns and employment patterns and added to the demographic information which I gained from church and chapel records. As I and other historians have noted however the censuses give unreliable information about the employment of women, grossly underestimating the number of women engaged in economically productive labour, the prevailing notion being that men earned enough to provide for a family.[49] Furthermore, there is little consistency between the decennial reports. Although wives of inshore fishermen were involved fully in household production and might be expected to have been included in the censuses of 1861 and 1871 – the pattern for other industries in which household production prevailed – in Northumberland at least, they were not. The only women listed as having occupations were the full-time fish hawkers. Curiously, the 1881 census designated widows of inshore fishermen and of agricultural labourers as wives of fishermen and wives of agricultural workers, though this designation was lacking when their husbands were alive. This practice was limited to the 1881 census and may have been a product of the proclivities of the enumerators, which was always a factor in the accuracy of the returns. The recording of women assisting their husbands, as fisher women did, was to await the 1951

---

[49] For a detailed discussion of the deficiencies of the census records, see Nigel Goose, 'Working women in industrial England' in Nigel Goose, ed., *Women's Work in Industrial England: Regional and Local Perspectives* (Hatfield, 2007), pp. 1–28; Edward Higgs, 'Women, Occupations and Work in the Nineteenth Century Censuses', *History Workshop Journal* 23 (Spring, 1987), pp. 59–80; Bridget Hill, 'Women, work and the Census: A Problem for Historians of women', *History Workshop Journal* 35 (1993), pp. 78–94; S. Horrell and J. Humphries, 'Women's labour force participation and the transition to the male-breadwinner family, 1790–1865', *Economic History Review* XLVIII (1995), pp. 89–117.

census.[50] Throughout the period 1861 to 1901, wives of agricultural labourers who worked full-time appeared as full-time workers, as did daughters. The seasonal work of hinds' wives however performed at times other than when the census was taken – in spring – though substantial, went unrecorded. Higgs has estimated that in the country as a whole, women amounted to as much as 25 percent of the agricultural workforce in 1861 and he, along with Miller, have found female day labourers in the southwest of the country in the turn of the twentieth century after they had disappeared from the southeast.[51] As for mining communities, there is no mention in the censuses of miners' wives' entrepreneurial efforts to augment the family income.

The various reports to parliament, especially those on agriculture and fishing, gave me valuable information about women. The decennial censuses which give aggregate data, as opposed to the individual data given by the Enumerators Books, and the Registrar-General's reports, which cover districts in the various counties, were most useful, as were those which deal with the various occupational groups on a national basis. Also, the reports of medical officers of health and sanitary officials gave me valuable information about mortality rates, disease rates and living conditions, and about the struggles by officials to improve conditions.

The records of organisations of various kinds held outside the archives were also important. Political organisations such as the Women's Cooperative Guild, the Women's Labour League and, after the First World War, the Women's Section of the Labour Party were important for mining women. Unfortunately, social and geographical isolation and a very burdensome work schedule put such organisations beyond the reach of the fishing and agricultural groups.

I am indebted also to many secondary works. The books and articles on women's history are too numerous to list. They have however formed the background to my thinking about my topic. I will mention only the main secondary sources that apply specifically to the three groups of women. Those dealing with politics, such as Pamela M. Graves' *Labour Women: Women in British Working-Class Politics 1918–1939*,[52] have been particularly relevant for my study of mining women in the twentieth century. For a sense of the mining community, Bill Williamson's *Class, Culture and Community: A Biographical Study of Social Change in Mining*[53] is unrivalled. The most

---

[50] T.J. Hatton and R.E. Bailey, 'Women's Work in Census and Survey', *Economic History Review* LIVI (2001), pp. 87–107.

[51] Edward Higgs, 'Occupational Census and the Agricultural Workforce in Victorian England and Wales', *Economic History Review* 4 (1995), pp. 700–16; C. Miller, 'The Hidden Workforce: female fieldworkers in Gloucestershire, 1870–1901', *Southern History* 6 (1984), pp. 139–61.

[52] Pamela Graves, *Labour Women: Women in British Working-Class Politics 1918–1939* (Cambridge, 1994).

[53] Bill Williamson, *Class, Culture and Community: A Biographical Study of Social Change in Mining* (London, 1982).

useful of the older books is the autobiographical study *A Man's Life*, by Jack Lawson.[54]

There is a paucity of books on inshore fishing. The main secondary work on fishing in general is Paul Thompson, Tony Wailey and Trevor Lummis' *Living the Fishing*[55] but it deals mainly with offshore fishing. David Clarke's *Between Pulpit and Pew: Folk Religion in a North Yorkshire Fishing Village*,[56] though not dealing with Northumberland, is an insightful sociological study of a fishing community. The articles of the anthropologist Jane Nadel-Klein have been of great use. They include 'A fisher laddie needs a fisher lassie: Endogamy and work in a Scottish fishing village',[57] 'Occidentalism as a cottage industry: Representing the autochthonous "other" in British and Irish rural studies',[58] 'Reweaving the fringe: Localism, tradition, and representation in British ethnography',[59] and 'Granny baited the lines: Perpetual crisis and the changing role of women in Scottish fishing communities'.[60] Also invaluable were local studies of fishing communities in Northumberland and in Scotland. In the case of Northumberland, Katrina Porteous' *The Bonny Fisher Lad* is an insightful and sensitive analysis of fishing people in North Northumberland.

Although there are several general works on agriculture in England which deal in part with women, such as *Women, Work and Wages in England, 1600–1850* and Nicola Verdon's *Rural Women Workers in Nineteenth-Century England*, by far the most useful for my purposes of studying Northumberland is Jane Long's chapter on bondagers in *Conversations in Cold Rooms*,[61] Karen Sayer's *Women of the Fields* and Tom Devine's 'Women Workers, 1850–1914' in *Farm Servants and Labour in Lowland Scotland, 1770–1914*,[62] because they deal specifically with female agricultural labourers, and Judy Gielgud's PhD thesis, 'Nineteenth-Century Farm Women in Northumberland and Cumbria'. Most recently, Dinah Iredale's *Bondagers*, produced by Wooler Local History Society, has added interesting detail to the picture. I have also consulted numerous nineteenth-century books which describe the system of farming in Northumberland, but will mention only a few: Hastings

---

[54] Jack Lawson, *A Man's Life* (London, 1944).

[55] Paul Thompson, Tony Wailey and Trevor Lummis, *Living the Fishing* (London, 1983).

[56] David Clark, *Between Pulpit and Pew: Folk Religion in a North Yorkshire Fishing Village* (Oxford, 1999), pp. 111–34.

[57] Jane Nadel-Klein, 'A fisher laddie needs a fisher lassie: Endogamy and work in a Scottish fishing village' in Jane Nadel-Klein and Dona Lee Davis, *To Work and to Weep: Women in Fishing Economics* (St John's, 1988), pp. 290–310.

[58] Jane Nadel-Klein, 'Occidentalism as a Cottage Industry: Representing the Autochthonous "Other" in British and Irish Rural Studies' in James G. Carrier, ed., *Occidentalism: Images of the West* (Oxford, 1995), pp. 109–32 .

[59] Jane Nadel-Klein, 'Reweaving the fringe: Localism, tradition, and representation in British ethnography', *American Ethnologist* 3, Vol. 18 (August 1991), pp. 500–15.

[60] Jane Nadel-Klein, 'Granny baited the lines: Perpetual crisis and the changing role of women in Scottish fishing communities', *Women's Studies International Forum* 3 (2000), pp. 363–72.

[61] Long, *Conversations in Cold Rooms*, Ch. 4.

[62] T.M. Devine, 'Women Workers, 1850–1914' in T.M. Devine, ed., *Farm Servants and Labour in Lowland Scotland, 1770–1914* (Edinburgh, 1990), pp. 98–123.

M. Neville, *Under a Border Tower*;[63] *The Agricultural Labourers of North-umberland: their physical and social condition* by Samuel Donkin;[64] and Mrs Williams, 'The Bondage System' in *Voices from the Plough*. The value of these nineteenth-century works is the insight they give into contemporary attitudes to the women farm labourers.

On the basis of a careful analysis of these sources I have, in the following pages, drawn a picture of the lives and work of these three groups of North-umberland women: wives of coal miners; wives of inshore fishermen; and women agricultural labourers. I have sought to show how divergent their experiences were and that what it meant to be a woman varied within class as well as between classes. As in the case of all social historians, I have aimed to shed light on people hitherto 'hidden from history'.

I have made the decision to leave most of the comparisons to the end of the book so as not to disturb the story of the work and lives of these women. To do otherwise would have left the pictures fragmented. Where relevant, I draw comparisons and contrasts through the book. This study therefore is organ-ised into three parts, the first dealing with coal mining women, the second with inshore fishing women and the third with female agricultural labourers. Each part has two chapters. The first chapter focuses upon mining women in the period 1860–1914. In it, I describe their work, their demographic patterns and the unique burdens that they faced, emphasising their domestic role, though showing that they did add to the family income in small ways. I also deal with the beginnings of their political activity. In the second chapter, I continue the story of the miners' wives into the inter-war years, stressing both the changes and continuities in this difficult economic era. I examine the effects of depression in the coal industry, the changes and continuities in their demographic situation and the flowering of political activity of mining women in the Labour Party. I refer to the 'curious contradictory role' of mining women; the intense domesticity on the one hand and the avid political activity on the other, stressing the clear public/private divide which existed in this one working-class group.

The second section of the book, beginning with the third chapter, deals with inshore fishermen's wives, noting throughout the differences in life expe-riences and roles between them and mining women. I address their impor-tant role in the fishing industry, the existence of a family economy in that industry, and gender relations. The fourth chapter deals with the relationship between the fishing community, women in particular, and the wider society, stressing the contradictory feelings towards the fisher people: admiration for their bravery but, on the other hand, suspicion of them such that they were seen as 'a race apart'.

---

[63] Hastings Neville, *Under a Border Tower* (Newcastle upon Tyne, 1896).
[64] Samuel Donkin, *The Agricultural Labourers of Northumberland: their physical and social condition* (Newcastle upon Tyne, 1869).

The third section of the book addresses female agricultural labourers, a unique group of women. In the fifth chapter, I stress how different their experience and role was from that of mining women and fisher women, and of course from middle-class women. I describe their arduous and often dirty work in the fields and barns and the question of the sexual division of labour. I also assert that, despite what was regarded outside the area as their being employed in 'masculine' work, they were not seen as having lost their femininity but were instead depicted as embodying a 'muscular femininity'. I cover a variety of topics in the sixth chapter. I deal first with the domestic duties of wives, many of whom worked in the fields, at least intermittently, and their contribution to the family economy; I also address the degree of autonomy enjoyed by the various groups of women – the wives, the bondagers, the cottars and the daughters – arriving at an ambiguous conclusion. The next subject I tackle is the high level of illegitimacy in these rural districts. I trace the pattern up through the inter-war years and try to give an explanation for it. In my conclusion to the chapter, I stress the importance of these women to farming in the county of Northumberland and their pride in their work. I note also their out-migration in the twentieth century as the cities beckoned.

PART I

WOMEN IN COAL MINING COMMUNITIES

1

1860–1914: 'Stay at home and look after your husband'

Women in coal mining communities have been largely 'hidden from history', appearing briefly in a single chapter in works which focus upon miners or on the economics of the coal industry. Miners, on the other hand, have long drawn the attention of scholars and literary figures. Historians, particularly labour historians, have been attracted from as early as the nineteenth century by their volatile industrial relations which often ended in violence.[1] The emergence of stable trade unions in the late nineteenth century, born of a remarkable solidarity which, in turn, grew out of the uniquely difficult conditions in which miners worked, led to a proliferation of studies of trade-union histories dealing with virtually every mining region in England, Wales and Scotland.[2] Northumberland too has its chronicler, though the story is limited to the post-World War One period.[3] Unlike the other studies, which focus on labour relations alone, both the *Derbyshire Miners: A Study in Industrial and Social History* by E.W. Williams written in 1962 and, more recently, Carolyn Baylies' *The History of the Yorkshire Miners 1881–1919* (1993) have tried as far as possible, in what are trade-union histories, to include women.[4] That the miners in the 1920s became the backbone of the Labour Party was a further incentive for studies dealing with miners, as was the bruising six-month lock-out in 1926.[5] Economists have been attracted to the coal industry by its great success before the First World War as the leading industry in the country and by its rapid decline in the inter-war period, which earned it the name of the sick industry of modern Britain. Many books have been written about this subject. The most comprehensive has been the Oxford Series *The History of the British Coal Industry*, for our purposes volumes 3 and 4, both of which included women briefly.[6]

[1] Richard Fynes, *The Miners of Northumberland and Durham* (Sunderland, 1873).
[2] I will mention only a few here. Sidney Webb, *The Story of the Durham Miners 1662–1921* (London,1921); E. Welbourne, *The Miners' Unions of Northumberland and Durham* (London, 1923); W. Garside, *The Durham Miners, 1919–1960* (London, 1971); Raymond Challinor, *The Lancashire and Cheshire Miners* (Newcastle upon Tyne, 1972); A.R. Griffin, *The Miners of Nottinghamshire Vol. 1* (Nottingham, 1956).
[3] Jack Davison, *Northumberland Miners History* (Newcastle upon Tyne, 1973).
[4] E.W. Williams, *The Derbyshire Miners: A Study in Industrial and Social History* (London, 1962); Carolyn Baylies, *The History of the Yorkshire Miners 1881–1919* (London, 1993).
[5] G.D.H. Cole, *Labour in the Coal Mining Industry* (Oxford, 1923).
[6] Roy Church, *The History of the British Coal Industry, Volume 3: Victorian Pre-eminence* (Oxford, 1986); Barry Supple, *The History of the British Coal Industry, Volume 4: The Political Economy of Decline* (Oxford, 1987).

Sociologists, too, have been attracted to the mining community. The classic sociological study is Dennis, Henriques and Slaughter's *Coal is Our Life* (1956),[7] which describes the male culture and gender relations in a Yorkshire coal mining community in the immediate post-World War Two period. More recently, Martin Bulmer's 1978 work *Mining and Social Change: Durham County in the Twentieth Century*[8] points to the very close links between community life and the work sphere, links which allow us to see mining communities as 'occupational communities'. This concept implies that men who worked together spent their leisure time together, whether in the pub or the working-men's club, the sports field or in their allotments. The result, as verified by many accounts of miners themselves – such as George Parkinson[9] and Sid Chaplin[10] – was a vibrant male social life from which women were excluded. Such connections gave men the necessary support they needed to work in difficult and dangerous conditions underground. Novelists, such as Richard Llewellyn in *How Green was My Valley,* stressed the difficulties of life and work in mining communities and the danger.

Women have been excluded from study largely because coal mining was a quintessentially masculine industry and they did not show up in the payrolls of the industry. Prior to the late eighteenth century, when operations had been small scale, women in Northumberland and Durham, like women in other mining areas, had helped their husbands by hauling the coal, but at the end of that century the industry in these northeastern counties had excluded women from the mines, even from work at the surface. Thus mining there became a totally male industry, with miners achieving the male-breadwinner ideal which was based on the notion that men should earn enough to support their families without a financial contribution from their wives and children.[11] And miners for the most part were successful in this. In 1842, the Coal Mines Regulation Act had removed women from underground work in the rest of the country, though they continued to work at the surface in a few counties, Lancashire in particular. In Northumberland and Durham, such was the bias against women working in the mines in any capacity that men would turn back home if they met a woman on their way to work, considering the sight of a woman a bad omen. Miners in these counties also looked down on their counterparts in areas where women still worked at the surface of the mine, calling the practice of employing women in this way 'slavery'. Women

---

[7] Norman Dennis, Fernando Henriques and Clifford Slaughter, *Coal is our Life* (London, 1956).
[8] Martin Bulmer, ed., *Mining and Social Change: Durham County in the Twentieth Century* (London, 1978); Martin Bulmer, 'Sociological models of the mining industry', *Sociological Review* 23 (1975), pp. 61–92.
[9] George Parkinson, *True Stories of Durham Pit Life* (London, 1912).
[10] Sid Chaplin, 'Durham Mining Villages' in Bulmer, ed., *Mining and Social Change*, pp. 59–82.
[11] For a discussion of the male-breadwinner wage norm, see Wally Seccombe, 'Patriarchy stabilized: the construction of the male breadwinner wage norm in nineteenth-century Britain', *Social History* 11 (1986), pp. 53–76; Sara Horrell and Jane Humphries, 'Women's labour force participation and the transition to the male-breadwinner family, 1790–1865', *Economic History Review* 48 (1995), pp. 89–117.

also faced exclusion from the mining community's rich masculine social life, which was an extension of the work in the pit, though they were able to craft a social life of their own. Mining communities were therefore more divided along gender lines than any other communities. Yet the pit permeated the lives of women at every level such that they were, in essence, part of the capitalistic enterprise of mining. The pit influenced their demographic patterns; its profitability determined their standard of living, living conditions and housing policies and its shift system structured their daily routine. All worked together to mould an identity which was for most a largely non-remunerative, domestic one.

Domesticity

Mining women were however no mere products of the pit or ordinary domestic women. They determined much about their own domestic role, creating standards that defied the dirt and grime of the outdoor environment. While they appeared to fit the lifestyle favoured by the middle class, in that they were almost wholly dependent on their husbands' wages and were confined to the domestic sphere, they were far removed from the middle-class ideal. While sharing many of the features of other working-class women, they differed in subtle ways, even from those who had a wholly domestic role. They differed also quite markedly from women in inshore fishing and agricultural labouring communities, diverging from the latter two groups and from most other working-class women by virtue of their political awareness. Although some other working-class women, most notably textile workers, engaged in political activity they were, unlike mining women, generally women doing waged work outside the home.[12]

Long before the beginning of our period in 1860, mining women, despite their limitation to the domestic sphere, joined with their husbands in militant action in the industrial disputes which grew out of the numerous sources of conflict in the coal industry. They developed a political consciousness which, if not quite as strong as that of their husbands, certainly surpassed that of other women. By the turn of the nineteenth century a minority of them were enthusiastically joining political organisations. Thus we find mining women being, at one and the same time, the most domestic of working-class women and the most politically conscious.

Further, they had a definable culture which, though much less visible than that of their husbands, was distinctive. The legendary solidarity which miners exhibited in their industrial relations and in their social life had its parallel among their wives, furthering the division of the community along sex lines. The female group, though lacking the organisational structure of the miners' group, was an important force in the mining community and functioned to

---

[12] See, for example, Jill Liddington and Jill Norris, *One Hand Tied Behind Us: The Rise of the Women's Suffrage Movement*, 3rd edn (London, 2000).

give much-needed mutual support. It is true that neighborhood networks were not unique to mining communities. Elizabeth Roberts and others have described them and we find them in agricultural labouring communities, as we shall see.[13] Yet such neighbourhood networks were particularly significant in mining communities where the insecurities of life were great. If the realm of the men was the pub, the working-men's club, the sports field and the allotment, then that of the women was the washing lines, the communal water tap and the fireside where they would exchange gossip and information.

The economic structure of the mining towns and villages added to the male-dominated nature to limit further the opportunities for economic activity on the part of women. Such communities, like those in Durham County and in South Wales, were virtually all one-industry towns. The sparseness of jobs for women in these towns contrasted with those in counties such as Lancashire where mining was interspersed with the textile industry and in the midlands with the pottery industry. The employment statistics in Northumberland mining communities reveal the lack of jobs for women. In 1911, for instance, only 12 percent of women over the age of fourteen were employed outside the home.[14]

Girls and young women had limited options and, at times, suffered exploitation. If the family included several male workers, the mother often kept the eldest daughter at home to help. She became what observers, even people from the mining community itself, called the family 'drudge', overwhelmed, along with the mother, by the heavy routine of the pit household, and often restricted from opportunities for socialising and courtship.[15] This situation was true of Jack Lawson's sisters whom he pictured 'slaving with mother – caring for a family of many small children and several working sons'.[16] It is unclear whether any of these 'family drudges' resented their situation. None of my respondents had been in that position but several, both men and women, commented sympathetically on the phenomenon. The burdens on such daughters and daughters in general were very great and exceeded those of boys.[17] Girls were rarely free of caring for younger siblings while mothers carried out their domestic tasks. If they were allowed to leave the home

[13] Elizabeth Roberts, *A Woman's Place: An Oral History of Working-class Women, 1890–1914* (Oxford, 1984). For some autobiographical accounts, see J. Burnett, ed., *Useful Toil: The Autobiographies of Working People from the 1820's to the 1920's* (London, 1974).

[14] *Census of England and Wales, 1911, County of Northumberland* (London, 1914), Table 24; *Census of England and Wales, 1921, County of Northumberland* (London, 1923), Table 16; *Census of England and Wales, 1931, County of Northumberland, Classification of Industries* (London, 1934), Table 3.

[15] It was common in other working-class households with several male wage earners for daughters to be kept at home to help mothers. See Selina Todd, *Young Women, Work, and Family in England 1918–1950* (Oxford, 2005), p. 60; Leonore Davidoff, *The Family Story: Blood, Contract and Intimacy, 1830–1960* (London, 1999), Ch. 8; R. Roberts, *The Classic Slum*, 2nd edn (Harmondsworth, 1974), p. 53.

[16] Jack Lawson, *A Man's Life* (London, 1944), p. 34.

[17] For a discussion of this point, see Miriam Glucksmann, *Cottons and Casuals: The Gendered Organisation of Labour in Time and Space* (Durham, 2000), Ch. 4.

after finishing school, they would 'go to place' – take a position in domestic service usually in a nearby town or country house. Some girls helped in the homes of miners who had no daughters and had several working sons.

A few others were more fortunate. Employment in small stores increased as the period progressed. Large communities such as Ashington, for instance, whose population by 1911 exceeded 23,000, registered more than one hundred girls employed in general retail, clothing and drapery.[18] The problem was that such jobs were beyond the reach of most miners' daughters because they required being 'spoken for', usually by someone in the retail trade. A more likely and desirable option were jobs in the Cooperative Wholesale Society, a workers' organisation, which provided benefits such as training, education, subsidised health care and good wages.[19] Yet, they demanded that the candidates pass examinations before gaining entry and that they had, what respondents called, a 'connection', usually through a father who was involved in the cooperative movement. Another handful of girls became dressmakers. Daughters of dressmakers themselves or of officials in the mine dominated these jobs because they demanded an apprenticeship which was generally unpaid, and thus beyond the reach of daughters of regular workmen. A new opportunity was the scholarships to secondary schools which became available at the turn of the twentieth century through the Northumberland County Council. The Education Committee of the Council, for example, reported in 1912 that five to ten miners' daughters won scholarships to secondary schools or pupil teacher colleges in the first decade of the century.[20] The problem was however that many families could not afford the cost of uniforms and books and the loss of wages involved in a daughter accepting a place.

Few girls worked for long because marriage featured heavily in the lives of young women in mining communities. Most women married early. Indeed, mining communities showed very high rates of marriage. In 1911, for instance, at an average of 70 percent in Ashington and 75 percent in Bedlingtonshire, the proportion of women aged fifteen to forty-five who were married exceeded that of women of the same age in neighbouring towns by fully 20 percent.[21] Illegitimacy rates were low in comparison to the national average and many Northumberland districts, especially rural ones. Low illegitimacy rates had long been a characteristic of mining communities.[22] Medical officers of health frequently commented on the fact that many girls were pregnant before marriage, often to lodgers.[23] Describing sexual patterns

[18] *Census of England and Wales, 1911, County of Northumberland* (London, 1913), Table 24.

[19] For a discussion of this general pattern, see Todd, *Young Women*, p. 41.

[20] Minutes of the Education Committee of the Northumberland County Council, Vols I–XI, NRO NCC/CM/ED.

[21] *Census of England and Wales, 1911, County of Northumberland* (London, 1913), Table 27.

[22] Jane Humphries, 'Protective Legislation, the Capitalist State and Working Class Men: The Case of the 1842 Mines Regulation Act', *Feminist Review* 7 (1981), pp. 1–34.

[23] Comment of the Medical Officer of Health for Ashington, 1903, but repeated by many of his colleagues. Annual Report of the Medical Officer of Health for Ashington, 1903, Wansbeck Environmental Health Office.

in the neighbouring district of Bedlingtonshire, the medical officer for that district noted that a section of the population practised a 'certain amount of license as regards sexual intercourse before marriage' and when a 'fruitful outcome' was assured, arrangements were made for the young couple to establish a household.[24] The following table suggests that the medical officer was correct.

Table 1.1. Percentage of illegitimate births in two Northumberland mining communities compared to the percentage for England and Wales, 1900–1914

Year	England and Wales	Ashington	Bedlingtonshire
1900	4.14		4.5
1901	3.8		3
1902	3.8	3.4	2.63
1903	4	3.5	4
1904	4	2.7	3.9
1905	4	3.6	2.9
1906	4	3.1	3.1
1907	4.46	9.2	4.9
1908	4.1	2.7	3.1
1909	4.3	3.7	3.9
1910	4.2	3.3	3.3
1911	4.4	2.9	5
1912	4.2	4.5	4.3
1913	4.5	3.9	4.9
1914	4.4	4	3.2

Source: Annual Reports of the Registrar General of Births, Deaths and Marriages in England and Wales for 1900–1914 (London, appropriate years).

While unable to find full-time employment, mining wives did augment the family income, as did many other working-class women, including fisher women and women in farming communities. So common was this practice that it could be said that they were, in a sense, casual workers. Most often this took the form of taking in lodgers. In this period – the last part of the nineteenth century and the early twentieth century – the mining industry was expanding rapidly and the provision of housing was not keeping up with the expansion of labour. Thus around 25 percent of wives kept lodgers, adding 15p per week to the family income, a significant contribution which often represented as much as 10 percent of the miner's wage.[25] This pattern was particularly true of newly burgeoning communities such as Ashington. The activity of wives was a classic example of wives using the home as a

---

[24] Annual Report of the Medical Officer of Health for Bedlingtonshire, 1910, Wansbeck Environmental Health Office.

[25] A.L. Bowley and A.R. Burnett–Hurst, *Livelihood and Poverty* (London, 1915), pp. 147 and 153.

resource.[26] As Humphries has suggested, and as later respondents verified, some of the families' lodgers had distant kin connections.[27]

Women also contributed by entrepreneurial efforts which John Benson called 'penny capitalism'.[28] Such activity included taking in laundry, baking bread or doing sewing for people. Some women hung wallpaper for neighbours while others worked on farms at harvest and potato picking times, joining fisher women who lived near farms. The money earned from such activities, which Higgs notes was seen as 'topping up the family wage',[29] could be crucial when deprivation ensued from the breadwinner earning a low wage because of a bad working place leading to a poor output, and when the pits were working intermittently due to bad winter weather. The economic situation could reach a crisis point when workers sustained injuries resulting in absence from work and loss of wages, an occurrence that one ex-miner estimated to have happened to 80 percent of miners over a lifetime.[30] Although the greatest proportion of miners injured were absent from work for no longer than four weeks, about 10 percent were disabled for twenty weeks or more.[31] Payments from the trade-union fund, friendly societies and, on a very few occasions, compensation through the Workmen's Compensation legislation passed in 1896 and 1907 made up only partly for losses of wages. Workmen's compensation, which required the services of a lawyer, was extremely difficult to achieve. Thus we see the importance of women's earnings, however meagre. It is however extremely unlikely that they were given much credit for their contributions in this hyper-masculine culture. Trade-union officials frequently extolled the ability of the northeastern miners to earn a family wage and compared them favourably to miners in districts in which wives were engaged in employment.[32]

The nature of work in the mine and the culture of the miners meant a heavy domestic role for wives, making work outside the home impossible, even if it had been available. Work in the pit was both dangerous and arduous and was conducted in terrible conditions. Regardless of whether they were cutting coal in low seams which caused them to lie on their side or whether they had to work in water, miners had to wield their picks at breakneck speed, with all the strength they could muster, because their wages were dependent on how much coal they produced. Then explosions of gas, falls of stone, or

[26] For a discussion of lodgers, see Leonore Davidoff, '"The separation of home and work?" Landladies and lodgers in nineteenth and twentieth century England' in Leonore Davidoff, ed., *Worlds Between: Historical Perspectives on Gender and Class* (Cambridge, 1995), pp. 151–79.

[27] Jane Humphries, 'Class struggle and the persistence of the working-class family', *Cambridge Journal of Economics* 2 (June, 1977), pp. 241–58.

[28] John Benson, *The Penny Capitalists: A Study of Nineteenth Century Working-Class Entrepreneurs* (London, 1983).

[29] Edward Higgs, 'Women, Occupation and Work in the Nineteenth Century Censuses', *History Workshop Journal* 23 (Spring, 1987), pp. 59–80.

[30] Chaplin, 'Durham Mining Villages'.

[31] Northumberland Coal Owners Association Minute book, 1897–9, NRO 00263/B.

[32] Miners Federation of Great Britain, Ashington Branch Records, Miners' Offices, Ashington.

Figure 1.1. Miner bathing in a tin bath in front of the fire having just returned from work. His wife will have already scrubbed his back, which would have been black with coal dust. Illustrates the ritual nature of the miner's bath and one of the many services his wife had to perform.
Place unidentified, c.1950

inundation by water were constant threats. As a result of such conditions, miners felt they had to be treated like 'kings' at home, and women were brought up to support the notion that they were 'kings'. The routine of the household revolved around the routine of the pit and the needs of the miners. That routine required physical strength on the part of the women, as did the work of fisher women and women agricultural labourers. Mining women were expected to have the tin bath ready in front of the fire for each worker as soon as he came home from work, black with coal dust. This necessity involved carrying water in buckets from the water-barrel outside or from the standpipe in the street, heating it in the set pot or in a pot on the fire, scrubbing at the dust encrusted on the backs of the workers, emptying the bath and cleaning up the kitchen (Figure 1.1). Frequently, the house included several workers. If there were no working sons, one or two lodgers might be present. One observer, noting the drudgery involved and echoing the comments of many medical officers of health, said the wife had 'no end of trouble'[33] fulfilling this task. Tragically, many accidents were associated with this process. Very frequently the local newspapers reported toddlers falling

---

[33] H. Stanley Jevons, *The British Coal Trade*, 2nd edn (London, 1920), p. 618.

Figure 1.2. 'A little palace.' Typical interior of a mining woman's house, with new batch of baking cooling and hearth and brasses shining. Woman dressed in a pinnie for the evening instead of the everyday overalls. Illustrates the extreme cleanliness the miner's wife was able to achieve in spite of the filth outside.
Newcastle upon Tyne, 1928

into the tub of hot water and being scalded, sometimes fatally.[34] The problem was that the wife, in addition to getting the bath ready, was also rushing to prepare the meal because the workers were ravenous after their shifts and needed to eat before they collapsed, exhausted. Most wives were involved in preparing a succession of meals and baths from early morning until late at night. Jack Lawson remembers his mother rising at 3 a.m. to see her husband off and then again at 5 a.m. to prepare for her sons' departure.[35] In addition, workers were notoriously intolerant of any failure to meet these demands. Each day, women had to 'dad' pit clothes, a process which involved beating them against a wall to get rid of the worst of the grime and dust from the pit. Then they had to dry and rub them soft, for they would have hardened in the process of drying. In addition, they had to clean pit boots rigorously.

Yet miners' wives were not just the victims of their husbands' demands; they played a large role in determining the nature of their own domestic role. An important part of their self-image was a self- imposed regime of rigorous cleanliness and exemplary housewifery. Miners' wives scrubbed, cleaned and

---

[34] See, for example, *The Morpeth Herald*, 23 October 1909.
[35] Lawson, *A Man's Life*, p. 33.

Figure 1.3. Typical scene in unpaved back lanes in both Northumberland and Durham. The coal waiting to be sorted is making the lane even more filthy, as is the smoke belching from the burning pit heap at the end of the lane. Illustrates the difficulty of keeping houses and washing clean.
Easington, County Durham, date unspecified

polished assiduously such that their houses were what one medical officer of health called 'little palaces'[36] (Figure 1.2). This result was no easy feat because the environment of the mining villages and towns was filthy with coal dust, made worse at times by the red dust emanating from slag heaps which sometimes caught fire. Unpaved back lanes were dusty in summer, 'clarty' (muddy) when it rained and further dirtied by the weekly delivery of coal which was stacked up against the coal-house doors until it could be stored (Figure 1.3). Children's feet dragged the resulting coal dust and clarts into houses. It is no exaggeration to say that these women waged war on dirt and dust every bit as much as their husbands waged war on the coalface. When not cleaning, washing the men and readying work clothing, they were cooking, baking, mending, knitting or sewing. They worked so hard that medical officers of health said that they laboured harder than their husbands did in the mine.[37]

Each day was consumed by a laborious task. Monday was for 'washing', a heavy and time-consuming task, described as 'all hell'. It involved carrying more water, heating it in the copper or a pot on the fire and boiling the whites

[36] Annual Report of the Medical Officer of Health for Bedlingtonshire, 1910.
[37] Ibid.

Figure 1.4. Mrs Sally Thompson 'possing', the laborious method of washing clothes. Hard work; medical officers of health blamed the many miscarriages on it. Ashington, late 1930s

in it. Women then 'possed' the whites, that is, beat them with a 'poss' stick in a barrel to get out the dirt and, after rinsing, fed them through the mangle to squeeze out excess water before hanging them out to dry (Figure 1.4). They followed the same process, except for the boiling, with coloured articles. No woman who valued the opinion of her peers would hang out laundry that was less than spotless. If the day was dry and the dust minimal drying the laundry was no problem, but often dust and dampness necessitated that laundry be hung indoors on pulleys and clotheshorses in the small crowded kitchens/ living rooms. Ironing, which took up much of the next day, involved heating irons in the fire, and starching the whites: men's dress shirts, tablecloths and embroidered doilies.

An equally rigid schedule was followed for the rest of the week. Wednesday was baking day. A good wife baked not only bread and pies but also scones and cakes of various kinds. Housework occupied Thursday but Friday was the real 'turning out day', when everything was scrubbed until it 'shone like brass'. Jack Lawson's description captures the frenzy of the weekly spring clean: 'And how they worked: Clean! They rubbed and scrubbed, washed and dusted from morning till night.'[38] On Saturday, women prepared for the big day: Sunday. One task was a fresh batch of baking and the preparation for the big Sunday meal. They polished the brasses and took out the best

---

[38] Lawson, *A Man's Life*, p. 30.

mats, fenders and fire irons to replace the everyday ones. On the big day, which took on ritual proportions, the family sat down to a sumptuous meal of three courses, the middle one of which was roast beef with the appropriate accompaniments.

None of these special tasks took account of the day-to-day responsibilities. Women had to feed and take care of children on a different schedule from the menfolk, who worked on shifts. Most of the time, wives would be pregnant or would have a nursing infant to care for. They rarely had free hands. Each day, they black-leaded the fireplace, polished the step, and washed out the back-door area and also the shared outhouse – called the 'nettie' – if it was their turn to do so. In addition, they made soups, stews, pot pies and various kinds of puddings from scratch. When supper was finished and the children were in bed, the women mended clothes, made larger clothes into ones to fit the smaller children, knitted pit socks and crocheted the edges of pillow-cases and doilies. On winter evenings they made rag rugs, called 'hooky' and 'proggy' mats, from scraps of material left over from old clothing, curtains and bed covers, prodding strips which they had cut from the material through canvas. These mats, made according to home-made designs, added warmth, colour and comfort to the rough floors.

Such efforts on the part of wives were of great significance. They created order and even beauty in a filthy and disorderly environment and thus ensured a measure of control which was important given the many insecurities of mining life. The beauty and cleanliness was also a welcome contrast to the otherwise filthy environment in which the miners worked. We find the Medical Officer of Health for Ashington puzzling over an epidemic of enteric fever in 1895 because 'Cleanliness was the order of the day in every home not only in but around the dwelling.'[39] The women set the tone of the household and helped the miners improve their reputation and even achieve a measure of respectability. In working-class terms that meant cleanliness and order in household management, well-turned-out children, and a moderate lifestyle.[40] Miners needed an improved image, having previously had a reputation for drinking, gambling and brawling unequalled in the nation in the early to mid nineteenth century. While the spread of Methodism into the mining communities in the 1840s had undoubtedly improved the miners' reputation, the miners' wives' domestic achievements in the face of difficult conditions furthered the process. As in many working-class communities, women set the tone of the home and thus, in part, the community, helping to offset the more negative aspects of the male culture. Their efforts played into the campaign to persuade the Liberal Party to allow a Northumberland miner, Thomas Burt, to run for Parliament in 1874 as one of the pioneer working-

[39] Statement of the Medical Officer of Health for Ashington, quoted in *The Morpeth Herald*, 13 July 1895.
[40] There are numerous descriptions of working-class respectability. See, for example, Ellen Ross, '"Not the sort that sit on the doorstep": Respectability in pre-war London neighbourhoods', *International Labor and Working-Class History* 27 (Spring, 1985), pp. 39–59.

class members, and the beginning of what became known as the Lib/Lab Alliance – an alliance between the Liberal Party and Labour leaders, which was to lead to the onset of increasingly stringent safety legislation. It also helped to persuade the Northumberland mine owners to recognise the miners' unions and enter into collective bargaining with them.

Women also had the important task of managing the family budget, a task that was common to working-class wives. Miners' wives had some advantages over other working-class wives. Many miners had allotments on which they grew vegetables that were a valuable supplement to the diet. Rent-free houses or rent allowances and free coal were further advantages.[41] Also, wages in coal mining, especially for hewers who cut the coal, were relatively higher, though often fluctuated even in this period of general prosperity for the coal industry.[42] Piece rates were the method of payment and wages varied according to the skill and physical strength of the individual miner and the ease with which the coal was cut in any particular seam. Productivity changed according to the geological conditions in which the miner was working – the thickness of the seam and the presence of water. If the miner had a bad working place, wages would be low. Further, if the mining company exported its product, as many did in Northumberland, winter weather could disrupt the sale of the coal and the working of the pits and therefore cause additional fluctuations in wages. In these circumstances, miners' wives' informal economic activities took on added importance. When these did not suffice, wives made use of the pawn shops which prospered in the larger mining communities.[43]

The actions of the miners themselves were at times the cause of budgetary problems for wives. While many miners 'tipped it up' – gave the whole pay packet to their wives and received back some pocket money – others kept back a sum of money before handing over the wage packet. These men used this sum, called the 'keepie back', for drinking or gambling and deprived the family of needed money. It is impossible to tell how common this practice was but the many jokes about the 'keepie-back', which included the money being hidden in the outhouse, suggests that it was not uncommon. Though the majority of married men seem not to have been drunkards or gamblers who deprived their families of needed resources, and looked down on the men who did, most men participated in the legendary male sociability to one degree or another, even if only consuming a few drinks in the club on a Sunday morning.

Large families added to financial problems and to the workload of mining women. Mining couples had the nationally highest rates of fertility and were also slower to engage in the decrease in family size that was occurring among other groups. Historian Simon Szreter has suggested that, until the 1920s,

---

41 Return as to Houses, Rent and Coal, 1900, National Coal Board Records, NRO NCB/AS/35.
42 J.W.F. Rowe, *Wages in the Coal Industry* (London, 1923).
43 *Kelly's Directory of Northumberland and Durham* (London, 1897), pp. 60–2.

mining families in the nation as a whole exhibited unrestricted fertility.[44] His finding does not however agree with other evidence. *The Census of Fertility* of 1911 suggests that, in the years 1881–6, mining couples had an average of around 8.71 births, with those women married before twenty having 8.8 births.[45] These numbers were the highest in the nation. By World War One, completed family size seems to have declined to about 4.00, with women marrying below twenty having a family size of 4.32.[46] It is somewhat problematic comparing these figures because the latter take account of infant and child mortality while the former do not. The actual number of births may be around 4.75. It is clear however that Szreter underestimates the period at which miners began to reduce their birth rate, and that mining women by the first decade of the twentieth century were doing so and were therefore less burdened by childbearing. Local medical officers of health in Northumberland, by that point, were commenting on the restriction of births.[47] Further, Ethel Elderton's 1914 *Report on the English Birth Rate* supports this finding.[48] Yet, in the period up to the First World War, mining couples' fertility was still 132 percent of the national average and more than half of my interviewees born before the First World War came from families of more than eight children. Jim Bullock writes that his mother told him that 'never since her first born arrived could she remember when she was not either suckling a babe or expecting one'.[49]

The reasons for such relatively high fertility patterns are complex. One certainly was the early age of marriage, which allowed for many years of childbearing. Miners in the nation as a whole married on average at twenty-two, two years younger than the average. Local marriage records reveal the same pattern, with many brides below the age of twenty-one.[50] The sex ratio, which averaged around 987 women to every thousand men, encouraged early marriage as did the ability of young men to earn full wages at an early age and gain a colliery house.[51] A number of working sons could assure the families of the larger houses. Also, as Sid Chaplin notes, 'lads not only brought in money, but added to status'.[52] A further factor in high fertility was the

[44]   Simon Szreter, *Fertility, Class and Gender in Britain, 1860–1940* (Cambridge, 1996), p. 388.
[45]   *Census of England and Wales, 1911, Vol. XIII, Fertility of Marriage* (London, 1917), Table 31.
[46]   *Census of England and Wales, 1961, Fertility Tables* (London, 1966), Table 16. There is a problem with assessing the fertility of any group because of the different ages at which wives married and the different durations of marriage. The results therefore are rough estimates.
[47]   Annual Medical Officer of Health Report for Ashington, 1903; Annual Medical Officer of Health Report for Bedlingtonshire, 1910.
[48]   Ethel Elderton, *Report on the English Birth Rate. Part I. England North of the Humber* (London, 1914), p. 88.
[49]   Jim Bullock OBE, *Bowers Row: Recollections of a Mining Village* (Wakefield, 1976), p. 4.
[50]   See, for example, Ashington Primitive Methodist Chapel Marriage Records, NRO M11/94; Bedlington Primitive Methodist Chapel Marriage Records, NRO M11/72, 74, 75, 77; St Andrews Newbiggin-by-the-Sea Parish Records, NRO 4455.
[51]   For statistics on sex ratios, see *Census of England and Wales, 1911, Occupations and Industries* (London 1912), Table 8.
[52]   Chaplin, 'Durham Mining Villages'.

heavy labour demands of the coal industry in a period when the industry was expanding and both coal cutting and haulage remained largely un-mechanised.[53] It was no accident that hewers who cut the coal registered the highest fertility, 2 percent higher than the average miner. Particularly when young they were the highest-paid coal workers, for whom there was the greatest demand.[54] The very high rates of infant mortality, which we will discuss later, may have further encouraged higher-than-average fertility.

The burdens of maternity on miners' wives were often great. Some women who had started bearing children in their early twenties were still becoming pregnant and nursing children in their mid forties. *Maternity: Letters from Working-Women Collected by the Women's Co-operative Guild* gives us an indication of the problems faced by women who had large families and several miscarriages.[55] Though none of these letters came from mining women, they are applicable to miners' wives with their high fertility. One woman spoke of having ten children and two miscarriages. While complaining about the difficulties of caring for a home, husband and many children, and often suffering ailments such as varicose veins and other repercussions of multiple pregnancies, virtually all the women seemed to take their multiple pregnancies as part of life, although one said that her denial of sexual intercourse would result in her husband turning nasty.

Often mothers of large families lost children, but none more so than miners' wives. At the turn of the twentieth century, death rates of miners' children over one year of age in Northumberland were 10 to 15 percent higher than the national average. This situation prevailed in mining communities nationally. The main causes were infectious diseases, such as scarlet fever, measles, diphtheria and whooping cough, and the various diseases, such as enteric fever, brought on by insanitary conditions.[56] Ashington in 1914, for instance, recorded a death rate of children over one of 2.9 per thousand, compared to the national average of 1.21.[57] This statistic represented a considerable improvement from earlier decades which was largely attributable to the better control of scarlet fever through isolation hospitals and a decline in virulence of the disease. Another factor was reduced death rates from enteric fever.

The high rates of infant mortality in mining communities in Northumberland and in mining communities nationally were even more significant.[58] A

---

[53] The Ashington Coal Company was virtually the only company in Northumberland to have begun the mechanisation of coal cutting before the First World War (Ashington Coal Company's Directors' Minutes, NRO ZMD/54/4).

[54] *The Census of Fertility, 1911* separates out the hewers from other miners and they consistently have higher fertility.

[55] Margaret Llewelyn Davies, ed., *Maternity: Letters from Working-Women Collected by the Women's Co-operative Guild* (New York and London, 1978), Intro. by Linda Gordon.

[56] Annual Reports of the Medical Officer of Health for Northumberland, 1893–1914, NRO 3897/1–3; *Registrar-General's Supplement to 65th Report, 1904* (London, 1905).

[57] Annual Report of the Medical Officer of Health for Ashington, 1914, Wansbeck Environmental Health Office.

[58] Annual Reports of the Medical Officer of Health for Northumberland, 1893–1914; *Registrar-General's Supplement to 65th Report, 1904.*

comparison of the infant mortality rates of the two main mining communities of Northumberland – Ashington, the most concentrated of the large mining communities in the county, and Bedlingtonshire, somewhat more diversified – with the rates for the country as a whole indicates the seriousness of the problem (Table 1.2).

Table 1.2. Number of deaths under one year per one thousand births in two Northumberland mining communities and England and Wales, 1901–1914

Year	Ashington	Bedlingtonshire	England and Wales
1901	233.48	182	156
1902	136.04	134	169
1903	153.11	172	132
1904	223.16	142.8	146
1905	185	155	146
1906	188.6	158	133
1907	146.7	174	118
1908	202.7	174	121
1909	132.9	116	140
1910	163	157	106
1911	212*	113	130
1912	101	172	95
1913	150	172	108
1914	148	164	105

* Hirst, the section of Ashington in which most of the miners lived, registered an infant mortality rate of 336 in 1911, the lower rate of Ashington as a whole being the result of the non-mining population in the other section of the town.

Source: Annual Reports of the Medical Officer of Health for Ashington and Bedlingtonshire, 1901–1914, Wansbeck Environmental Health Office.

Ashington in particular therefore registered much higher infant mortality rates than communities in the nation as a whole. They peaked in 1904, 1908 and 1911 because of hot summers and the resulting incidence of diarrhoea. Deaths from diarrhoeal causes, pulmonary causes, developmental causes and infectious diseases were all higher than average in mining communities – in Northumberland and elsewhere – and neo-natal deaths (those of children up to four weeks of age) were considerably higher. Though declining between 1911 and 1921 they remained significantly higher than average up to the Second World War and beyond.[59] Indeed, as the Registrar General noted in his decennial report of 1901–10, 'of all industries, mining was the one associated with the highest infant mortality'.[60] While improvements had been made

[59] 'Social and Biological Factors in Infant Mortality', *The Lancet* Vol. 268 (March 12, 1955), p. 554.
[60] *Registrar-General's Decennial Supplementary Report, Part III, 1901–10*, PP 1914–16 VIII, pp. 663–67.

since the mid nineteenth century, the infant mortality rate of miners' children exceeded the rate in the nation as a whole by 32 percent.[61]

As in the case of high fertility, the causes of high infant mortality were complex. High on the list were environmental problems which led to diarrhoeal diseases. Such diseases accounted for a large proportion of infant deaths.[62] While water supplies were gradually cleaned up and rendered sufficient during the period, standpipes in the street serving ten to twelve families were still the only source of water. The treatment of sewage was another problem. The predominant method of sewage collection to begin with was dung heaps. Following that came privy middens, large pits which collected the sewage draining from outhouses. A major problem with such middens was that the farm servants sent by the farmers usually emptied them by carrying the contents through the houses. Further, the middens often lacked concrete floors and thus leaked their contents into the subsoil. In addition, they were often uncovered and were thus a breeding ground for flies, which were a source of summer diarrhoea. Another attraction for the flies was the spillage that occurred on the back lanes when the farm servants emptied the middens. Invariably, children tracked some of this spillage into the houses on their boots. A further factor in infant mortality was the method of feeding babies. A study of six mining communities, none of them in Northumberland, but one in Durham County, found that approximately 30 percent of babies were fed partially or wholly by bottle, most of those being the long-necked kind which were difficult to clean and, given the problem of flies, were often a source of infection. The diarrhoeal death rate of babies artificially fed was substantially higher than that of babies who were breastfed, sometimes twice as high. Hot summers exacerbated the problem.[63] The environment also caused pulmonary complaints. Constantly burning coal fires and slag heaps which periodically caught fire, spewing red dust into the atmosphere, which was often already damp, produced conditions dangerous for the lungs of infants, causing a high death rate from pneumonia and bronchitis.[64]

Inadequate housing also loomed large as a cause of infant mortality in mining communities though not, as we shall see, in rural districts. Given rent-free by the management, most colliery houses were small. From the 1870s onwards, the houses built by the coal companies were generally two rooms with an attic, though older houses with one room and attic were still common.[65] Houses for large families or for officials had three or four rooms. Although houses at the end of the century were built to better standards,

[61]   Ibid.
[62]   Annual Reports of the Medical Officer of Health for Northumberland, 1893–1914.
[63]   Ian Buchanan, 'Infant Feeding, Sanitation and Diarrhoea in Colliery Communities' in Derek J. Oddy and Derek S. Miller, eds, *Diet and Health in Modern Britain* (London, 1985), pp. 148–77. Medical officers of health frequently complained about artificial feeding and urged mothers to breastfeed.
[64]   Annual Reports of the Medical Officer of Health for Northumberland, 1893–1914.
[65]   Interview by author, Mr E. 8 February 1978.

many from 1870s and 80s that were still being used were damp, poorly ventilated and overcrowded. Jack Lawson writes of ten children and two adults
in a two-bedroom house, four to a bed: 'Two at the bottom, two at the top',
the result being 'finding a foot in your face'.[66] Clearly the practice of giving
large families the bigger houses did not apply in this case. Jim Bullock talks
of how he and his eleven brothers and sisters would sit at the table, six on
one side and six on the other.[67] When anyone was ill, that person or child had
to lie in the all-purpose kitchen surrounded by the family.

Governmental reforms had made inroads into the worst of these environmental conditions by the First World War. These reforms included the Public
Health acts of 1875 and 1890, the Private Streets Act of 1892 and the Housing
of the Working Classes Act of 1890 which set standards for housing and
street lay-out, systems of sanitary and medical inspection and even allowed
for the provision of public housing for the working class. The Public Health
Amendment Act of 1907 and the Housing and Town Planning Act of 1909
provided further powers to effect better standards of sanitation and living
conditions. While none of the local authorities in Northumberland had taken
advantage of all the powers at their disposal to improve the environment of
their districts, because of their unwillingness to increase the local property
taxes, most had adopted a proportion of them. A major factor in encouraging
their adoption was the attitude of the medical officers of health and sanitary
officials who, in Northumberland as elsewhere, took their responsibilities to
improve health and the environment very seriously and waged a constant war
against filth and other impediments to good health in the communities under
their care. Once men from the Labour Party were elected to the local authorities in the early twentieth century, the call for the adoption of the legislation
became vociferous. We find them constantly referring in the early years of the
century to the areas with high infant mortality rates, such as the Hirst section
of Ashington, as 'death traps'.[68]

Thus we see a steady improvement in most, though not all, conditions up
to the First World War, leading to an increase in the survival rates of infants
and children. One of the most important improvements was the establishment of isolation hospitals, which were instrumental in reducing deaths from
infectious diseases, particularly scarlet fever. Further, as we have seen, local
authorities had mostly solved the problems of contaminated water and insufficient water supplies by the turn of the century, though most families were
still forced to carry water from standpipes in the street. Tighter standards
of construction had led to an improvement in the problem of dampness in
houses. The privy-midden system of sewage collection, though not eliminated,
saw improvement through proper cementing and covering and more careful
emptying of most, that responsibility having been taken over by the local

---

[66]   Lawson, *A Man's Life*, p. 224.
[67]   Bullock, *Bowers Row*, p. 33.
[68]   Issues of *The Morpeth Herald*, 1908–1914.

councils. Even in Ashington however, known to be a progressive community, 30 percent of the privy middens were still in a 'delapidated and insanitary' condition in 1914. At the same time, a few of the dreadful old netties had been replaced by ash closets and even water closets. Also, the more progressive local authorities had begun to take over responsibility for improving the back streets and eradicating the filth that resulted from the mixing of midden spillage and 'clarts'. Overcrowding however had not decreased. Although newer houses were generally larger, in-migration of labour occasioned by the rapid expansion of the coal mining industry led to housing shortages and perpetuated the habit of taking in lodgers and even of subletting sections of the larger houses. A common pattern was for newly married couples to live with their parents. Ashington, one of the most progressive collieries in the county, had one of the highest rates of overcrowding in the nation in 1911, with 6.1 persons per house.[69] Yet infant mortality rates, with the exception of the years 1908 and 1911, did see a steady decrease, caused largely by declines in deaths from diarrhoeal diseases. Deaths from pulmonary causes also declined. However the continuing high death rate from developmental causes, especially prematurity, that occurred in the first month of life caused concern and puzzlement in official circles.

The recognition by the authorities of the effects of the environment on the health of infants and children did not prevent them from blaming mothers for high death rates, a standard theme in middle-class and official circles not only in Britain but in other parts of Europe. As we have seen, medical officers of health railed against young mothers for failing to breastfeed their babies and for using the long-tube feeding bottles. In reality however overworked wives, with several children and men on shift work, were often unable to breastfeed babies and had to leave daughters to bottle feed them. Further, the long-tube feeding bottle made feeding easier because of its flexibility. A further complaint made by officials was the habit of 'quieting the wailing of the suffering child … by using whisky or patented medicines containing opiates', which, according to the Medical Officer of Health for Newburn, caused 'wasting disease'.[70] Another complaint was that mothers fed infants with adult foods, believing that they 'should live as we do', the results being 'stomach complaints and debility'.[71] One medical officer of health blamed the high rates of infant mortality partly on 'the carelessness, ignorance and occasionally willful neglect' of young mothers whom he considered too immature to bear maternal responsibilities.[72] It is true that the highest rates of infant mortality were in Hirst, which was populated by young couples. While some of the blame may be attached to them, mothers could not help the fact

---

[69] *Census of England and Wales, 1911* Vol. VI (London, 1913), Table 5.
[70] Annual Report of the Medical Officer of Health for Newburn, 1902, Wansbeck Environmental Health Office.
[71] Annual Report of the Medical Officer of Health for Northumberland, 1895, NRO 3897/1.
[72] Annual Report of the Medical Officer of Health for Bedlingtonshire, 1909.

that colliery districts were breeding grounds for infection. As we have seen, women were generally excellent housekeepers.

The authorities intervened to improve the supposed maternal deficiencies. One step was the appointment of nurses to visit mothers of newborns, the belief of medical officers of health being that 'old dames' aggravated matters by offering old-fashioned, harmful advice on such matters as the feeding of infants. At the same time, with the passage of the Midwives Act of 1902, the councils created a class of professional midwives to replace the 'good women' who had formerly delivered babies. The effect of such interventions on health is unclear. Probably, the most important factor in the decline in the death rates of infants and children was the improvements in sanitation and the environment generally.

However other factors played a role in the birth of unviable babies who died in the first month of life, a situation which, as we saw, caused great concern in medical circles. Some medical officers of health blamed miscarriages, premature babies and unviable babies on the hard work of women, in particular on 'possing', the method of laundering clothes and linens. While other working-class women also 'possed', the filth of the mining environment made this task particularly difficult in mining households. At times, women would help each other by 'double possing', each wielding a 'poss stick' in the same barrel.[73] The carrying of heavy baths of water several times a day was probably a greater cause of miscarriage than 'possing'. Yet the other two groups, inshore fishing women and female agricultural labourers, also carried heavy loads and 'possed' and did not appear to have the same high rates of miscarriages and prematurity. Other medical officers of health suggested poor health and nutrition on the part of young mining mothers, noting their propensity to subsist on tea, bread and jam and, consequently, to suffer from anaemia. Yet other medical officers of health rejected the notion of poor nutrition, saying that there was little evidence of poverty in mining districts. Yet, it was well known that miners consumed the bulk of the food, particularly protein, because of the extreme physical demands of their job. Next came the needs of the children and only then, if there was anything left, were the wives' needs met. Women thus sacrificed themselves for their husbands and children. This pattern had been observed in the evidence to the 1842 Royal Commission on the Employment of Women and Children in the Mines, which saw it leading to 'the misery of the family'.[74] Given that women, when pregnant – a frequent condition – needed a lot of protein, this division of food was nonsensical.

Even if the miner's wage was adequate in normal circumstances, it was often deficient when it came to the costs of pregnancy and childbirth. When

[73] Interview by author, Mrs M. 6 October 1977.
[74] Royal Commission on the Employment of Women and Children in the Mines 1842, PP XVII, p. 246. See Jane Humphries, 'Protective Legislation, the Capitalist State, and Working Class Men: The Case of the 1842 Mines Regulation Act' *Feminist Review* 7 (1981), pp. 1–34.

she gave evidence as part of a Women's Co-operative Guild deputation to the House of Commons in 1911, a Mrs Layton, drawing from her own experience as a midwife, said that, even if the husband gave over all his wages, 'the only way a wife could pay for her confinement was by going short herself, as the man had to be kept going for the work's sake, and it would break her heart to starve the children'.[75] If miners had the habit of depriving wives of the full pay packet, then wives would pay the price in insufficient food. Although the available statistics do not provide us with such information, we can suggest that frequent pregnancies were another cause of unviable babies. The ill health of working-class mothers caused by this was well documented in *Maternity: Letters from Working-Women Collected by the Women's Co-operative Guild*.

Whether as a result of frequent pregnancies or not, the ill health of mothers was a matter of concern in public-health circles. A study conducted for the Carnegie United Kingdom Trust in 1917 on the physical welfare of mothers and children in England and Wales found that half of the deaths of children under fourteen days was due to the physical weakness of mothers during pregnancy.[76] This pattern of ill health continued into later life. Evidence from *The Report on Occupational Mortality in 1931* suggests health problems on the part of mining women, who had death rates that were 20 percent higher than their husbands who bore the risk of mining accidents, while a study conducted in the post-World War Two era found miners' wives with higher-than-average morbidity and mortality rates from a number of diseases such as pleurisy, bronchitis, anaemia, blood diseases and cancer.[77]

Then there was the issue of abortion. We can probably assume that some criminal abortions took place, even though the records of the Assizes and Quarterly Sessions, which heard such cases, show no indication of women from mining communities being indicted for such crimes. Such indictments almost always involved domestic servants employed in the cities. Yet such abortions only came to the attention of the authorities if a serious injury was sustained. Also, women generally saw criminal abortions as a last resort.[78] The use of drugs was by far the most common way to induce abortion. The Medical Officer of Health from Bedlingtonshire, for instance, complained about the use of abortifacients during pregnancy, describing the practice as 'a false conception of the obligations of matrimony'[79] which he said resulted

---

[75] Gillian Scott, *Feminism and the Politics of Working Women: The Women's Co-operative Guild, 1880s to the Second World War* (London, 1998), p. 112.

[76] E.W. Hope, *Report on the Physical Welfare of Mothers and Children in England and Wales*, Vol. I (Liverpool, 1917), p. 5.

[77] *Registrar-General's Decennial Supplement, England and Wales, 1931, Part IIa, Occupational Mortality, Fertility and Infant Mortality* (London, 1938), p. 169; John Fox and Peter Goldblat, *Longitudinal Study: Socio-demographic Mortality Differentials* (London, 1982).

[78] Jane Lewis, *Women in England, 1870–1950: Sexual Divisions and Social Change* (Sussex, 1984), p. 17.

[79] Annual Report of the Medical Officer of Health for Bedlingtonshire, 1905, Wansbeck Environmental Health Office.

in mothers becoming weakened and producing 'premature and immature children' who were not viable.[80] It is more than likely that abortifacients were also the cause of many miscarriages in other Northumberland mining communities, as they were in working-class communities in Britain as a whole. Although it is impossible to estimate the incidence of abortion, all indications are that it was common. Ethel Elderton's findings support this conclusion. In her *Report on the English Birth Rate* in 1914, she notes that some of her respondents estimated that 'seven and probably eight in ten' working-class women took abortifacient drugs.[81] Many of the letters in *Letters from Working-Women* mention women taking drugs to abort, though the writers never admit to having done so themselves. Abortion was a means of birth control when *coitus interruptus*, the traditional method, failed, and it was not regarded as a sin if done in the first three months of pregnancy. Also, abortifacients were readily available, advertised widely in women's magazines and on offer by specialists. The following advertisement, which appeared in the *Newcastle Chronicle* on 30th March 1910, was typical:

> Madame J. Jacobson LADIES SPECIALIST. Treats all common complaints incidental to her sex successfully

When families were already large and wives already middle-aged, as in mining communities of Northumberland and indeed in Britain as a whole, abortion was a strategy for survival. As Barbara Brookes notes, 'Use of abortifacients was part of an enduring tradition of self-medication among working-class women which allowed them to make choices free from outside interference.'[82] Jane Lewis also maintains that abortion was 'very much part of a female culture'.[83] Women had no control of the other method of contraception, *coitus interruptus*, and, according to Barbara Brookes, they shared information and helped each other procure abortion. The close female networks found in mining communities promoted the spread of relevant knowledge. Yet, while understandable, the use of abortifacients had downsides. As Margaret Llewelyn Davies, editor of *Maternity: Letters from Working-Women*, claimed, 'it was ruinous to the health of mothers and produced weakly children'.[84] It is likely that the high death rate of infants from developmental diseases in Northumberland mining communities, as in other mining communities, was linked to drugs taken to induce abortion.

In addition to the hardships that women faced in dealing with the losses of children, they suffered from the constant dread of the dangers of the pit and the loss or maiming of husbands and sons. The disaster of 1862, when 204 men and boys from the village of Hartley perished, took the greatest toll and remained in the memory of the mining communities of Northumberland. The

---

[80] Annual Report of the Medical Officer of Health for Bedlingtonshire, 1910.
[81] Elderton, *Report on the English Birth Rate*, p. 3.
[82] Barbara Brookes, *Abortion in England 1900–1967* (London, 1988), p. 5.
[83] Lewis, *Women in England*, p. 18.
[84] Davies (ed.), *Maternity*, p. 15.

pit gear fell down the one shaft of the mine, trapping all who were below, many of them fathers and sons. The tragedy left 163 widows and 257 children without the support of their male breadwinner. One particularly badly hit household lost four sons.[85] Fortunately, this tragedy was the only one of its kind in Northumberland during the period under study. Awful though this event was, the weekly toll of accidents was also bad. Northumberland miners at the turn of the century were twice as likely to be killed in an accident than other workers.[86] Further, barely a day passed where someone, a man or a boy in Northumberland, was not badly injured in a pit accident. In the case of men, the accident was usually caused by a fall of stone when the man was cutting coal.[87] Boys and youths, engaged in haulage work, were frequently crushed to death by tubs of coal and sustained scrapes, bruises and broken bones in hauling tubs through narrow passageways at breakneck speeds. A survey done in 1925 found that between one-third and one-quarter of young transport work in the mines of Northumberland were involved in accidents in that year.[88] If widowed by an accident suffered by her husband, the miner's wife could find herself in difficult straits, given that she lived in a company house. Where there was no scarcity of houses, the coal company might allow the widow to stay and open a small shop to earn a meagre living, and if she had working sons, such generosity was ensured. The coal company would evict her if houses were scarce and she had no working sons.

In times of need, the affection and regard between women played an important role. Though not unique to mining communities, the bonds were tighter and operated more often in mining, given that tragedy struck more frequently. While much has been made of the mutual support among miners and their legendary solidarity, these qualities were no less strong among their wives, for whom a reputation for neighbourliness was much valued. Douglas Pocock describes the process when families faced difficulties: 'any confinement, illness or injury brought an instant parceling out of the cooking, cleaning and child minding'.[89] Other examples of a sense of community abounded. That the ritual of housekeeping which we have previously described was followed in unison, the same tasks being done on the same days, enabled support to be given to members of the group and standards kept up. The group also gave the women a social outlet. Restricted from visiting pubs and working-men's clubs, they visited each other's homes to take part in mat making, sharing

---

[85] Report of the South Shields Committee on Accidents in the Mines, Pamphlets XXIVb, Institute of Mining Engineers, Newcastle upon Tyne.

[86] *Registrar-General's Decennial Supplement, England and Wales, 1921, Part II, Occupational Mortality, Fertility and Infant Mortality* (London, 1923).

[87] Annual Reports of the Inspectors of Mines, 1895–1914, PP 1896 XXII 1–PP 1914–16 XXVIII 341; 'Return as to young and married hewers', Northumberland Coal Owners Association Minutes, Vol. 3, 1896, NRO 00263/B.

[88] Return: Employment of boys between 9 p.m. and 5 p.m. National Coal Board Records, NRO NCB/AS/31.

[89] Douglas Pocock, *A Mining World: The Story of Bearpark, County Durham* (Durham, 1985), p. 37.

a pot of tea and a pan of home-made toffee rather than the beer imbibed by their husbands. The mat making combined a casual social event, to which they could bring their children, with a practical outcome and reinforced the sense of belonging and mutual support. One 1878 event reveals the depth of the women's solidarity. Forty women flogged a wife beater and dragged him to a pond. Only the intervention by some men saved him from a ducking.[90] We shall see later that same community spirit among women expressed in the area of politics.

Clearly, these mining women were prodigious workers who took great pride in caring for their homes, husbands and children. They looked down upon anyone who failed to live up to the rigorous standards they had set. These standards of domesticity were quite remarkable, especially given the grime of the colliery villages. 'Housewives' is therefore an inadequate description of them. They made housekeeping into an art. And many, using their homes as a resource, were able to add to the family coffers by taking in lodgers or by entrepreneurial activities in the home. But their role was not limited to a domestic one. Like their husbands they had long had a political role which, if, in the beginning, was only exercised intermittently, became more formal by the beginning of the twentieth century.

The political role of mining women

Industrial relations in coal mining were, as we have indicated, the most volatile of any industry and miners the most militant of workers. Women were affected by this atmosphere and also by the decreases in wages which led to strikes, and often took the initiative in riots. During the Chartist struggles of the 1830s and 40s when working men in the North East, as elsewhere in the nation, fought for the Charter – a list of ten political demands which would have given working men political power – miners' wives in one Northumberland community refused to do business with shopkeepers unless they promised to sign the Charter.[91] In periods of industrial unrest they often engaged in riotous actions and physical force, echoing a well-established pattern from earlier times. The local press commonly represented them as a threat to the social order and referred to them as 'amazons'.[92] While women, at times, were confused with men, as men dressed in women's clothing to avoid severe punishment, there is no denying that throughout most of the early to mid 1800s mining women exhibited violent behaviour at times of strikes and lockouts. Such actions were not unique to Northumberland. Rosemary A.N. Jones has shown that Welsh mining women had a long tradition of communal action both against people who transgressed local norms and

---

[90] *The Blyth News*, 17 August 1878.
[91] Fynes, *The Miners of Northumberland and Durham*, p. 169.
[92] *The Newcastle Journal*, 9 June 1832.

during strikes against blacklegs[93] and, as Carolyn Baylies has noted, mining women in Yorkshire were at times more militant than the men. Like medieval women in food riots, they appeared to believe that they had a particular right to fight physically if their family's welfare was threatened.[94] They were particularly active if the owners sent out what were called candymen (men employed to evict families from homes) to evict them and their families from their rent-free homes, as often happened in times of strike. The removal of furniture was done with little care for the sanctity of the family's property and it provoked considerable rage, if not violence, on the part of miners' wives.

Such actions continued on into the period under study. On one occasion, in October 1865, the police had to intervene in a Northumberland community but were unable to prevent the candymen getting 'very considerably mauled'. Often the case in protests, the women

> got out their blazers – pieces of sheet metal used as blasts to draw up the fire – and accompanying their shrill, treble yelling with an incessant and discordant banging on these iron plates, they created a perfect panic and terrified the horses of the policemen which plunged and kicked.[95]

The end result was a 'perfect riot' and the candymen fled. On another occasion in the 1880s, they urged the miners to arm themselves with pick-shafts.[96] Women were particularly active against blacklegs, frequently attacking them. On other occasions, they intimidated the men by following them to and from the pit, hooting at them.[97] Three women were charged with intimidation in 1882.[98] During a strike in 1887 the women of Bedlingtonshire, along with the young men of the colliery, protested the policies of the coal owners by banging on pot lids.[99] Such action on the part of men and women became less frequent in the next decades as industrial relations became more orderly with the Northumberland coal companies agreeing to collective bargaining. Even the nationwide strike of 1912, made possible by the joining together of all the county unions, Northumberland included, passed over without a repeat of these kinds of disturbances, largely because of the speedy intervention by the government. A repeat of riotous action on the part of women was to await the industrial warfare of the 1920s.

Another activity that, though not strictly political, certainly allowed a minority of women leadership and had political ramifications was their work in the Methodist Chapel and to a lesser extent in the Anglican Church and Roman Catholic Church. These women belonged to the families which, in the

93 Rosemary A.N. Jones, 'Women, collective action: the *ceffyl pren* tradition' in Angela V. John, ed., *Our Mothers' Land: Chapters in Welsh Women's History 1830–1939* (Cardiff, 1991), pp. 17–42.
94 Carolyn Baylies, *The History of the Yorkshire Miners, 1881–1918*, 1st edn (London, 1993), pp. 109–13.
95 Fynes, *The Miners of Northumberland and Durham*, p. 249.
96 Welbourne, *The Miners' Unions*, p. 264.
97 Ibid., p. 275.
98 Ibid., p. 216.
99 *The Morpeth Herald*, 23 April 1887.

case of the Methodist chapels, virtually ran the establishments forming, in the persons of the husbands, not only the lay officials but also the lay preachers and, in the case of the Anglican Church, the sidesmen and trustees. The women, in both the churches and chapels, ran the Women's Owns, helped with the Sunday Schools, the Women's Classes and many other organisations and raised money. In the case of the Methodist Chapel, their fundraising was extraordinary. They baked, sewed, held sales of work, teas, concerts, bazaars and garden parties – three of the latter in Ashington in the summer of 1898 – to raise money to build the chapels and equip them with organs.[100] Many in the community, whether Methodist or not, would attend such events, especially the local anniversary. The proceeds from one single bazaar, organised by the women of the Guidepost Methodist Chapel – with a relatively small membership of 88 – netted £8. Further, it was reported in 1911 that the women had raised half the money for the chapel's missionary efforts.[101] Social or religious events at the chapel took up many of their evenings. It is noteworthy that, by the end of the 1890s, the chapel began appointing a handful of women as class leaders, a position which involved leading the class meeting at which each member would stand up and tell of some experience from the previous week and the leader would reply. Even more significant, the Ashington Circuit in 1908 appointed a woman for the 'putting on plan', which prepared a person to be local lay preacher.[102] This achievement marked a change from previous decades when the only women allowed to preach were the occasional female evangelical preachers. A suggestion in 1880 that a woman be ordained was met with derision.[103] The experience of working in these organisations, both as leaders and as fundraisers, gave women training in leadership and created confidence. Further, it frequently led to participation in the political organisations that were forming and, as several daughters of chapel women asserted, influenced them to get involved in politics.

At the turn of the twentieth century, we see the establishment of national women's political organisations and, at that point, political activity for a minority of mining women became more formal. One can surmise that the spread of trade unionism among the men in this era was an encouragement to this development. The first organisation to draw in miners' wives was the Women's Co-operative Guild which had been established in 1883. An offshoot of the male workers' Co-operative Wholesale Society, it was unique before 1900 not only in its feminist and class focus but also in its membership, which was composed of working-class wives though its leader,

[100] The Ashington Primitive Methodist Circuit Minute Book, No. 1, NRO M3/16.
[101] The Ashington Primitive Methodist Circuit Minute Book, No. 2 NRO M3/11; Ashington PM Circuit Yearly Reports 1895–1909, NRO M3/20. The Ashington PM Circuit included Ashington, Choppington, North Seaton, Guide Post, Stakeford, Morpeth, Pegswood, Longhirst and New Hirst.
[102] The Morpeth Herald, 22 September 1908.
[103] Reported in The Morpeth Herald, 18th June 1880.

Margaret Llewelyn Davies, was middle class. As Gillian Scott asserts, 'it was a self governing organisation of working-class housewives'.[104] It drew attention to the concerns of working-class women, especially married women, joining for instance in the campaign for maternity centres and baby clinics, for divorce reform and for the new maternity benefits to be paid to women not men. It also fought for votes for women and to get women onto the Boards of Guardians.[105] In addition, the Guild highlighted, through its publication of *Maternity: Letters from Working-Women* in 1915, as *The Times* described it, 'the distresses, hardships, suffering, and enfeeblement, which poverty and maternity between them inflict on women'.[106] The publication of *Letters* moreover brought attention to the plight of women burdened by too many pregnancies, opened up the private area of married life and shed light upon the area of working-class sexuality as never before. The book even addressed the taboo subject of men's sexual demands upon women, suggesting that they were unreasonable and the cause of distress to women and their families. Furthermore, it made mention of women's recourse to abortion, previously a taboo subject.

By the early years of the twentieth century, the Guild had active branches in the mining communities, including in Northumberland. In all mining communities, it attracted principally women from political families, generally the wives and daughters of men involved in the overlapping organisations of the trade union, the Co-operative Wholesale Society, the Permanent Relief Fund and the chapel, of which they themselves were usually a part. These men were more likely to be supportive of their wives becoming involved in political organisations. Yet, not all men involved in the Wholesale Cooperative welcomed the participation of their wives. As Gillian Scott has shown, it was not until the early twentieth century, when branches were forming in mining communities, that Guild women came to accept fully their right as citizens to participate in public affairs. Though the Guild never attracted more than a minority of women in any community (many women when approached to join being apt to say, 'Oh Thank you! I never go out'[107]) it was still of great significance, being the first organisation to take women out of the home and offer them a wider horizon. Through it, they became well versed in issues of public policy, especially those dealing with the health of women and children. Like other women's organisations it made great and supportive efforts to train women, unused to public speaking, to lecture on these issues. We find them for instance reading papers to each other on the 'The Labour Movement', 'Local Government in Relation to Maternity', and 'Syndicalism', to name just a few of the topics addressed. Members received

---

104 Scott, *Feminism*, p. 4.
105 Annual Reports of the Women's Co-operative Guild, 1892–1920, Co-operative College, Manchester.
106 Quoted in Scott, *Feminism*, p. 118.
107 Eileen Murphy, 'A Democracy of Working Women: The Women's Co-operative Guild, *North West Labour History Journal* 28 (2003), pp. 67–80.

training in public speaking and the proper format for holding meetings and running organisations. The Guild was arming its members for taking part in public life when the vote had been gained. Fortified with their new skills, members of the Guild lobbied for seats on the committees of the Cooperative movement. While unable to make headway on major committees, these being monopolised by men, Guild women, by the onset of the First World War, had made inroads in the movement by gaining seats on the Education Committees. An important achievement of the organisation's focus upon the health of mothers and children was its effect on the growing Labour Party, which took on many of these issues.

Women also made contributions to the Labour movement through membership in the Independent Labour Party (ILP). Though not a women's organisation, such as the Guild and the Women's Labour League Party (WLL) which was formed in 1906 and which we will discuss later, the ILP did attract women. Formed in 1896, it established quite a strong following in mining communities in Northumberland in the early years of the century among younger miners and younger women who wanted to supplant the alliance between miners and the Liberal Party, and who believed in the socialist aims of public ownership of the means of production. Unlike the Guild and the WLL, the ILP was run by men. Although its female members stressed that they were treated equally in the organisation, and though they emphasised feminist issues such as women's suffrage and the engagement of female factory inspectors, their real role within the ILP was as auxiliaries responsible for all of the constituency and election work.[108] Women prepared election material, delivered it, and canvassed in support of the men running for office in the local councils. Through their canvassing, and their help in organising the Sunday evening lecture series in the parks, they promoted the propaganda of socialism, promising a better world for all. They also spent a great deal of time organising social events and sales of work to fund these election efforts and to keep the branches going, and were thus fundamental to the organisation. These social events were an important part of the calendar and an attraction, especially for young people. A further attraction were the cycling groups and the theatrical groups, which were particularly popular for their renditions of George Bernard Shaw's plays, with their strong social message.[109] But the ILP never had the supportive, educative role of women that the Guild and the WLL had because, though supporting women's suffrage, it was not a feminist organisation. For the ILP women, class dominated over gender.

As we have noted, another organisation which attracted mining women in the early twentieth century was the WLL. Formed in 1906 to ensure that the Labour Party did not ignore issues concerning women, it was a socialist, feminist organisation which never lost its feminist character even though it

---

108   Clare L. Collins, 'Women and Labour Politics in Britain, 1893–1932' (PhD thesis, London School of Economics, 1991), p. 64.
109   *Northern Democrat*, Issues 1909.

affiliated with the Labour Party in 1908. After that, it spread rapidly in the mining communities of Northumberland, as in those of other districts, as an alternative to the alliance between the trade union and the Liberal Party, established in 1874. Its focus was on many issues which were of importance to mining women and overlapped with many of the Guild's aims. These included equal divorce and marriage laws, a campaign for miners' baths, baby clinics, school meals and the medical inspection of schoolchildren.[110] After 1913, under the stewardship of Marion Phillips, it fought for women's suffrage. As Christine Collette has noted, it was the caring, social-welfare image of its earlier years that was the League's biggest contribution to the Labour movement.[111] In addition, it did very important electioneering work for the Labour Party which, because of this, gave the organisation a grant of £100 per year starting in 1911. This grant was justified, for the women did indeed carry out valuable work in that area. One of their most important tasks was to get the electoral rolls up to date and get voters registered.[112] Then came the task of persuading voters to vote for Labour Party candidates. Members prepared literature and canvassed voters in homes, explaining the policies of their candidates and, in so doing, helping Labour Party men gain seats in local councils. Further, Lisbeth Simms, organiser of the WLL branches in the North East, won a seat on the Board of Guardians for Gosforth in 1908.

Between elections, WLL members spent their time raising money and educating themselves on public-policy issues. In order to fund their election efforts and their branches, they held many sewing circles, the products of which they sold at sales of work, and held innumerable musical and literary evenings and teas. Fundraising in this way for political causes was to become a hallmark of Labour women's efforts. While seemingly frivolous, these events had a strong communal component and, in addition, served an important purpose. They allowed the wealthier members of the organisation to contribute to its upkeep but also kept the morale of the group up and brought new members in. The joy and the profound sense of purpose that would become so much a feature of the Women's Sections of the Labour Party in the difficult inter-war era was born at this time. The WLL members spent most of the rest of their time educating themselves on theories of class and gender politics, Labour Party policies, and ways of explaining these to others, especially when they were canvassing. Like the Guild women, they read papers on public-policy issues ranging from socialism and infant mortality to women's suffrage, following the Guild's pattern of educating the women in ways that were not threatening to the uninitiated. At times, such hefty political readings would be combined with sewing circles. Again, like the Guild women, the WLL members were taught how to speak in public, hold meetings, and run

---

110 Records of Women's Labour League, London School of Economics Library, COLL MISC 0268.
111 Christine Collette, *For Labour and for Women: The Women's Labour League, 1906–18* (Manchester, 1989), p. 185.
112 Ibid., p. 98.

their branches. Both the Guild and the WLL were solidly feminist, stressing, as well as the franchise, the interests of working-class women such as their health, the high rates of infant mortality and the need for family allowances. They, like their Guild counterparts, felt they were preparing their members to take a place in public life equal to men. Though certainly feminists, who should be considered part of the first movement of feminism, they differed at points from middle-class feminists who, though focused on the franchise, were – with a few exceptions, such as Eleanor Rathbone – less interested in the social problems of the working class, focusing mainly on such issues as better employment opportunities for middle-class girls and the legal rights of married women.[113] Each strove however to persuade their membership of their right to engage fully in public life.

Both the Guild and the WLL transformed their members. They created confidence in mining women, as in their other working-class women members, who had never before reached out of the home and what one WLL member called their 'narrow, monotonous lives'.[114] It is no exaggeration to say that membership of both organisations changed women's outlook across the board. Both groups came to see that they were citizens in every sense of the word, with responsibilities. One woman said, 'I feel more and more what an immense power united action can be.' The Guild 'has brought us out'.[115] Lisbeth Simms said that they could not be proper home-makers if they did not take on wider responsibilities. The leadership of both groups urged their members to pay less attention to their housework, a necessary admonition to house-proud mining women. The rhetoric of these movements was designed to make the members aware of their value. The same Lisbeth Simms was to say in September of 1909 that

> We need the sympathy and service and experience of these women whose homes are patterns of orderliness and good management. She who can carry on the wonderfully complex duties involved in the private home life in a manner conducive to the health and happiness of the whole of the inmates is the very woman we need in the public affairs of our towns.[116]

While those who were most transformed were the leaders, even those who did not care to take on a leadership role could find a place in both the Guild and the WLL, whether by helping to raise funds or by becoming involved in election work. The sense of pride was palpable. One reported 'of the joy of a male comrade (member of the Labour Party) in the awakened intelligence of his wife who, through the Labour League meetings, for the first time, now

---

113   Olive Banks, *Becoming a Feminist: The Social Origins of "First Wave" Feminism* (Athens, Georgia, 1987), Ch. 4.

114   *Northern Democrat*, February 1909.

115   Scott, *Feminism*, p. 77.

116   *Northern Democrat*, September 1909.

discussed the labour problems in which he was interested with sympathy and understanding'.[117]

Conclusion

The early political activity of mining women, which took the form of rough music, thus became more organised and formalised in the years before the First World War, though, by that point, women had still not won the right to vote in national elections. In this period, the average mining woman was likely, as one member of the Northumberland WLL said, 'to think we are a queer lot when we go about selling tickets – they think we must neglect our homes'.[118] Though such participation in political organisations involved only a minority of mining women, it was nonetheless significant as a precursor of what was to follow. There was no doubt that it was feminist although, while certainly supporting the vote for women, it often had different priorities from those of middle-class, equal-rights feminists. Both groups however believed fully in women's right to public office and the basic equality of women. Although it was going to become much more pronounced in the inter-war period, we can already see among mining women the public/private divide between those who stayed in the home, creating 'little palaces', and those who ventured out into the public sphere to deal with matters of both local and national concern.

The activist trend was to become much more developed in the inter-war period after women got the right to vote and, with the decline of the Liberal Party, the Labour Party became the second major political party in the nation. At that point, the average mining woman came to accept the activists and voted for them, asserting her own political role in the difficult economic and political situation of the new era. But women faced prejudice from men. When Lisbeth Simms was running for the seat on the Gosforth Board of Guardians, for instance, she was told by the men to 'stay at home and take care of my husband'.[119] Yet she won. There was a growing appreciation that the work done by the Guardians which involved care for the poverty-stricken was well within the province of women. This idea was going to be extended to other tasks for which women were suited in the years following the war.

[117] Ibid., February 1909.
[118] Ibid., February 1909.
[119] Ibid., May 1908.

2

The Inter-War Years:
The Contrasting Roles of Mining Women

The inter-war years brought many changes to the mining community and to mining women. After a boom during the war, the industry sank into depression. One problem was the loss of markets during the war, particularly severe in exporting districts such as Northumberland, and a slowness to mechanise the cutting and haulage of coal. The return to the gold standard in 1924 which plunged the United Kingdom into depression five years before the 1929 Crash further added to the problems of the coal industry. The combined result was that what had been known as 'King Coal' before the war became the 'sick man' of industry in the 1920s and 30s. This change in the fortunes of the mining industry had major effects on mining families. A related feature of the inter-war period was the nationwide industrial strife in the coal industry, first in 1920 and 1921 and then, much more severely, in the six-month lock-out in 1926. The onset of the Great Depression in the 1930s furthered the difficulties of the industry and added to the woes of mining families. Not until the eve of the Second World War did the situation begin to improve. Yet the inter-war period was not all doom and gloom for mining women. Some of the burdens of the women's lives were lifted in this period as a result of official actions and the actions of mining families, especially women.

We see many continuities with the prewar period however. The male-breadwinner pattern having remained, gender roles continued to be very distinct, most women retaining an almost wholly domestic role which, as before, was all-consuming. They continued their informal economic activities which became all the more important in the depressed conditions of the era. While fertility rates declined and infant mortality rates improved, the latter still ranked poorly with most other working-class groups and the nation at large. The earlier pattern of spontaneous action by women in times of industrial strife reappeared in the economically troubled times of the 1920s. Further, in this period, the formal political role of women which began at the turn of the century became enlarged with the 1918 winning of the vote for women over twenty-eight, the extension of the vote to women over eighteen in 1928, the rise to power of the Labour Party in 1918, and the emergence of women's sections of that Party in the same year. So involved did some women become in politics that their political role superseded their domestic role. The contrasting picture which we had begun to see in the prewar period – with most women limited to the private sphere and all-consuming domesticity, and a minority enthusiastically and aggressively striking out into the public sphere in the formerly male preserve of politics – now became much more apparent.

Retention of a domestic role

As before, the miner's wife was responsible, in her domestic role, for managing the family budget, a difficult matter given the industry's decline in this era. While the wages of miners had always fluctuated, they had been generally sufficient compared to those of many workers, if the miners had had a good working place and if the pay packets were handed intact to their wives. Now, in the inter-war period, outright unemployment and underemployment bit into the housekeeping budget. Low wages and intermittent work began in the early 1920s, long before the onset of the Great Depression of the 1930s.

The situation was at its worst during the six-month lock-out in 1926. Jack Davison indicates the difficulties faced by Northumberland families, as by mining families elsewhere. Families with two children subsisted on £1 per week awarded by the Boards of Guardians, with the addition of 30p from the trade union for the first four months and then 15p for the next two months.[1] Such payments usually proved inadequate and women had to resort to the soup kitchens, many of which were run by the working-men's clubs, and to provisions bought on credit from the Co-operative Wholesale Society stores. Fortunately, coal companies did not adopt the nineteenth-century practice of evicting families from their colliery houses. After the lock-out ended in November 1926, families had to pay back the relief they had been given and the money they owed the Co-operative Wholesale Societies. Even in 1930, the debt owed to the poor law unions in Northumberland was still £228,314.[2] Adding to the situation, the miners went back to work facing a further reduction in wages, while some faced unemployment and short-time work. By 1929, wages in mining in the nation as a whole were 12 percent lower than what they had been in 1924. According to Barry Supple, miners were the only industrial group whose wages had fallen in real terms.[3]

The onset of the Great Depression in the 1930s spread these conditions to more mining families. Many men suffered outright unemployment. At its highest point, unemployment in Northumberland reached 21.2 percent of miners and remained high until 1935.[4] An unemployed miner with a wife and two children was entitled to £1.35 per week, an amount that was reduced slightly in 1931 and then increased to £1.40 in 1934. Employed men might only be slightly better off, earning sometimes 6p to 8p per shift, so only

[1]   Jack Davison, *Northumberland Miners, 1919–1939* (Newcastle upon Tyne, 1973), p. 71.
[2]   Barry Supple, *The History of the British Coal Industry Volume 4: The Political Economy of Decline* (Oxford, 1987), p. 463.
[3]   Ibid., p. 443.
[4]   Ibid., pp. 450–1, Table 10.3.

£1.40p to £2 per week. Even the most skilled earned only 40p to 50p per shift, £2 to £2.20p per week.[5] Employed men however had no guarantee that they would work five shifts per week. Work was often intermittent and an employed man might take home less than an unemployed one. Although these difficulties were felt by mining communities throughout the nation Northumberland, as an export district, suffered particularly badly from short-time work. To make matters worse, 1931 brought the imposition of the hated Means Test which led to the allowances of families being reduced if the examining official considered that they owned items of any value. Further, if one person in the household got a job the whole family was denied assistance, causing that person, usually a son, to leave the home.

While men certainly felt a great deal of pressure during these years, the burdens of feeding and clothing the family fell on women. Many reputedly often 'went without' to provide for their families. Their management skills, always important to their families' survival, were at this point tested to the limit. The home-made pot pies and bread, soups and puddings were all the more important in this period and women sacrificed clothing, boots and furniture to feed the family. Interviewees remember their mothers reinforcing their shoes with newspaper as the soles became worn out. Though the local newspapers repeatedly reported a decline in male drinking during the depression, the problems of men using up valuable money on alcohol did not stop entirely. Some men continued to be what was described as 'clubmen': men who spent a great deal of time and money on alcohol and gambling at the club. Interviewees recounted how women would go down to the working-men's club, where their husbands had gone instead of coming home with the pay packet, the intention being to get their housekeeping money before it was spent. Cissie Charlton's mother, for example, regularly took her children down to the club and waited for her husband to come out 'addled by drink'. She would then force him to go to the shops with her to buy items for the children.[6]

Women continued their informal economic activities role in this period, their contributions to the family income being even more crucial than in the past. The traditional method of taking in lodgers, which had been an important source of their extra income, was limited in the inter-war period because the labour force was contracting, not expanding as before. Some families, who lived in the new, larger council houses, sublet part of their homes, but this usually helped pay the higher rents rather than adding to the family income, and perpetuated the problem of overcrowding which the council houses were meant to allay. Some new options for part-time work for wives with grown children or older children had opened up. Although mining communities continued to be one-industry towns, the largest of them had developed quite large service sectors involving, in the case of towns

[5]   Ibid., pp. 453–4.
[6]   Cissie Charlton, *Cissie* (Newcastle upon Tyne, 1988), p. 48.

such as Bedlington and Ashington, numerous shops, cinemas, dance halls and places of business. Oral evidence suggests that a few married women were able to augment the family income by cleaning offices and shops and the houses of middle-class people on a part-time basis. Many women resorted to small-scale entrepreneurial activities, as before. Some used their skills as dressmakers. Adeline Hodges recalls how her mother made a little money at home by sewing 'bait pokes' (bags for carrying food underground) and 'pit flappers' (miners' flannel body shirts) and, through a contract with the local bedding shop, sewing sheets.[7] One of my respondents recalled how her mother baked bread for people.[8] These women, like those before them, were unlikely to have seen their role as wage earners. While evidence is lacking, we can assume that their husbands were more appreciative of their efforts than before, much of their confidence in being able to provide for their families shaken by the economic situation.

The employment options for young women had improved a little also but there was much continuity. The increase in the number of shops offered employment for some who were 'spoken for' but, as before, it was low paying. Department stores had increased in number slightly and the Cooperative Wholesale Society, located in every mining community, offered better conditions but had the same barriers to entry as in the prewar era. According to respondents, girls regularly attended the Cooperative classes, at which they learned the theories of cooperation and the history of the movement, hoping to increase their chance of gaining this much sought-after position. It is possible that a very small minority gained employment in the few offices that existed in the larger communities, probably as typists. We can deduce this from the records of the girls who attended the evening classes in commercial subjects organised by the Ashington Coal Company in cooperation with the Northumberland County Council.[9] A few others, as before, won scholarships to secondary school, but, in the depressed conditions of the inter-war period, were unlikely to be able to attend.[10]

Others followed traditional patterns. Many young women, especially oldest daughters, still stayed at home to help mothers care for workers and younger siblings. The 'family drudge' thus remained a reality. Yet others, the bulk of those who sought employment, went into domestic service as many of their mothers had done, sending home virtually all of their paltry wages. The continued lack of factory options together with the tendency for girls to follow the employment patterns of their mothers, to which Todd

---

7   Adeline Hodges, 'Up the Ladder', Tuesday Club Occasional Paper No. 2, N.D. Pit flappers were flannel body shirts which men wore to protect them from catching cold coming out of the hot pit. Women had sewed bait pokes in earlier decades. See Jane Humphries, 'Protective Legislation, the Capitalist State, and Working Class Men: The Case of the 1843 Mines Regulation Act', *Feminist Review* 7 (1981), pp. 1–34.

8   Interview by author, Mrs W.T. 6 July 1980.

9   Ashington Mining School Minutes, NRO CES/1.

10 Northumberland County Council Education Minutes, Vols XXXI–XXXVI, 1930–1939, NRO NCC/CM/ED.

has pointed, determined the persistence of this habit.[11] Some girls continued to find employment in the homes of other miners who had more than one worker but no daughters old enough to help their wives.

Sometimes, accidents depleted the income of the family, making the contributions of women all the more essential. Though not equal to the Hartley disaster of 1862, an accident killed sixteen men in Ashington in 1916. Further, newspaper reports indicate that one or two men or boys in Northumberland died every other week in single accidents. Though workmen's compensation was easier to win in this era, it did not prevent families from suffering deprivation. Boys, as before, were particularly susceptible to accidents with haulage tubs. We hear of a pony driver aged fifteen, killed in November of 1932 when he was caught between the tub and the roof, his pony having jerked forward.[12] A retired miner recounts an accident in Choppington Pit:

> Once a pony strayed into a gallery which contained a heavy concentration of carbon monoxide or black damp. A young putter in charge of the animal followed it. In these days a pony was considered to be a valuable asset down below. When the youth failed to return, the deputy without any thought of danger, followed. When the alarm was raised, a rescue operation was mounted, only to find the missing trio in their last sleep.[13]

The accident rate actually increased in the inter-war years. In the period 1922–6, 0.40 men per 100,000 manshifts worked were killed. By 1932–6 this had risen to 0.44.[14] The men attributed this increase to the progress of mechanisation. The problem was that the noise of the coal-cutting machines drowned out the creaking noises which warned of the imminence of a fall of stone.[15] If fatal accidents were the most serious, non-fatal accidents were most common. Almost one-fifth of Northumberland miners suffered non-fatal accidents during the 1930s.[16] Every mining community had its share of amputees who worked at the surface on light jobs.

For women the dread of accidents remained very real. Even though it had happened many years before, the Hartley disaster was a common subject of conversation and its anniversary was noted every year. Bill Williamson, in his biographical study of the mining community of Throckley, Northumberland, in which he grew up, describes the fear of accidents among women:

[11]   Selina Todd, *Young Women, Work, and Family in England 1918–1950* (Oxford, 2005), p. 89.
[12]   *The Morpeth Herald*, 24 November 1932.
[13]   Tom Wilkinson, 'Choppington Pit' in Mike Kirkup, ed., *Pitmen Born and Bred: Award Winning Stories from Britain's Coalfields* (Ashington, 1994), p. 21. A putter is a young haulage worker aged 14 to 17. A deputy is an official in the mine.
[14]   Supple, *The History of the British Coal Industry*, p. 428, Table 10.1.
[15]   Oral interview by author, Mr L. 26th October 1977. For a description of the effects of machine cutting, see B.L. Coombes, *These Poor Hands: The Autobiography of a Miner Working in South Wales* (London, 1939).
[16]   Bill Williamson, *Class, Culture and Community. A Biographical Study of Social Change in Mining* (London, 1982), p. 86, Table 5.3.

… my grandmother's life was lived in the shadow of the pit.… Like other wives in Throckley, she was extremely attentive to outside noises. The bustle of the street, the crunch of hob nailed boots, children playing, the calls of hawkers, the intermittent clanking of the tubs from the dilly line, the throb of the pumping engines of the pits – all implied normality. But an unexpected blow from the pit buzzer could penetrate the normal noise immediately spreading alarm and anxiety through every house. Saturday and Sunday were the only days she was free of the subliminal threat. Only then could she feel that she was safe.[17]

Yet there were some general improvements for the mining communities of England in the inter-war years. One was the decline in fertility rates in mining families which rendered mining women less defined by maternity. The average size of family, which had been about 4.1 children in the early twentieth century, had declined by the 1930s to approximately 2.75–3.00 children, with women married under the age of 20 who generally had more births, having a slightly larger family. We see a slight rise in family size in the late 1930s, due probably to an easing of the depression of that decade.[18] The above statistics take into account the deaths of infants and children. The average number of births to mining couples however was probably just over 3.1 and around 3.4 for women married under twenty years.

Yet demographic patterns showed continuity. In 1939, the birth rate of miners' wives was still 37 percent higher than the national average. Marriage rates had remained high in comparison to other communities. In 1931, for instance, Ashington and Bedlingtonshire registered 70 and 75 percent of women respectively between the ages of fifteen and forty-five married, proportions 25 to 28 percent higher than a non-mining town of comparable size in Northumberland.[19] In 1931, in Ashington, the sex ratio was still skewed: for every 100 females there were 107 males.[20] Males still married two years younger than the average: 22.5 instead of 24.6.[21] Contemporaries commented on the persistence of some families of ten children, mostly, though not always, among Catholics. By that point however agricultural workers and general labouring couples had overtaken mining couples in numbers of children born.[22] One cause of this decline was the decrease in economic opportunities in the coal industry. Miners and their wives could no longer assume that a son could begin earning high wages at eighteen. Further, with the increase

---

[17] Ibid., p. 124.

[18] These figures, due to the nature of the official records, are very rough estimates. *Census, 1951 England and Wales, Fertility Report* (London, 1959), p. 208; *Census of England and Wales, 1961, Fertility Tables* (London, 1966), Table 16.

[19] *Census of England and Wales, 1931, County of Northumberland* (London, 1935), Table E.

[20] *Census of England and Wales, 1931, Industry Tables* (London, 1934), Table D.

[21] *Registrar-General's Decennial Supplement, England and Wales, 1931, Part IIb Occupational Fertility, 1931 and 1939* (London, 1953), p. 9.

[22] Ibid., Table 4.

in the school-leaving age to fourteen, the cost of children had increased. The culture of the 1930s was probably another factor in the decline.

This decline in fertility was achieved through birth control. The general consensus among interviewees was that the most common method of birth control was withdrawal, so much so that there were many jokes about it. In addition to the joke common in working-class communities about 'getting off the train before arriving at the destination', miners in Northumberland spoke of 'jumpin aff gangin'.[23] Historians such as Diana Gittens and, more recently, Simon Szreter and Kate Fisher, reinforce the conclusion of the widespread use of the withdrawal method, also noting that, by the inter-war period, men had assumed responsibility for birth control.[24] Szreter and Fisher also point to the periodic use of abstinence, especially if there was a particular fear of pregnancy, and to the unpopularity of condoms in working-class communities in the north of England where only the thick variety was available. Then there was their cost. Jane Lewis has noted that they cost an average of 10p to 15p per dozen, a considerable sum when wages during the depression often amounted to only £1 per week.[25] While a few birth-control clinics did appear in Northumberland mining communities in the 1930s, such as in Ashington, it is unlikely that they had much effect upon limiting the birth rate of mining couples. According to Barbara Brookes and Szreter and Fisher many working-class couples regarded mechanical methods of birth control as not being 'natural'.[26] A London magistrate commenting in 1933 on women's reluctance to attend birth-control clinics noted, 'contraception is not … considered "respectable" but harmful methods of birth control and even abortion, are'.[27] It is likely that abortion was still being used as a means of birth control and was partially responsible for a decline in the birth rate of mining couples. Jane Lewis reports that 'As late as 1938, a governmental interdepartmental committee on abortion found that "many mothers seemed not to understand that self-induced abortion was illegal. They assumed that it was legal before the third month (before quickening), and only outside the law when procured by another person."'[28]

The national pattern was for abortion to increase in the 1930s.[29] Jane Lewis noted that a practising midwife in a small colliery village in the 1930s believed that of 227 miscarriages amongst 122 women over a period of seven years, few were accidental.[30] And mining communities in Northumberland

---

[23] Interview by author, Mr C. 1st March 1977; Mr S.M.M. 1 October 1977.
[24] Diana Gittens, *Fair Sex, Family Size and Structure, 1900–1939* (London, 1982); Simon Szreter and Kate Fisher, *Sex Before the Sexual Revolution: Intimate Life in England 1918–1963* (Cambridge, 2010), Ch. 6.
[25] Jane Lewis, *Women in England 1870–1950: Sexual Divisions and Social Change* (Sussex, 1984), p. 17.
[26] Barbara Brookes, *Abortion in England 1900–1967* (London, 1988), p. 16.
[27] Quoted in Brookes, *Abortion in England*, p. 4.
[28] Quoted in Lewis, *Women in England*, p. 18.
[29] Brookes, *Abortion in England*, p. 9.
[30] Lewis, *Women in England*, p. 18.

appear to have been part of this trend. In 1932, the Medical Officer of Health for Bedlingtonshire raised the possibility of attempts on the part of mothers to effect 'criminal abortion'.[31] Although he rejected this thesis, it is probable that women, if not resorting to criminal abortion, did continue to seek the same end via abortifacients. There were hints of efforts to induce abortion, as in the earlier period. One interviewee spoke of the 'black bottle' which was 'hush hush'.[32] We can assume it was penny royal or quinine, two abortion-inducing compounds. Also, there were plenty of incentives to resort to abortion if *coitus interruptus* failed, since mining communities in Northumberland, as elsewhere, were suffering unemployment and underemployment. Undoubtedly, many wives who already had several children were desperate if they found themselves pregnant again. As in the earlier period, abortion was a way for women to have a measure of control over their bodies, independent of men. Encouraging a decline in the birth rate, despite the relatively early age of marriage, was the decrease in infant mortality. Fewer lost babies made multiple births less necessary to attain a target family size.

The decrease in infant mortality, which began before the First World War, gained momentum in the inter-war period. Sanitary, environmental and medical improvements led to a decrease in infant mortality across the whole population. Begun before the First World War, they now sped up. Every year saw the progressive substitution of water closets for privy middens in each district. In Newbiggin-by-the-Sea, Northumberland, for instance, by 1938 only 158 privies were still in existence, the place of the others having been taken by 2,312 water closets.[33] Though the old rent-free colliery housing continued to predominate, district councils, despite the economic difficulties of the inter-war years, began to build commodious houses. Unfortunately, most families could not afford the rents. The result was usually sub-letting and continued overcrowding. A further improvement was the introduction of piped-in water to roughly half of the houses by the mid 1930s. The rest of the houses were still served by taps in the street.[34] A further third had piped-in water by the end of the 1930s. By that same date many, though not all, of the urban district councils had taken control over and paved the unpaved back streets, which had been such a source of mud, associated with illness and extra domestic labour. A further improvement was the establishment of Maternity and Child Welfare centres following the 1918 act of that name. After a slow start, women began attending them often and they were especially valuable during the Depression for their distribution of free milk and dietary supplements for children. Further, the establishment of ante-natal clinics in the mid 1920s proved popular with mothers. As a result of all these

[31] Annual Report of the Medical Officer of Health for Bedlingtonshire, 1932, Wansbeck Environmental Health Office.
[32] Interview by author, Mrs M.T. 7 June 1996.
[33] Annual Report of the Medical Officer of Health for Newbiggin-by-the-Sea, 1938, Wansbeck Environmental Health Office.
[34] *The Morpeth Herald*, 20 July 1934.

changes, infant deaths from diarrhoea declined to around forty per thousand births in the 1920s and 30s from around sixty at the turn of the century. A slight decline in other causes contributed to a total decline by the late 1920s and 1930s of 20 to 30 percent over the earlier rates.[35]

Yet the loss of children in mining communities was still greater than in other communities. The Registrar General noted in his 1931 report that the death rates of infants in mining families in the nation as a whole showed 'a large excess over the class average'.[36] An examination of the infant mortality rates for Ashington and Bedlingtonshire, both mining communities in Northumberland, reveals this pattern. Although the rates of both declined by 18.6 and 18.5 percent respectively from 1923–5 to 1930–2 they remained, shockingly, around 37 percent higher than the national average and were still apt to spike.[37] The following table comparing the infant mortality rates of Ashington, the most concentrated of the mining communities in Northumberland, and England and Wales illustrates the pattern.

Table 2.1. Deaths of children under one year per one thousand births in Ashington compared to England and Wales, 1921–1939

	Ashington	England and Wales
1921	121	83
1922	116.3	77
1923	92.24	69
1924	115.3	75
1925	103.2	75
1926	81	70
1927	73.5	69
1928	79.9	65
1929	134.3	73
1930	82.23	60
1931	85.53	66
1932	80.79	65
1933	87.78	64
1934	73.5	59
1935	103.8	57
1936	77.65	59
1937	73.12	58
1938	73.34	53

Source: Annual Reports of the Medical Officer of Health for Ashington, Wansbeck Environmental Health Office.

---

[35] Annual Reports of the Medical Officer of Health for Northumberland, 1920–39, NRO 3897/1–8.
[36] *Registrar-General's Decennial Supplement, England and Wales, 1931, Part IIa Occupational Mortality* (London, 1938), p. 169.
[37] Supple, *The History of the British Coal Industry*, p. 472, Table 10.4.

As the death rate from filth and diseases declined, medical officers of health began to pay more attention to the high death rates from prematurity and developmental causes in general. Medical officials focused upon the poor health of mothers as a cause of the high rates of prematurity. We have already noted evidence showing the poorer than average health of mining women. It reveals women to have mortality and morbidity rates 34 percent higher than the average woman and even higher than those of their husbands.[38] Local evidence supports the conclusion of poor health. The Medical Officer of Health for Bedlingtonshire for instance in 1923 noted seeing 'anaemia written on the faces of mothers'.[39] As we have already suggested, one reason may have been that women were weakened by frequent pregnancies. That seemed to be the conclusion of the letters sent to Margaret Llewelyn Davis.[40] As before, medical officers of health pointed to the poor nutrition of women, which deteriorated in the depression. It remained typical for women to give the bulk of the food to their husbands who, given the physical nature of their jobs, were thought to require protein. Wives then fed the children and, after that, ate the scraps that were left. It was no coincidence that medical officers still complained that wives subsisted on tea and toast. Such inequity was particularly harmful if wives were pregnant or nursing, as was frequently the case.

Domestic burdens, as before, defined the lives of women though they lessened somewhat in this period. Men still worked in shifts. Respondents noted that all women got up with their husbands regardless of the time the men started or finished work. Cissie Charlton, in her memoir, recalled her mother cooking leek puddings at 2 a.m. and, alternatively, when her husband was on a different shift, getting up at 4 a.m. to make a full meal for her husband beginning his shift at 6 a.m.[41] Wives still had to feed and take care of children on a totally different schedule. One medical officer of health noted how mothers were 'subject to the life of constant labour with irregularity in the hours of rest and sleep as a result of the different shifts among mine workers'.[42] The progress of the Maternity and Child Welfare centres in the 1920s indicates the women's crowded schedule. Although these institutions were much needed, they were well attended only in the six-month period in 1926 when the miners were locked out of work and the women were free of the burdens of caring for men on shifts.[43]

---

[38] *Registrar-General's Decennial Supplement, England and Wales, 1931, Part IIa Occupational Mortality*, p. 169 and Table IVc. These patterns persisted into the 1970s. See John Fox and Peter Goldblat, *Longitudinal Study: Socio-demographic Mortality Differentials* (London, 1982).

[39] Annual Report of the Medical Officer for Health for Bedlingtonshire, 1923, Wansbeck Environmental Health Office.

[40] See Chapter 1, p. 00.

[41] Charlton, *Cissie*, p. 39.

[42] Annual Report of the Medical Officer of Health for Bedlingtonshire, 1926, Wansbeck Environmental Health Office.

[43] *The Morpeth Herald*, 17 September 1926.

The establishment of pit-head baths, made possible by the Mines Act of 1920, did constitute a major improvement for miners' wives by ending the need for the filth of the pit to be washed off in the crowded colliery houses. When they became available, no longer did wives have to prepare the tin bath in front of the fire, 'dad' the pit clothes, clean the boots and deal with the coal dust that was dragged into the house. All these tasks were done at the pit head and the worker could come home clean and in his regular clothes. Yet, while they revolutionised the wives' lives, pit-head baths were by no means standard in Northumberland until after the end of the Second World War. One cause of the delay was the disagreement over payment, miners expecting owners to pay for the baths out of royalties and owners asserting that the money should come out of the Welfare funds set up by the Mines Act of 1920 to provide welfare and social facilities for mining communities.[44] As Davison, historian of the Northumberland miners, notes, out of a total of forty pit-head baths which had been installed in British collieries as a whole by 1930, seven were in Northumberland. The depression and then the war slowed down the construction of baths so that it was not until the nationalisation of the coal mines in 1947 that all the collieries in Northumberland were provided with pit-head baths.[45] Even when they were established, many of the older men refused to use the new facilities, preferring the traditional routine of bathing in the tin bath in front of the fire. Their wives remained burdened with not only cleaning up the dirt that came from the pit but lifting the heavy tubs of water for their husbands' baths.

Whether or not pit-head baths were available, the same old rigorous regime of house cleaning prevailed.[46] Oral evidence from the inter-war period and medical officer of health reports for Northumberland provide insight into the imposition of this regime by mining women's own system of approval and disapproval. Respondents noted how tasks were still performed according to a strict schedule which all but the few 'mucky' (dirty) women followed in unison and, as in the prewar period, comments of the medical officers of health attest to the standards of cleanliness. As before, each day of the week brought its own particular tasks. Monday was washing day, as onerous as ever, involving the laborious task of 'possing' the clothes. Wednesday was still baking day, when wives baked bread, scones, cakes and pies, and Friday was still 'turning out day' on which everything was scrubbed. As Williamson recounts, 'the flat irons and fender were polished with Brasso, the big brass line and the hearth whitened with a brush ... it was sparkling when finished. The furniture was polished with a wash leather, washed in vinegar and water, and clean covers put on'.[47] Saturday was, as before, consumed with prepa-

[44] Supple, *The History of the British Coal Industry*, p. 474.
[45] Davison, *Northumberland Miners*, pp. 244–9.
[46] For the emphasis on cleanliness among working-class women, see Jane Lewis, 'The working-class wife and mother and state intervention, 1870–1918' in Jane Lewis, ed., *Labour and Love: Women's Experience of Home and Family, 1850–1940* (Oxford, 1986), pp. 99–120.
[47] Williamson, *Class, Culture and Community*, p. 123.

rations for the big day: Sunday. The wives' tasks involved a fresh batch of baking and preparations for the large Sunday dinner; in addition, the best mats, fenders and fire irons were taken out to replace the everyday ones. The family consumed the sumptuous three-course meal, the high point of Sunday, as before, in a shining and spotless house.

The pressure to keep up standards had many positive elements. Echoing the sentiments of one of his predecessors, the Medical Officer of Health for Wheetslade said they allowed the miner's wife to turn 'a hovel into a little palace'.[48] It also compensated in part for the sanitary deficiencies, the all-pervasive dust and soot. Speaking of his grandmother, Williamson notes how important such standards were:

> My grandmother found that self respect in her diligent housework and the visible signs of that – the bright windows, the sanded steps, the line of white washing, the well turned out kids – each a simple yet powerful symbol of a powerful dignity which much in her environment threatened to destroy; and each amply compensating in its symbolic force for the deficiencies of its material worth.[49]

Yet, the regime could be overwhelming. Cissie Charlton recounts her mother's insistence on maintaining the standards even in the face of her increasing weakness and the strain they placed on her as the eldest child.[50] The regime moreover embodied a measure of competitiveness and was harsh to those who did not conform. Respondents talked of 'mucky families' being 'looked down upon'.[51] Yet, as in the prewar period, it did allow women to encourage each other to maintain order.

As before, neighbourliness was as central a component of the identity of mining women as camaraderie and solidarity were of men. Both Williamson and Carr, the wife of a miner, note that an important part of the role of women was to maintain the links between neighbours.[52] Indeed their reputation depended upon that characteristic. Williamson quotes a respondent who relates how people used to knock on the walls to see if their neighbours were all right.[53] Furthermore, interviewees, stressing how welcoming neighbours were, never failed to note how doors in mining communities were never locked, signifying availability, and how their mothers and grandmothers, as in the earlier period, helped neighbours out in times of need and, in turn, were helped out. Adeline Hodges talks of her mother baking and doing laundry for neighbours who were ill 'to put them over'.[54] Women still helped each other by laying out the dead and aiding in confinements. The popular saying that,

---

[48] Quoted in *The Morpeth Herald*, 8th September 1932.
[49] Williamson, *Class, Culture and Community*, p. 126.
[50] Charlton, *Cissie*, p. 40.
[51] Interview by author, Mrs R. 7 June 1995.
[52] Giselda Carr, *Pit Women: Coal Communities in Northern England in the Early Twentieth Century* (London, 2001), Ch. 9.
[53] Williamson, *Class, Culture and Community*, p. 137.
[54] Hodges, 'Up the Ladder'.

Figure 2.1. Mrs Molly Miles and neighbours getting the rags ready to begin
making a 'proggy' mat. Note the presence of the child. Illustrates the sense of
community between mining women which is usually overlooked, the emphasis
being put upon the camaraderie of the men.
Ashington, late 1930s

in times of trouble, people could depend on 'God and good neighbours'[55]
reflected their importance. As before, most women, lacking a social centre
equivalent to that of the men who gathered in the working men's club, met
informally. Usually this took place over the washing lines or at the water
tap. They still gathered in each other's homes, with their children in tow, to
make 'hooky' and 'proggy' rugs, these evenings made more agreeable by
pots of tea and home-made toffee (Figure 2.1). According to respondents,
rarely would a woman be without a frame set up in her home and, when a
neighbour dropped in, a cup of tea would be accompanied by a short stint at
the mat. The communal ties of women were nowhere as apparent as in election time. As we shall see, once women were nominated to fill town-council
seats, the women of the communities often voted as a block, ensuring that
their candidate would top the poll.[56]

Such close relations between women did not preclude occasional conflict,
any more than it did between miners. Newspapers occasionally reported fights
between neighbours, usually over children or over laundry which had been
fouled by children playing with balls. Sometimes these conflicts occurred

[55] Charlton, *Cissie*, p. 22.
[56] Interview by author, Mrs T. 23 June 1998.

between women, the result being a vicious fist fight in which husbands got involved and appearances in court by the parties. Interviewees explained such events by insisting that they were caused by the minority of 'rough families' in the mining community, perhaps those same families who did not follow the prescribed standards of cleanliness. These occasional fissures do not negate the conclusion that a strong sense of community existed among the women.

Despite the lack of social amenities for married women, for single women the inter-war years brought an improvement. Before the First World War, women had been excluded from the intellectual organisations, such as the literary and debating societies which were popular in mining communities, especially Ashington. In the inter-war period a few women, usually relatives of male members, joined these organisations, though never in large numbers. More young women, especially those involved in politics, were attracted to the new, more egalitarian debating societies, which catered to women. The Workers Education Association also loomed large among left-leaning women. As before the war, the Independent Labour Party offered many social events for young people.

Less intellectual young women also saw improvements in their leisure options. The larger mining communities shared in the great increase in commercial leisure which was apparent in the nation as a whole.[57] Despite the economic problems that emerged in the coal industry as early as the 1920s, cinemas and dance halls proliferated and drew young people from surrounding smaller communities. Given the straitened circumstances of families, it is curious that young women should be able to participate in these opportunities. It is probable that, as Marjory Rice suggests, mothers indulged girls with spending money to the extent that was possible.[58] Alternatively, young men who received more spending money than girls may have shouldered the cost of entrance fees. The facilities provided by the Miners' Welfare Fund, created by the Mining Industry Act of 1920, also offered some new opportunities, such as tennis. Parks helped more, providing clean places for children to play.

The church and chapel continued to consume the lives of some women. They taught in Sunday Schools, ran the Women's Home meetings and sang in the choir. They still organised teas, sales of work, bazaars, garden parties and other events which not only raised money but provided social events for the whole community. Chapel anniversaries were especially popular, even among families who were not avid chapel goers. So too were the Sunday evening concerts at the commodious Central Hall which was built in Ashington in 1925. While fundraising was more difficult in the hard economic circum-

---

[57] For a discussion of the general commercialisation of young people's leisure, see Selina Todd, *Young Women, Work, and Family in England 1918–1950* (Oxford, 2005), Ch. 7.

[58] Marjory Spring Rice, *Working-class Wives: Their Health and Conditions*, 2nd edn (London, 1981), p. 105.

stances of the 1920s and 30s, we still read of the Women's Auxiliary raising £52 for mission work in 1923–4. These activities provided leadership opportunities for religious women. More women by this time had been appointed class leaders and, by 1934, the Ashington Primitive Methodist Circuit had two female lay preachers.[59]

Within households patriarchy was the order of the day. Oral evidence suggests that wives for the most part deferred to their husbands. One respondent was adamant that men were 'the boss'.[60] Several others said that wives did as their husbands said and that some had to ask their husbands' permission to leave the house. The persisting tradition of the 'keepie back' indicates that many men continued to assert their authority over their wages. An indication of this is that some wives of drinkers had to go to the working-men's club to get their housekeeping money from their husbands before it was all spent on alcohol or gambling. In this period, as in the previous, court records reveal instances of husbands 'bashing their wives',[61] often when drunk. Wives would frequently go home to live with their mothers. At times, wives would fight back by throwing dishes and pots at their husbands. It is probable that the frequency of violence was greater than is suggested by the court records, women being likely to keep quiet about such events and, as Janet Lambertz has noted, resigned to them.[62] One interviewee was explicit about the number of women with 'bonnie faces', the result of 'bashings', and about the fact that the women would never refer to them.[63]

The evidence of gender oppression in the form of service is clear. While not unique to mining women, oppression was ritualised in their case. The oral history of the inter-war period tells us that women felt they had to anticipate their husbands' needs, even to the point of knowing when they wanted another cup of tea. Like other working-class wives, respondents attest to the fact that wives would forego food to make sure their husbands were well fed.[64] One interviewee from Newbiggin-by-the-Sea, Northumberland, recounted the advice given to her by her mother: 'You have to look after the lads for the terrible work that they do.'[65] Jack Lawson recalls how his mother's treatment of him changed as soon as he entered the pit at the age of fourteen. 'From that day', he states, 'his previously dominating mother deferred to him'.[66] Like the other men he got all the meat he wanted. An astute commentator referred to the 'divine right'[67] of men in mining communities who just sat and waited for their every need not only to be fulfilled,

[59]   Ashington Primitive Methodist Circuit book, NRO M3/16.
[60]   Interview by author, Mrs M. 7 June 1997.
[61]   Interview by author, Mrs H. 23 June 1998.
[62]   Janet Lambertz, 'The politics and economics of family violence from the late nineteenth century to 1948' (MPhil thesis, Manchester University,1984), p. 77.
[63]   Interview by author, Mrs T. 6 September 1997.
[64]   Interview by author, 'Over Sixties Club' of the Holy Sepulchre Church, Ashington, 5 April 1994.
[65]   Interview by author, Mrs J. 6 August 1997.
[66]   Jack Lawson, A Man's Life (London, 1944), p. 46.
[67]   Interview by author, Mrs M.T. 7 August 1998.

but to be anticipated. Interviewees were unanimous in stating that women 'waited on the men hand and foot'. Unfortunately, we do not have evidence of whether such service extended to the area of sexual relations, though that would explain the frequent pregnancies.

An important factor in making miners' expectations exceed those of other workers was the nature of their work: the peculiarly hard and dangerous nature of pit work; the sense of class oppression created by such work; and the constant struggle to receive fair remuneration under the piece-rate method of payment. Being treated 'like kings' when they came home fulfilled an almost childlike need for nurture, born of the danger and hardship that they faced.[68] At the same time, it gave them a sense of power that compensated for their work experience and fitted into the cult of masculinity which was bred from the arduousness and danger of their work and fostered by the camaraderie of mates in the pub, the club and the sporting field.

Yet it is still difficult to see mining women as mere victims. Relationships were complex. Oral evidence suggests that men admired women for their domestic skills, regarding them as hard working and frequently commenting that they 'had the thick end of the stick'. Home was a kind of haven for the men used to the terrible conditions underground, and they appreciated the women for their relentless efforts. Also, as Joanna Burke has pointed out of working women generally, their meticulous housekeeping and careful management of resources gave them status.[69] Further, their skills made them indispensable and rendered men totally dependent on them. Women made the home a centre of power for themselves, where they reigned supreme and where their husbands could not challenge them. This idea fits in with some evidence from the 1850s. John R. Liefchild, commissioned by the Mines Act of 1842 to examine the coal mines, wrote that women in some mining households 'were almost sure to rule in any case' when a decision was made and that, if there was any business to transact, 'she must either superintend or do it herself'.[70] This evidence and Burke's statements are difficult to reconcile with the assertion that men were the 'boss'. It may be that, though men had ultimate control, in families where men 'tipped it up' women did have such authority. Also many men, exhausted after a day's work, were probably relieved to leave most decisions to their wives.

The importance of the wife and mother at home cannot be overemphasised. Men felt incapable of living on their own and, if widowed, usually moved in with their sisters. Some obviously remarried but the skewed sex ratio made that difficult for men. Observers such as Bill Williamson, who grew up in a

---

[68] For the demands of workers in general, see Pat Ayers and Jan Lamberts, 'Marriage relations, money and domestic violence in working-class Liverpool, 1919–1939' in Lewis, ed., *Labour and Love*, pp. 195–219.

[69] Joanna Bourke, *Working-Class Cultures in Britain, 1890–1960: Gender, Class and Ethnicity* (London, 1994), Ch. 3.

[70] John R. Liefchild, *Our Coal and Our Coal Pits. The People in Them and the Scenes Around Them* (London, n.d.), p. 219.

mining community in Northumberland, commented on the importance of the women in the household in writing of the 'nostalgic mother-centred family image of the past'.[71] His comments fit with the evidence that Jane Humphries has garnered from her study of the autobiographies of working men, which, without exception, reveal great attachment to their mothers.[72] The reports by respondents that many women, except for making short visits to neighbours, never left the house, and never took off their pinnies (aprons), attests to their constant presence. Linda McCullough-Thew reinforces this idea by her observation that a house without the presence of the woman was always regarded as 'empty', regardless of who else might be there.[73]

As in the previous period, then, the domestic role of the women remained predominant but, as we have seen, they were no ordinary housewives. It was common to hear it said that 'they lived for their work'. Their polished brasses, brightly coloured rugs, embroidered doilies and the ritual of the Sunday dinner were just a few of the elements which added grace to the otherwise grimy mining communities. In the prewar period, the domestic role of some had been blended with a political role. The inter-war period saw that trend continue and indeed become stronger as economic and political stresses beset the mining community in Northumberland, as elsewhere.

The growing centrality of a political role

It is no exaggeration to say that in the inter-war period mining women in Northumberland, as elsewhere in the nation, took on a greater role in politics than virtually any other group of working-class women. For some, political action superseded their domestic responsibilities. These women, like their predecessors – though in greater numbers – operated in the public sphere, in contrast to the majority of miners' wives who remained largely in the domestic sphere. We see therefore an example of the private/public divide, made all the more unique by the fact that it operated within one group of women. Major factors in the increase in activists were the enfranchisement of women, the increase in strength of the Labour Party after the end of the First World War and the establishment of women's sections of that Party. As before, that political action had a distinctly feminist tone and, while conducted in the public sphere, had many connections to the domestic sphere. The efforts of these political women had their basis in the earlier efforts to fight for improvements in the health of women and children, maternity benefits and pit-head baths. The war itself further politicised women and allowed them to develop new skills. Throughout the four years, women organised relief for widows and women whose husbands were at the front. As was the case elsewhere, women

---

71   Williamson, *Class, Culture and Community*, p. 119.
72   Jane Humphries, *Childhood and Child Labour in the British Industrial Revolution* (Cambridge, 2010), pp. 137–150.
73   Linda McCullough-Thew, *A Tune for Bears to Dance To: A Childhood* (Newcastle upon Tyne, 1992), p. 156.

provided relief for families of men injured or killed, raised money by bake sales and teas for which they charged a small entrance fee, and knitted socks and sewed various other items for the war effort. One community sewed or knitted just short of one thousand articles of clothing for the troops in the first few months of fighting alone.[74] A prominent politician said in 1918, 'We would have gone under but for the women.'[75]

The end of the war brought further crises which raised the political consciousness of women. One was the industrial strife that began as the industry went into decline. The most serious event was a six-month lock-out in 1926 occasioned by the miners' refusal to accept a 40 percent reduction in wages. Women threw themselves into the fight. The role of the activists was to help feed and clothe the miners' families and their efforts were unremitting. The women ran the child-welfare centres, distributing items from a national fund organised in London by the Women's Committee for the Relief of Miners' Wives and Children.[76] Some of the most significant of the items were boots for children. One respondent remembers accompanying her mother to people's houses asking their needs and returning with clothing and boots.[77] Sally Johnson, a Northumberland miner's wife – who was to become a major political figure in the county – together with five other mining women and ten miners, formed a deputation which went to the Soviet Union during the lock-out to raise money for relief. For average miners' wives, the six-month period meant a daily struggle to feed their families. Soup kitchens, run by the working-men's clubs, and credit given by the Cooperative Wholesale kept them going. In order to gain coal to keep fires burning some wives, along with their husbands, stole coal from the pit heaps.

A much larger group of women resorted to the riotous behaviour so common in the nineteenth century, thus temporarily taking on a political role. Their chief target was strikebreakers. Believing in the morality of their cause, they joined with their men in threatening the strikebreakers, trying to prevent their working. At one point early in the strike, women were heard shouting, 'Kill the blackleg.'[78] A few weeks later, a group of pitmen and their wives 'threw missiles and used foul language' at a group of strikebreakers near Annitsford; shocking in the case of the women.[79] At the end of the lock-out, when a few of the regular miners began to drift back to work, feelings had reached fever pitch. Women in Ashington routinely lined the road as these men walked to the pit, haranguing them and banging pot lids. In November a menacing crowd of two thousand, many of them women, followed strikebreakers home

---

[74] *The Morpeth Herald*, 1 January 1915.

[75] Ibid., 8 February 1918.

[76] *The Labour Woman: A Monthly Paper for Women*, May–December 1926, January–March, 1927 and *The Morpeth Herald*, 18 March 1927.

[77] Interview by author, Mrs Q. 30 June 1999.

[78] *The Morpeth Herald*, 18 June 1926.

[79] Ian Turner, 'A spot of bother: Civil disorder in the north east between the wars', *Bulletin of the North East Labour History Society* 18 (1984), pp. 40–7.

while another crowd formed across a road to prevent a busload of strike-breakers from gaining access to the pits. The women were said to be urging the men on. They did not resort to violence because strikebreakers were better protected by the police than they had been in the previous century. Several women however were charged with 'doing an act likely to cause disaffection and using language calculated to stop certain workmen from following their employment'.[80] One woman, the leader of a group, picked up a stone and followed a strikebreaker to his house threatening to 'knock his head off'.[81] She was bound over by the court to be on good behaviour for six months. *The Morpeth Herald* depicted her and her fellow rioters as 'uncouth and unfeminine'.[82] The end of the strike that same month brought the resumption of peace in the mining districts of the county, as in other counties. While this was to be the last strike of the period, the activities of the rioters, women included, when added to the derailment of a train by miners at Choppington, had raised fear of social disorder.

Dramatic though they were, these activities were limited to the year 1926; the main political actions of the women in the inter-war period were peaceful and took place under the auspices of women's organisations: the Women's Co-operative Guild and Women's Sections of the Labour Party which had taken over from the Women's Labour League after women got the vote in 1918. Indeed with the winning of the vote, the political activities of women became much more extensive than they had been in the prewar period, such that politics became the centre of some women's lives. Some Guild members, who had legitimised their public role in the prewar period and had worked through the war to bring relief to the needy, exemplified this situation. As before, they brought a message of feminism which stressed the health and welfare of working-class women and children. By 1921, 531 Guild women in Northumberland were grouped into eleven branches, representing a small but significant core of politically active women in mining communities. A respectable number of them were Guardians. They were also the first women to be co-opted onto the Maternity and Child Committees, formed after the passage of the Maternity and Child Welfare Act of 1918. The organisation still strove to educate women on public policy and 'bring them out', holding weekend schools for that purpose.[83]

The prominence of the Labour Party after the war and the establishment of women's sections of that party meant however that it increasingly became the main focus of women's attentions, though at times membership of the party overlapped with membership of the Guild. The Labour Party was an obvious choice for political mining women. To begin with, mining members of Parliament were the backbone of the Labour Party throughout the inter-

---

[80] *The Morpeth Herald*, 5 November 1926.
[81] Ibid.
[82] Ibid.
[83] Annual Reports of the Women's Co-operative Guild, 1920–30, The Co-operative College, Manchester.

war years and beyond. Also, the party was committed to the nationalisation of the coal mines and other industries and, largely because of the efforts of the women's organisations, to the improvement of living and working conditions and health of the working class. Further, the Labour Party had supported the enfranchisement of women, if somewhat belatedly. By the mid 1920s, eighty Women's Sections of the Labour Party were in existence in Northumberland. Those in Bedlington and Ashington, the largest of the mining communities, averaged ninety members throughout the inter-war period. Membership in Ashington rose to 496 after the lock-out of 1926 before settling back down to a smaller number.[84] Out of the ninety members in the large communities, about thirty would be really active while two or three of these would be the leaders.[85]

Given the domestic burdens faced by mining women and the demands imposed by men, it is relevant to ask who these activists were and how they were able to pursue their political activities in a culture which stressed that women belonged in the house. While activists took pride in their domestic abilities, they rejected the rigorous housekeeping standards of most women and risked criticism. Paved roads, piped-in water and pit-head baths did eventually make conditions better, but these improvements did not materialise until almost the end of the 1930s and did not entirely mitigate the filth of the atmosphere. As Margaret Gibb, Labour Party Organiser for the North East, noted, political women had to be willing to rearrange their domestic schedule completely.[86] They often needed help and enlisted the aid of daughters, as one of my interviewees noted. She said, 'I had to do the cooking and the washing when my mother went to political meetings.'[87] Some women waited until their children were independent while others received help from their mothers in caring for young children. A key factor in women becoming politically active was the number of children they had. Although some activists in the 1920s had large families, this group of women appears to have been among the first to limit their family size to two or three children.[88] Such action required the cooperation of husbands – easier to achieve in the depressed conditions of the 1930s. The political activity of wives however required the cooperation of husbands generally. Male activists supported their efforts but so did some other men, so sacrosanct was the cause of Labour, particularly in the aftermath of the lock-out of 1926.[89] Some interviewees asserted how cooperative their husbands were, even though they were not involved in politics. One respondent noted, appreciatively, that her husband raised no objections to her

---

[84] Northumberland Labour Women's Advisory Council Committee Books, NRO 4415/1/1–2; Northumberland Labour Women's Conference Book, NRO 4415/7.

[85] Issues of *The Labour Woman*, 1920–1939.

[86] Margaret Gibb, 'Labour in the North East between the Wars', Margaret Gibb Papers, NRO 2973/4.

[87] Interview by author, Mrs Q. 7 June 1998.

[88] Ibid.; Also, Pamela Graves, *Labour Women: Women in British Working-Class Politics 1918–1939* (Cambridge, 1994), p. 66.

[89] This was true of Chester Armstrong – see his *Pilgrimage from Nanthead* (London, 1938).

using his money for her political expenses as a member of both the Guild and the Women's Section of the Labour Party.[90] A few men had self-serving reasons for tolerating their wives' frequent absences. One activist recalled how her husband made her political work an excuse to spend time at the working-men's club.[91]

But to become an activist also demanded creating a new self-image, much like the women of the Guild and the WLL had done before the First World War. It meant becoming assertive in a male-dominated society that was often unfavourable to the intrusion of women. It was no accident that only a few women chose this path. Many of them appear to have been influenced by family tradition.[92] Some had mothers who had been active in the women's organisations before and during the war. Indeed, some of these mothers were still active, though now quite old. Others had mothers who were active in the Methodist Chapel, while others had fathers who were prominent in labour organisations such as the trade union, the Labour Party itself, the Permanent Relief Fund and the Wholesale Cooperative Society. One noted how her family 'ate, drank and slept politics', the result of her father's involvement in the Labour Party.[93] Another recounted accompanying her father on his political work.[94] Some young women met their husbands through political activities and became political partners, while others' activist husbands encouraged them to become active. For yet others the crises in the mining communities, most notably the lock-out of 1926 and the depression of the 1930s, were catalysts for action. For two activists, the opportunity to 'get out of the house' was a further incentive.[95]

The first advances were made by members of the Guild. In the wake of the Maternity and Child Welfare Act of 1918, which was, in no small measure, a tribute to the work of the Guild and the Women's Labour League before the war, several of these women were asked to sit on the Maternity and Child Committees which developed from the Act. Such efforts helped improve the health of mothers and children in the inter-war period. With the formation of the Wholesale Co-operative Party in the early 1920s, one woman in Ashington won a seat on the Urban District Council in 1925.[96] Guild women also helped with relief during the six-month lock-out in 1926. Soon they began to win seats on the Board of Guardians in several of the largest communities in Northumberland, including Ashington, Bedlingtonshire and Newbiggin-by-the-Sea. While not the first women to sit on such boards, they were the first working-class women to do so. The Board of Guardians, being

---

90   Interview by author, Mrs C. 8 June 1997.
91   Interview by author, Mrs D. 7 June 1998.
92   Graves also makes this point. Graves, *Labour Women: Women in British Working-Class Politics*, p. 48.
93   Interview by author, Mrs T. 6.14 1998.
94   Interview by author, Mrs N. 6 May 1995.
95   Interview by author, Mrs N. 6 June 1995; interview by author, Mrs F. 5 July 1977.
96   *The Morpeth Herald* 23 July 1921, 20 November 1920, 22 April 1921, 10th April 1925.

responsible for welfare relief, was the scene of most of the first successes of women activists. For the entire inter-war period, Guild women lobbied tirelessly for issues regarding child and maternal health. In the 1930s, like Guild women elsewhere, they became a voice for peace.[97]

The greatest successes of mining women activists however lay in their work for the Labour Party. As historian Pamela Graves has noted of activist women in general, their contribution to the Labour Party was enormous.[98] In the case of Northumberland, they played a central role in the party's success in the parliamentary elections of 1923, 1928 and 1935 in the constituencies of Morpeth and Wansbeck. Furthermore, they were central to the election of Labour Party candidates to local councils and thus to the many improvements in housing and environmental conditions in the 1930s. The role of the Labour women was multifaceted. Most important was the ideological fervour that pervaded all their activities. One male town councillor described the Labour women as the 'most vital force' in the organisation.[99] They performed most of the essential services for the party, distributing party literature, canvassing, and overseeing the polls where, seemingly, 'the men talked and the women worked'.[100] According to Labour Party organiser Margaret Gibb, they regularly canvassed houses as far away as Newcastle upon Tyne, working in teams.[101] Two interviewees recounted how, if they failed to find an occupant of a house at home, they would tirelessly return to it and, on election day, would 'do anything to get people to the polls, even bathing babies and hanging out laundry'.[102] Robert Smillie, miners' leader, credited them for his success in winning the parliamentary seat for Morpeth, Northumberland, in 1928.[103]

Labour women's social and ceremonial activities were also of great value to the movement. As they had done in the prewar period, but now to a much greater degree, they organised frequent 'at homes', whist drives, home craft exhibitions, children's outings, and parties to raise money for the women's sections, the local party and a variety of causes. In so doing, they brought the Labour movement together, reinforcing its sense of purpose and keeping morale high. These contributions were crucial given the shocks of the period: the disastrous six-month lock-out of 1926; unemployment and then full-scale depression in the industry in the 1930s; the substitution of the National Government for the Labour government in 1931; the parliamentary defeat that same year in the constituency of Wansbeck which had been held by a

---

97 Jean Gaffin and David Thomas, *Caring and Sharing: The Centenary History of the Co-operative Women's Guild* (Manchester, 1983), pp. 109–13.
98 For roles of women generally, see Graves, *Labour Women: Women in British Working-Class Politics*, Ch. 6. For Ashington women, see *The Labour Woman*, January 1935. For mining women in the North East, Margaret Gibb, interview by author, 16 September 1980.
99 *The Morpeth Herald*, 18 December 1936.
100 Graves, *Labour Women: Women in British Working-Class Politics*, pp. 1–4 and Ch. 5.
101 Gibb interview, 6 August 1980.
102 Interview by author, Mrs M. 6 May 1988; interview by author, Mrs F. 6 August 1980.
103 *The Morpeth Herald*, 22 June 1928.

miner since 1885; and the humiliating Means Test imposed in 1931. The May Day marches and the women's yearly galas also fostered community. Led by brass bands, holding their banners aloft and decked in handsome hats, mining Labour women proudly proclaimed the cause of Labour and encouraged other women to join them. Such rituals kept resolve strong.

Yet Labour women's functions were not merely supportive: they exercised direct political power. Their first political successes came in 1927 when several were elected to the Morpeth Board of Guardians, joining their Guild colleagues. By the early 1930s, three of the seven Guardians from Ashington were women. Seats on the town councils came more slowly. Although from the early 1920s the Labour Party selected a handful of women to run for these positions, not until 1928 was one elected. Like Guild women, some Labour women were co-opted onto the Maternity and Child Committees of their local authorities. The experience and recognition gained through such work, together with the enfranchisement of women under twenty-eight in 1928, brought greater electoral success in the 1930s. After 1930, one or two women regularly sat on the town councils of the main mining towns, frequently topping the polls in elections. In 1937 one woman, Alice Johnson, was chosen to chair her town council. Another, Bella Horn, one of the most important of the Northumberland Labour women, was elected to the Northumberland County Council throughout the 1930s. These women and others sat as magistrates during the same period. By 1938, the Wansbeck Divisional Labour Party could count forty-two women on urban district councils and, in addition, one woman on the county council, twenty-five on rural district councils, two women aldermen and three out of twenty on the executive committee.[104]

These successes notwithstanding, the Labour men never accorded women an equal position in the party. Councillor William McLean, miners' leader and advocate of women's rights, complained that the all-important miners' trade unions, which were the backbone of the party, were 'not giving the necessary support to the women in our parties to secure for them places of advantage in the administrative machinery of the county'.[105] In a similar vein, Margaret Gibb noted that 'men were slow to give recognition to women',[106] while another interviewee noted that 'the men did everything in their power to make you feel you were not equal'.[107] Yet another remarked that 'men have been at the top for so long, you had to fight to show you were able to do the work'.[108] While nominating committees of the male-dominated local Labour parties selected women as candidates for local office, they kept women's numbers low. The exception was nominations for the Boards of Guardians

[104]   Wansbeck Division Labour Party Minute Book, NRO 527/A/13.
[105]   *The Morpeth Herald*, 18 December 1936.
[106]   Gibb interview, 6 August, 1980.
[107]   Interview by author, Mrs T. 23 June 1998.
[108]   Interview by author, Mrs F. 6 August 1998.

which, as the body determining relief in cases of poverty, was deemed suitable for women. In town-council elections, nominating committees sometimes bypassed women who had been successful and popular councillors, as was the case in Bedlingtonshire in 1934 and Ashington in 1937.[109] On these occasions, preference was given to inexperienced male trade-union officials. While one woman (Bella Horn) served on the finance committee of Ashington Urban District Council, the local party usually limited women to committees that dealt with health, housing and sanitation, areas in which women were thought to have particular expertise.[110] They were therefore never represented proportionately in official positions. Women made up about one-fifth of the executives at the divisional level of the party, but were given only token representation at the local level, where they were usually put in the position of secretary or treasurer.[111] Labour women were also often excluded from decision making.[112]

Political women did not accept such unequal treatment unquestioningly. Showing no deference whatsoever, the activists protested loudly at such unfairness – and at male dominance in general – and asserted their own importance in decidedly feminist terms, demonstrating considerable political skill in the process. One political interviewee explained how 'they refused to kowtow to men'.[113] When the party passed over Alice Johnson, an experienced councilwoman in Bedlingtonshire, as a Labour candidate for that council, she ran as an independent and not only won the seat, but also garnered the most votes. In Ashington, similar treatment toward veteran female councillor Sally Johnson prompted the women's section to withdraw its services from the polls at the next election.[114] As most of the work at the polls was done by women, this was a significant action. The women in the Parliamentary Division of Morpeth, of which Ashington was a part, then took advantage of the absence of men at a meeting to vote Sally Johnson chair of the Morpeth Divisional Labour Party, one of the most important political positions in the county. Labour women, moreover, often challenged men outright and complained loudly about being excluded. In speeches, they emphasised the equality of women, expressing confidence in a public role for women. When first elected to the Ashington Urban District Council, Horn made the following promise: 'I shall do all I can to make this town of ours into a garden.'[115] Several years later, she stressed the suitability of a public role for women: 'Women are more than child-bearing instruments. If given the opportunity, they could serve humanity usefully.'[116]

---

109 *The Morpeth Herald*, 2 March 1934, 2 January 1937.
110 Minutes of Ashington Urban District Council, NRO 1987/4.
111 Wansbeck Division Labour Party Minute Books, NRO 527/A/1–3.
112 Interview by author, Mrs E.T. 23 June 1998.
113 Ibid.
114 *The Morpeth Herald*, 30 April 1937.
115 Ibid., 26 September 1930.
116 Ibid., 16 March 1934.

Reinterpreting class in gender terms, Labour women consistently fought for working-class women's interests, especially those of mining women. They shared the municipal goals of the Labour Party which included building council houses, paving the streets, and cleaning up the polluted atmosphere. Like men, they protested loudly against the Means Test for unemployment benefits, instituted in 1931. Gender however shaped their class experience and their class experience shaped their feminism. Labour mining women, like other activist working-class women, in addition to fighting male predominance in office holding and struggling for socialist goals, also strove to right grievances specific to working-class women, especially women in mining communities: poorer than average health, greater than average fertility, and higher than average infant mortality.

While the problems of miners, particularly accidents in the mines, had been well documented, such female issues, with the exception of infant mortality, had received little attention. Labour and Guild women redressed that situation. They were strong advocates for child and maternal welfare, stressing the continuous improvement of the Maternity and Child clinics and the necessity of birth control, a contentious issue. The subject was anathema to many people, especially religious people, who saw it as a form of abortion. Further, many men were opposed to it and prevented their wives from using it.[117] Bella Horn was however successful in getting a clinic established in Ashington in 1933, the first one in the area. She also lobbied the town council for money for birth control devices.[118] Labour women, along with other volunteers, raised money for and helped staff this clinic and even discussed voluntary sterilisation. Evidence from Northumberland therefore does not support Pamela Graves' suggestion that Labour women in general de-emphasised gender issues in the 1930s.[119] Throughout the decade, Labour women lobbied for family allowances, argued for a change in the Labour Party constitution to give women more power, and agitated for more female parliamentary candidates.[120] They were clearly feminists, aggressively forcing their way into public life, all the while working on class issues such as the progress of the Labour Party and its programme of public ownership. As in the prewar period, they did not share all of the middle-class 'first wave' feminists' aims which, with the exception of the 'new feminists' such as Eleanor Rathbone, focused on middle-class issues such as ending the marriage bar on working, legal equality and equal employment opportunities.[121]

Several factors helped these Labour activists in Northumberland, as in other mining communities, in breaking out of the mould in such seemingly

---

117   Lewis, *Women in England*, p. 16.
118   *The Morpeth Herald*, 3 July 1931, 28 October 1932, 10 February 1933.
119   Graves, *Labour Women: Women in British Working-Class Politics*, Ch. 6.
120   Advisory Council Committee Book, NRO 4015/1/3; Advisory Council Conference Minute book, NRO 4415/7, NCO.
121   Lewis, *Women in England*, p. 103; Olive Banks, *Becoming a Feminist. The Social Origins of "First Wave" Feminism* (Athens, Georgia, 1987), p. 60.

Figure 2.2. Meeting of members of Women's Section of the Hartford Labour Party. Typical of political women's meetings of the 1920s and 30s. Illustrates the great sense of enthusiasm and unity among Labour women.
Hartford, c.1950

patriarchal societies. While the ideologies of guild feminism and socialism provided a rationale for action, more backing was needed. A further essential factor in their redefinition was the existence of a multilevel peer group, which gave moral and psychological support at the local, regional and national level. The Women's Co-operative Guild branches and the Women's Sections of the Labour Party provided this support locally. Lifelong bonds and relationships of mutual support and cooperation characterised both these groups and social events were important in solidifying such bonds between them (Figure 2.2). Women also worked in teams, sharing tasks and responsibilities, whether providing food for social events, canvassing, or working at the polls. Their processions, replete with brass bands and banners, were not only statements of support for Labour's cause, but also celebrations of these bonds of friendship and common purpose. This solidarity matched the legendary solidarity of miners and gave agency to mining women, as it did to miners.

Widening this relationship among political women and setting the stage for action were the regional and nationwide networks of Guild and Labour women. Through conferences and publications these organisations reinforced political women's self-image, cemented the group, and provided necessary fervour and confidence. Delegates to conferences came back well armed with all they had learned. Between conferences, monthly publications from the national organisation kept the commitment and group sense alive. Each month's edition of *The Labour Woman*, edited for most of the period by Marion Phillips, the Chief Woman Officer in the party, laid out the progress of the sections and councils, recent electoral achievements, and future goals. Practical advice sometimes followed. In December 1923, for example, the editor admonished activists to devote their time to canvassing work rather than having 'their brasses polished and floors scrubbed and everything spic and span'.[122]

Both Labour and Guild women were also unremitting in their efforts to gain training and confidence. Day schools, weekend schools and week-long summer schools were an important source of education on public policy. Women went to great lengths to attend them, sharing knowledge with their peers.[123] The summer schools, starting in 1925 and held in Yorkshire, offered the additional opportunity to get away from the domestic scene. The location, together with the social events in the evenings that provided 'the best fun in their lives' both widened and deepened women's relationships.[124] Classes in public speaking and in organising public meetings were an important part of the apprenticeship, as they had been for prewar women in the Guild and the Women's Labour League. Women reportedly took great pride in following proper procedures in meetings. At a more informal level women leaders functioned as mentors for younger members, allowing them to overcome their inexperience and lack of confidence by 'bringing them on'. One interviewee, who had not come from a political family, noted that she 'became right cheeky', under such guidance and became proficient at giving reports on policy issues.[125] The effect of these efforts is clear. At the weekend schools in the early 1920s it was generally the men who spoke on public policy. Soon however there were as many women speakers as men and, by the mid 1930s, women were lecturing not only on domestic policy but also on finance and even foreign policy. *The Labour Woman* made a particular note of the skill of the Ashington women in these areas.[126]

In privileging a public rather than a private life, these activists defined a new role for women in mining communities. Their predecessors in the Guild, the Women's Labour League and the Independent Labour Party had started that process before the First World War, but they had been limited in their actions by their lack of the franchise. The activists of the inter-war years were very conscious of their opportunities and their achievements. One said simply 'we had a push about us'.[127] They were extremely assertive and self-confident and clearly saw themselves as the backbone of the Labour Party. Yet they did not lose the connection with their roots in the mining community or as part of the female group. They saw their roles as perfectly natural, as did their counterparts in other working-class communities: extending women's care for their homes to the community and, as Bella Horn said, 'making it a

---

122 *The Labour Woman*, December 1923.
123 Gibb,'Labour in the Northeast between the Wars'.
124 Interview by author, Mrs F. 6 August 1977.
125 Interview by author, Mrs O. 6 May 1998.
126 *The Labour Woman*, February 1935.
127 Interview by author, Mrs Q. 6 August 1998.

garden'. Those on the town councils of Northumberland and on the county council worked tirelessly to hasten the improvement of the environment through the adoption of the available legislation and, in addition to many other issues, the mitigation of the effects of the Means Test. Although they refused to make housework the centre of their existence, urging their fellow workers to leave their brasses unpolished, political women took pride in using their domestic skills to organise social events and raise money. And average mining women, while regarding the activists as somewhat odd, nonetheless admired them and, persuaded by the activists' fervour and their assiduous campaigning, provided the bulk of their electoral support, further indicating the existence of a female community. After all, the women politicians took their message right into the homes of the electors and even helped hang out the washing and bathe the babies. One activist interviewee remarked 'they put us in' (office),[128] the general belief being that men did not vote for female candidates.[129] With some exceptions, even political men were ambivalent about women's roles in the party. They were glad of their help but unwilling to give them their due. One interviewee described the men as being 'afraid of being overtaken'.[130]

Much has been said about miners being the backbone of the Labour Party in the inter-war years, but these female activists showed a diligence, commitment and fervour which outshone that of the miners, and this was true not only of mining women in Northumberland. *The Labour Woman*'s monthly reports indicate that miners' wives in other regions were also active in Labour's cause, as were working women in many communities. These women, like their prewar predecessors, continued to keep gender issues alive in an often inhospitable environment and make women-centred issues, such as child and maternal health, an important part of the Labour Party agenda. All their efforts came to fruition in the creation of the Welfare State after World War Two.[131]

Conclusion

The inter-war years therefore brought changes to the lives of the mining women. By the end of the 1930s, some of the burdens and hardships they had faced in the late nineteenth century and early twentieth century had been alleviated. Fertility and infant mortality had both declined though they were still higher than average. Mining women still had worse than average health, probably the result of more frequent pregnancies and poor nutrition on the part of a section of the population. At the same time, depression in the coal

---

128 Interview by author, Mrs T. 23 June 1998.
129 Interviews by author, Mrs F. 6 July 1980; Mrs N. 14 July 1995; Mrs L. 14 July 1998.
130 Interview by author, Mrs L. 15 July 1998.
131 Graves, *Labour Women: Women in British Working-Class Politics*, pp. 220–25.

industry had brought unemployment, short-time work and uncertainty. The continuities thus are just as apparent as the changes.

The role of mining women became more complex in the inter-war period. For most, it remained a domestic one defined by intensive homemaking and child-rearing along with a women-centred neighbourliness. At the same time, the political role obvious in the prewar period became more striking. The most obvious and consistent political activity of the women was that connected to formal political organisations. It created a marked public/private divide, made all the more extreme by the all-consuming domesticity of the majority of mining women and the political fervour of the activists. Clearly to the latter, politics were central. It could rightly be said that they 'were steeped in politics'. But politics did intrude at brief intervals into the lives of the domestic women. That the votes of average mining women allowed the political women to top the polls at times speaks to their involvement and to their confidence in their activist counterparts. They no longer regarded the political women as 'a queer lot' (the observation made by a political activist in the pre-World War One period).[132] Also the participation of so many in the agitation against strikebreakers in 1926 reveals a well-developed political consciousness. It echoed the nineteenth-century riotous actions in times of industrial strife. If reactive rather than proactive, it spoke to the deep sense of moral outrage in the mining community as coal owners passed on the problems of the industry to the miners in the form of wage decreases, and reinforced the argument in the ranks of Labour for ending private owner-ship in the coal industry. And mining women were fully conscious of the importance of this outcome. The wives of inshore fishing women, whom we will study next, though apt, like mining women, to react in riotous fashion to grievances, were generally much less politically conscious.

[132] See Chapter 1, p. 49.

PART II

WOMEN IN INSHORE FISHING COMMUNITIES

3

A Household Economy in the Modern Era

Inshore marine fishing had some similarities with coal mining but also many differences. Both were long-standing, dangerous, quintessentially male industries, but, whereas mining was a heavily capitalised industry with an all-male workforce, inshore fishing involved petty commodity production in a family based system that also involved women and children. Not to be confused with deep-sea fishing, it was conducted by small entrepreneurs operating their own boats – called cobles – and was a holdover from preindustrial times.[1] The exception to this was the heavily capitalised summer herring fishing industry, in which wives and young fisher girls were involved from the mid nineteenth century. While rarely far apart geographically, these coal mining and inshore fishing communities in terms of their environment could not have been more different: the mining communities set in a grimy, dusty environment over which loomed pit gear and slag heaps, the latter often burning; the fishing communities crouched around picturesque bays, the view that of white beaches, rocks, and charming small fishing vessels. The experience of inshore fisher women was as dictated as that of mining women by the industry in which their husbands worked. Like mining women, they were not allowed actually to participate in the craft, the men fulfilling the most skilled and dangerous part of the trade and gaining all the status. The typical pattern of women being denied access to machinery, in this case the fishing boat, was thus apparent. Yet unlike mining women, who had no part in the mining industry, fisher women were intimately involved in the fishing industry, in particular with line fishing. Indeed this activity, which was carried out between autumn and spring, and after the First World War year round, needed women's participation in order to be pursued, such that women's identity was more as fishwives than housewives. Marilyn Porter makes this same point in regard to Atlantic fisher families.[2] A further factor which differentiated them from mining women was political involvement. While they could be stirred to engage in the kind of 'rough music' common to mining women, fisher women took no part in formal political organisations, as mining women did. The only exception was the young, full-time fish

---

[1] For a discussion of the persistence of the household economy see Jane Humphries, '"Lurking in the wings": women in the historiography of the industrial revolution', *Business and Economic History* Second Series, 20 (1991), pp. 32–46.

[2] See Marilyn Porter, *Place and Persistence: the Lives of Newfoundland Women* (Avebury, 1993), pp. 16–18.

hawkers around Newcastle upon Tyne who participated in suffrage marches in 1912 and 1913.

To be a woman in fishing

To be a woman in inshore fishing meant not only being responsible for the normal domestic and maternal skills but also being adept at several tasks associated with the craft itself. The sexual division of work was therefore very different from that in mining in Northumberland. So too was the domestic role. The primary task of the fisher women was preparing bait and baiting the lines for line fishing which was conducted by the men on a daily basis in small cobles, several miles off the coast. The women performed the baiting in the houses, which were workplaces as well as dwellings. While the work might sound straightforward, it was anything but. The first part of this task involved gathering mussels or limpets for bait. At best, this task meant digging up mussels from the mussel beds beside the village where the mussels had been laid. At worst, the women walked miles to the cliffs, dug limpets off the rocks and walked home with them in baskets. In some communities, such as Newbiggin-by-the Sea , men or boys usually gathered the bait. Before the lines could be baited, the women or sometimes the men had to 'redd' the lines – clear them of old bait and pieces of fish from the day before.

Then the women had to 'skein' (shell) the mussels and limpets before baiting the lines. A Northumberland woman explains the process of shelling the mussels, when the weather was bad and the mussels and limpets frozen:

> we used to carry the pails in (of mussels) ... ye put your pokers in the fire, and ye used to push them in among the mussels to thaw them. And then you took each one, and ye took your knife, and ye opened your mussel, and scooped it out into a jar (the water in the jar fattened the mussel). Ye had a tray on your knee: and ye had all these to shell, and the limpets – ye did them with a spoon – ready for them (the fishermen) coming back from the sea. And that's when the work started, when ye had to start and bait – 1,200 heuks (hooks). Sometimes more.[3]

The women had to take care to ensure that the mussels came out of the shell whole, otherwise they would not stay on the hooks and no fish would be caught. A hook that was snagged – caught onto another hook – as the line was being shot at sea, could be wasteful of time and possibly dangerous.[4]

Another Northumberland fisher woman explains the process of baiting, which required considerable skill and experience and had to be done quickly:

---

[3]   Quoted in Katrina Porteous, *The Bonny Fisher Lad: Memoirs of the North Northumberland Fishing Community* (Seaham, 2003), p. 65, evidence of Mrs May Douglas.

[4]   Peter Frank, 'Women's work in the Yorkshire inshore fishing industry', *Oral History* 4, I (Spring 1976), pp. 57–72.

Figure 3.1. Older woman baiting lines while daughter is 'skeining' the mussels ready to be put on the lines. Illustrates the family nature of work and the importance of women to line fishing.
Newbiggin-by-the-Sea, c.1920

Baiting the lines had to be done very carefully but also quickly as the men would be waiting for them. When ye placed the mussel on the hook, no part of the hook could be left showing. Sometimes ye had to put two or three mussels on each hook if they were small. That meant it took ye twice as long to finish a line. It took as much as four hours to bait a line.[5]

Each line, of which there were two, had seven hundred hooks and the women had to be careful the line curled in such a way that it would unfurl properly and not snag. The process took seven to eight hours per day (Figure 3.1). If the husband had a bad catch he would blame it on his wife's baiting. One female respondent, interviewed in the late 1990s, remembers how the resulting anger would be 'terrible'.[6] A health hazard of the baiting was many cuts on the wife's fingers. The hours were long because, after the wife had finished baiting – usually around midnight – she would scrub out the kitchen to get rid of the pieces of mussels and limpets and, only then, go to bed.

The women also had to perform tasks which demanded considerable physical strength and endurance, reminding us of the physical burdens of mining women. At 4 or 5 a.m., sometimes even at 2 or 3 a.m., wives, with only a few hours' sleep accomplished, would help their husbands carry the fishing gear – which included baskets of coiled-up baited lines, and oilskins – to the boats which were drawn up on the beach. Once they had helped load the boats, the women would assist in pushing them on their wheels to the shore, putting their backs under the side of the boats and heaving, wading into the sea, often up to their waists until the boats were afloat and, in the process, soaking their long skirts. While the practice of women launching the boats had died out in the fishing communities of North Northumberland by the end of the nineteenth century, it continued in Newbiggin-by-the-Sea and probably in the south of the county until the end of line fishing in the 1950s. Speed in launching was of the essence because the men who got to the fishing ground first would get the best place and ensure themselves a good catch. The fishermen competed fiercely for a good place. Stories abound about families creeping out as silently as possible, often using flashlights, to avoid alerting their neighbours to their early start. The women started baiting again in a few hours, and getting their children ready for school. In the afternoons, after watching for the boats to return, they performed the task in reverse, helping haul the boats high above the watermark to ensure against damage from the waves (Figure 3.2). They then carried the fish up the beach, a particularly onerous task if the tide was out (Figure 3.3). One respondent who suffered from asthma said she had been unable to help launch the boat and had had to get her mother, who was particularly robust, to perform this task. No conces-

---

[5]   Interview by author Mrs R. 7 August 1998
[6]   Interview by author, Mrs R. 6 September 1998.

Figure 3.2. Fishwives helping pull in the boats; a laborious task undertaken daily after the men had finished fishing. Illustrates the importance of the women to inshore fishing and their need for physical strength.
Newbiggin-by-the-Sea, c. 1950

Figure 3.3. Fishwives carrying heavy boxes of fish up from the boats which have just landed. Another example of the contribution of the women to the fishing work and their need to be physically strong.
Newbiggin-by-the-Sea, c. 1950.

sion was made for sickness, which was considered weakness and, as in other industries, women worked until the last moment when pregnant.[7]

The hard work of assisting took precedence over every other responsibility, including care of children. In fact, all respondents agreed that the preparatory work for line fishing dominated the house. One woman interviewee noted that 'It was Work! Work! Work! Life was consumed with work and there was no time for leisure – O, they worked hard,' she said.[8] When the weather was bad and the fishermen were unable to go to sea, the lines had to be 'redded' again and baited again in the evening ready for the next day. As it was, winter evenings were always taken up with baiting, women not finishing the task until midnight. Looking back from the vantage point of the late twentieth century, respondents were vociferous in their condemnation of the fishing work, both men and women, using descriptions such as 'awful work', 'murder on women', and 'real slavery'. Women complained particularly about carrying boxes of fish and pushing the boats in and out while pregnant.[9] One interviewee, who gave birth to a badly deformed child, attributed his deformities to these tasks. It is interesting that, when line fishing ended in the 1950s, some fishermen said that men's concern for women had been the reason. By that time, men seemed to have developed an awareness of how bad the lot of women was, one fisherman saying how 'for the men at sea, it was a good job, as far as fishing jobs go, but for the ladies it could be hell on earth'.[10] Reflecting in the late twentieth century, another fisherman said: 'It's a good job it's finished.'[11] Yet other men said that line fishing stopped because the women would no longer tolerate it.[12] The reality was that line fishing was no longer viable. By that point the supply of white fish, the catch of line fishing, was being sorely depleted by both trawlers and seine fishing boats which, operating further out to sea, dragged the smaller fish from the ocean floor leaving few mature fish for the inshore fishermen who fished seven or eight miles from shore.

When it came to fish processing, women also had a direct economic role. In the herring season – the summer months up until the First World War, the off season for line fishing – and in a few communities after the war, such as Berwick upon Tweed, Seahouses, Beadnell and North Shields, they worked in the herring yards. Some worked for the coopers. The herring workers and those who worked for the coopers were employed directly by the fish merchants, becoming temporarily part of a capitalised industry. Their task was to gut, salt and pack the herring in barrels as quickly as possible so that they not spoil before transportation. Though not as physically hard as some of women's other tasks this job had its own set of difficulties, in particular

[7]   Ibid.
[8]   Interview by author, Mrs A. 6 August 1998.
[9]   Ibid.
[10] Quoted in Porteous, *The Bonny Fisher Lad*, p. 63.
[11] Tom Douglas, Recording NRO T/141 7 January 1978.
[12] Interview by author, Mr A. 6 May 1999.

Figure 3.4. Women packing herring in barrels for export; a common summer occupation, especially before the First World War. Illustrates the economic contribution of women to the family economy.
North Shields, date unspecified

the likelihood of hands getting cut and then stinging because of working with salt and brine. As a result, women had to work with their hands bandaged in cloths, or 'cloots', as they were called in Northumberland. The pace of work was fast and hours were long, usually twelve per day (Figure 3.4). Andrew Rutter, a fisherman from Seahouses and a local historian, notes how his mother told him that the women took their babies to the herring yards, wrapped them in woollen shawls and laid them in barrels that were stored on their sides. He also relates that, before the shoals of herring reached Northumberland, single women from Northumberland travelled north to Shetland to join the Scottish girls working their way down the coast, all the while lodging with local families.[13] After the shoals had passed Northumberland, the women continued from there south to Yorkshire, ending up in Yarmouth by early autumn. Others, who lived in Seahouses, Berwick-upon-Tweed and North Shields, were able to carry on working full-time with the herring, it being landed continuously in these ports from boats fishing far off-shore. They designated themselves as 'herring workers'[14] in the census returns, indi-

---

[13] Andrew Craig Rutter, *A Seahouses Saga* (Stockport, 1998), pp. 18–19.
[14] Census Returns for Seahouses, 1881, RG11/5127.

Figure 3.5. Fishwives, wearing their traditional costume, waiting at the shore for the boats to come in so that they can load up their creels and baskets and set off selling the fish. Another example of the economic contribution of women to the family.
Cullercoats, c.1900

cating an occupational identity which was absent in the daughters and wives who baited the lines.

Fishermen's wives and daughters made other cash contributions to the family. As in all coastal regions of the country, Northumberland women in the line-fishing months sold this fish in nearby towns and villages. While this activity was most prevalent up to the First World War, it continued until at least the end of the period under study, women still waiting at the shore for the boats to come in so that they could get their fish to sell (Figure 3.5). The quality of the newly caught fish ensured a ready market in the settlements within reach. Not only was the fish very fresh, having just been taken from the seas but, as line-caught fish, it lacked the bruising of net-caught fish.[15] It was also cheaper than that bought from the merchants. It is difficult to tell how many women hawked fish in nearby towns and villages. As we have discussed, the census returns were deficient in registering the part-time work of women.[16] In Newbiggin-by-the-Sea in 1901, for instance, only two women – widows – designated themselves as fish hawkers in the

[15] Ministry of Agriculture and Fisheries, Committee of Inquiry into the Fishing Industry PRO MAF 383/11 1958; James and Liz Taylor, *Harvests of Herring* (Frazerburgh, 1992), p. 82.
[16] For a discussion of the deficiencies of the census returns, see pp. 12–13.

Figure 3.6. Fishing girls in traditional dress sorting out fish to fill their baskets and creels, before leaving to sell it.
North Shields, c.1900

census returns, possibly because they worked on a full-time basis.[17] We find a few such widows in other communities.[18] We can assume from the remarks of respondents that non-widowed women also sold fish, though on a more part-time basis, devoting the rest of their time to the family fishing work. Regarding the latter as their occupation, they did not enter their hawking work in the census returns (Figure 3.6).[19] They formed part of the invisible workforce found in many occupations, in agriculture for example, as we shall see. The 'fish hawkers' on the other hand obviously were not involved in baiting lines, worked full-time in hawking and saw themselves as having an occupational identity. In Cullercoats, further down the coast, twenty-two women designated themselves as fish hawkers or fish workers in the 1901 census and only seven of these were widows.[20] They moved within a radius

[17] Census Returns for Newbiggin-by-the-Sea, 1901, RG13/4836.
[18] For example see Census Returns for Craster, 1901, RG13/4842.
[19] For the under-recording of women's employment in the census returns, see Edward Higgs, 'Women, occupations and work in the nineteenth century censuses', *History Workshop Journal* 23 (1987), pp. 59–82; Nigel Goose, 'Working women in industrial England' in Nigel Goose, ed., *Women's Work in Industrial England: Regional and Local Perspectives* (Hatfield, 2007), pp. 1–28.
[20] Census Returns for Cullercoats, 1901, RG13/4804.

Figure 3.7. Fishwives coming from the train having sold their fish in neighbouring towns and villages. Illustrates the economic activity of fisher women. Given the small size of the village of Cullercoats, their numbers were significant. Cullercoats, 1920s

of forty miles into Newcastle upon Tyne, up the River Tyne and down into County Durham.[21] Clearly, the other fifteen did not combine selling with baiting lines and were full-time hawkers.

The image that these women fish hawkers presented was unique. They carried a basket called a creel, which fitted on their backs, and a basket on their arm. Their clothing was equally distinctive: heavy skirts which were pleated in such a way as to add warmth, to stay firm and to avoid getting caught in the creel or basket. Blouses and shawls completed the attire. The quaint, picturesque appearance of these women belied the difficulty of the task in which they were involved – a task that demanded a great deal of physical strength and fitness. Taken together, the combined weight of the creel and the basket when full was 57.2 kilograms (126 pounds). Like mining women and, as we shall see, female agricultural labourers, they were required to have considerable physical strength. At the beginning of our period, when transportation was limited, women would walk miles with that heavy load on their shoulders to sell their fish to their special customers for whom they would gut and clean the fish. Once their daughters had left school – first at twelve and then, in the inter-war period, at fourteen – they would accompany their mothers carrying their own special small creels. By the First World War, trains had made travel easier (Figure 3.7).

[21] *A Brief History of Cullercoats* (Newcastle upon Tyne, 1984), p. 10.

Women performed other subsidiary economic activities to boost the family income, especially at times when the fishing was poor. These activities fitted the pattern of petty capitalism which Benson has described, and which was carried on in different forms by miners' wives and wives of agricultural labourers, as we shall see.[22] In fishing communities which were holiday resorts (such as Newbiggin-by-the-Sea) some fisher women took in summer boarders for several weeks at a time, a practice which was found in fishing communities elsewhere in the nation, especially Cornwall. The pattern was for the boarders to bring their own food which the fisher women then cooked. In times of depression, the money earned from this activity could be crucial. One man, cited in Porteous' study of North Northumberland fishing communities, remembers the situation in his household in the early 1930s when 'his father was about past himself, wondering where the next shilling was coming from to feed his brood'.[23] His wife helped him by taking in summer boarders. Another remembers that a wife could earn £2 looking after a family for a week, a substantial sum in the depressed 1930s.[24] Wives also sold dressed crabs and crab cakes on the doorsteps in summer time. Further, anecdotal evidence suggests that fisher women and their children worked in the fields on nearby farms at harvest time when line fishing was not practised, and at potato picking time.

As important to the economics of the family was the wife's role as money manager. While such a role was the norm in working-class homes, it took on a special form in inshore fishing households. In addition to the usual budgeting for food and clothing, fisher wives had the task of continuous saving due to the peculiarities of the fishing economy. Before the First World War, and for some time after that point, fishermen could often make a good living.[25] Many owned their own boats, fishing gear and houses, and were able to lend their sons and daughters money to make down payments on their houses in turn or to purchase cobles. But fishermen's income was subject to severe fluctuations and, consequently, families had a profound sense of insecurity which caused them to save compulsively. One reason for this was the frequent damage and destruction to boats and fishing gear which resulted from stormy weather. Boats could be damaged at sea or even when drawn up on the beach, and crab and lobster pots were often destroyed. Lines too were frequently spoiled by storms or by other vessels, usually trawlers. In 1896 for instance, a fisherman complained that a steam trawler had damaged his lines to the cost of £8, a small fortune in the day.[26] And such was the frequency of damage to boats and fishing gear that insurance companies would not insure

---

[22] John Benson, *The Penny Capitalists: A Study of Nineteenth-Century Working-class Entrepreneurs* (London, 1983).

[23] Quoted in Porteous, *The Bonny Fisher Lad*, p. 75.

[24] Ibid., p. 26.

[25] Oral evidence of Bill Smailes, NRO T/70; Interview by author, Mr J.L.R. – retired fisherman and local historian of inshore fishing – 8 July 1997.

[26] *The Berwick Advertiser*, 6 November 1896.

either.[27] The fishermen did not get relief until the 1950s, when the government began to offer insurance. And even if boats were not damaged or lost in storms, fishermen still had to replace them, sometimes as often as every ten years and involving a considerable outlay of money.

Women saved 'painfully and laboriously' for new boats, for losses and for times when the fishing was poor, according to the Blyth newspaper and many respondents.[28] They typically kept their savings in the house, often in the kitchen drawer. Respondents were adamant that those fisher families who failed to save for a rainy day became impoverished. The term 'good wife' in inshore fishing communities included the concept of 'good saver'. As one might expect from their role in saving, women had an important role in financial decisions such as when to buy a house or purchase a new boat. As several fishermen respondents noted, their wives were their business managers. One fisherman described his wife as the 'Chancellor of the Exchequer'.[29]

The economics of the inshore fishing industry also required careful saving. While it could bring good profits, the industry was notoriously unpredictable because of the shoaling patterns of the fish and because of the weather. If the weather was bad for several weeks, as frequently happened, and the fishermen could not venture out to sea, fishing families suffered deprivation if they did not have a nest egg. In February 1886, in Newbiggin-by-the-Sea, *The Morpeth Herald* reported that soup kitchens had had to be set up, 'the unusual nature of this action having been caused by the fishermen being brought low by continuous bad weather and the resulting inability to go to sea to ply their craft'.[30] Hardship struck again in 1897 in North Shields as neither the salmon nor the herring were running the coast. According to the local newspaper, the *Shields Daily News*, 'the hard working population have experienced poverty and distress very unusual with them'. This situation necessitated the town setting up soup kitchens to feed the 'notoriously proud and independent fishing population' who were facing real hardships.[31] The gradual decline and then end of the availability of herring at the turn of the twentieth century made inshore fishing a less lucrative employment, except for those who were very skilled fishermen. Many had to leave fishing and find alternative employment in the mines, quarries and industry. A few returned, liking the independence that inshore fishing assured them. The census records from 1901 however show that, by that time, many of the sons of fishermen were choosing other occupations. In one community, Newbiggin-by-the-Sea, a large mining operation that opened in 1908 attracted fishermen who could work in the mines and continue to live in fishing housing.

After the First World War, the economic situation of many inshore fishermen deteriorated further, except for the very skilled minority. Paul

---

[27] Interview by author, Mr J.L.R. 5 July 1997.
[28] *The Blyth News*, 30 August 1912.
[29] Interview by author, Mr J.L.R. 6 July 1997.
[30] *The Morpeth Herald*, 6 February 1886.
[31] *The Shields Daily News*, 29 January 1897.

Thompson estimates that the industry in the nation as a whole declined 40 percent between 1913 and 1938.[32] One issue was the failure of the herring to shoal any more.[33] For most women who had worked in the herring yards, that work ended. Only in Seahouses, North Shields and Berwick-upon-Tweed, as we have seen, did the work continue, some of the herring being landed from Scottish boats fishing further out, the rest being caught by ring-net boats operating out of the Northumberland ports. For the most part, fisher families were now dependent on white fish, salmon, crabs and lobsters. As we have noted, in fishing communities generally a scarcity of white fish due to steam trawlers which fished far out and gathered up all the fish on the bottom, including small fish, and disturbed the spawning grounds made it difficult to earn a living. Many more inshore fishermen left fishing in the inter-war period therefore. As before the war, they tended to go to the mines or the quarries. Some men came back to the fishing when it was good but many then returned to the mines. It is true that inshore fishermen in Newbiggin-by-the Sea continued to do well, resorting to line fishing year round, it having traditionally been practised only in autumn and spring. The result of this extension of line fishing was more work for the women who, previously, had had a break from baiting in the summer months. The amount of white fish landed at other locations however declined markedly, leaving men dependent on crabs, lobsters and salmon caught in the summer. The following table gives an indication of the decline in landings of white fish, in the 1920s and 30s, in two of these communities, Beadnell and Cullercoats:

Table 3.1.   Amount of white fish landed at Cullercoats and Beadnell, 1923–1937

	Cullercoats	Beadnell
1923	5,027 lbs	1,795 lbs
1924	4,330 lbs	2,285 lbs
1925	8,507 lbs	5,807 lbs
1926	488 lbs	2,260 lbs
1927	923 lbs	2,856 lbs
1928	2,404 lbs	1,576 lbs
1929	1,922 lbs	1,394 lbs
1930	1,933 lbs	1,190 lbs
1931	587 lbs	1,248 lbs
1932	428 lbs	733 lbs
1933	514 lbs	850 lbs
1934	1,020 lbs	897 lbs
1935	464 lbs	425 lbs
1936	157 lbs	204 lbs
1937	95 lbs	278 lbs

Source: Ministry of Agriculture and Fisheries, Sea Fisheries Statistical Tables published yearly by His Majesty's Stationery Office (London, 1923–37).

[32]   Paul Thompson with Tony Wailey and Trevor Lummis, *Living the Fishing* (London, 1983), p. 91.
[33]   *Ministry of Agriculture and Fisheries Report of the Departmental Committee on Inshore Fisheries Vol. I* (London, 1914) App. XIV.

Like mining women, fishing women suffered the loss of men and boys. Indeed their losses may have been greater than those of mining women, though nothing in fishing compared to the Hartley Disaster of 1862. Unfortunately we do not have statistics which apply only to inshore fishermen, their fatalities being combined with those of deep-sea fishermen. It is clear however, from the numbers of reports in the newspapers of fatal accidents, that losses in inshore fishing were great and particularly tragic. Typically, a father and perhaps two or three sons, one usually a teenager learning the craft, or two brothers and their sons or some other family combination formed the crew of a coble. All too often, when a storm arose and the coble could not make it back to shore, the men having stopped to pull in their lines, the male members of a family would be wiped out. The following, which lists only the worst of the tragedies, indicates their persistence throughout the nineteenth century and into the twentieth century. The sea almost wiped out the Robinson family of Newbiggin-by-the-Sea in 1808 when, of the nineteen fishermen lost that day, seven were Robinsons. Five of them were George Robinson and his three sons and his grandson. In 1848, seven men from Cullercoats drowned in a storm. These tragedies continued into our period and beyond. In 1885, one Fawcus and his three sons from Beadnell drowned, while in 1889 Beadnell lost John Stephen, George Stephen and William Markham.[34] In one tragic episode in 1904, seven cobles went to rescue a boat only to overturn themselves. Six of the men immediately drowned; the seventh was able to hang on only for a short time.[35] March 18, 1915, was another bad day; fourteen men in central Northumberland lost their lives when four cobles overturned in a storm. The loss of the *Mary Scott* was particularly tragic, involving the drowning of the skipper, William Liddle Senior, and his three sons, Robert, Thomas and John. Hardly less wrenching was the overturning of the *Lily and Margaret* of Newbiggin-by-the Sea and the loss of the skipper, William Taylor, his uncle, George Taylor, and the skipper's two sons, William Taylor, aged eighteen and Harry Taylor, aged fifteen, and the capsizing of the *Excel* which left a father, his son and grandson dead. Further, two brothers and another man died when their coble, the *Mary Twizell*, overturned.[36] Similar disasters punctuated the 1920s and 30s. To list but two, James Scott, known as Pigeon, his son James, and William Taylor drowned when their coble capsized in a storm in 1929; brothers George, twenty-six, and Albert, nineteen, from Amble , drowned in 1934 when their coble, *Morning Star*, overturned.[37] *The Berwick Advertiser* had noted accurately in 1890, that 'scarcely a year passes without some fishermen met with a watery grave'.[38] This observation remained as applicable at the end of our period in 1939 as it had been in 1890.

---

[34] Unpublished ms., Mr John Lisle Robinson 'Fishing Disasters', in possession of author.
[35] *The Morpeth Herald*, 6 December 1904.
[36] *The Newcastle Chronicle*, 20 March 1915.
[37] Ms. 'Fishing Disasters'.
[38] *The Berwick Advertiser*, 31 January 1890.

The effect of such danger on wives was great. Reportedly, when the boats were out fishing, the women were 'in and out' all day, watching for changes in the weather. At the slightest sign of danger they rushed to the water's edge, anxiously peering out to sea. Respondents noted that frequently they agitated for the lifeboat to go out and, on some occasions, took the initiative of pushing it down into the water themselves, without official permission. And their fear was not without basis, as we have seen. At times, tragedies took place in sight of the wives, mothers and children, who watched in horror from the water's edge as their husbands, sons and fathers drowned.

When husbands were lost at sea wives were left to bring up their children with no breadwinner until a surviving son was old enough to begin fishing. Though the community would rally round and set up a fund, this was not a long-term solution. Further, institutional relief or compensation was weak. The inshore fishermen were not included in the National Insurance Act of 1911 because they were seen as partners in a venture.[39] And even when a wife was awarded an accident benefit from a friendly society into which the husband had paid, it rarely amounted to much. We hear of the Prudential Insurance Society in 1904 paying out £100, to a widow who had lost not only her husband but also her son.[40] Another policy paid out 25p per week to a widow and 12p for each child under twelve years for the first six months, then nothing thereafter.[41] Such widows usually had to eke out a living baiting lines for another household, often that of a brother or uncle, and maybe taking in summer boarders if her house was sufficiently large. According to one respondent, when Margaret Brown lost her husband, brother and nephew in 1922 and was left to bring up four small children, she helped bait lines for another brother who had married a woman with no experience of the work.[42] When herring was still plentiful, some women, as we have seen, became full-time herring workers, and listed themselves as such in the census returns.[43] Others became full-time fish hawkers. Widow Isabella Brown, according to the 1901 census, supported her five children in this way.[44] She too listed her occupation on the census returns.

Not surprisingly, lifeboat service was a major activity in coastal communities both in Northumberland and elsewhere. From as early as the mid nineteenth century, most fishing villages had their own lifeboat which was provided by the Royal National Lifeboat Institute, an organisation patronised by upper-class people who lived along the coast. Fishermen and a launching crew of fisher women made up the lifeboat crew. Both were responsible for

---

[39] *The Fishing News*, 7 April 1913.
[40] *The Morpeth Herald*, 9 December 1904.
[41] *The Berwick Advertiser*, 28 February 1890.
[42] Interview by author, Mrs R. 6 October 1998.
[43] See, for instance, Census Returns for Beadnell, 1881, RG11/5127.
[44] Census Returns for Newbiggin-by-the-Sea, 1901, RG13/4836.

rescuing not only fishermen from the villages but also any boat which was in danger close to the shore. Some indication of the value of the lifeboat is gained from the success of the Holy Island lifeboat in 1922 in pulling the *Hartlepool* off the rocks, thereby saving two hundred lives.[45] Men considered it an honour to be part of the lifeboat crew, a tradition which was passed down by generations of the same family. The women launchers were also an important part of the operations and took their role very seriously. Like the lifeboat men, they would typically serve for twenty to thirty years and would regularly train for rescues. Mitchell's study of Cresswell lifeboats records that one woman, Margaret Robinson, took part in rescues for fifty years, and another, Mrs James Brown, for thirty years.[46] When a boat was in danger, the call was not only 'men to the boats' but also 'women to the ropes'. The work of the women launchers involved pushing the lifeboat down on its wheels to the shore line and then into the water, often through heavy waves, until it was afloat. Next, they pulled it in when it had finished its task, often helping the survivors. The launchers generally considered themselves part of a long tradition that went back to Grace Darling. This revered girl had, decades before, along with her lighthouse father, helped rescue fourteen people, at great risk to herself. She was regularly feted. In addition, the launchers and the fisher women generally regularly raised money for the Royal National Lifeboat Institute, walking the streets in their fisher outfits.[47]

Given the importance of woman's work to success in fishing, the demands on the women in the family were great and they started from an early age. Like boys, girls were 'brought up to the fishing'. As soon as possible, they learned to skein the mussels and were set to assisting mothers in that task before going to school in the morning and after coming home from school. Further, even more so than in other working-class communities, mothers required daughters to look after younger children when they were busy with the fishing work. Respondents referred to them as 'little mothers'. After leaving school, they became full-time workers in the household, except for those in places such as Seahouses, North Shields and Cullercoats where they became herring workers or full-time fish hawkers, as we saw, listing their occupations in the censuses.

If the family did not require their services, they entered the households of other fisher families to look after children while the mother did the fishing work. Census returns of 1901 from Newbiggin-by-the-Sea and Cullercoats show that around 8 percent of households included teenage girls from other fisher families.[48] The likelihood is that some of these girls returned to the family home if the fishing work became greater due to an additional worker, perhaps a brother who had grown up. By that point, they would be inured to

45   *The Berwick Advertiser*, 20 January 1922.
46   Jill Mitchell, *The Story of the Cresswell Lifeboats* (Cresswell, 1956), pp. 5–6.
47   For a description of these outfits, see p. 90.
48   Census Returns for Newbiggin-by-the-Sea, 1901, RG13/4836; Census Returns for Cullercoats, 1901, RG13/4804.

the fishing work, but, as we have seen, some became fish hawkers or herring workers. The usual pattern then, it seems, was for a young woman – who was by that point trained in the fishing work – to marry a fisherman, usually from the same community, and perform the preparatory work for him. The thinking was that it was right 'to marry one of yer ane' (your own)[49] because a wife had to be used to fishing work. Oral evidence suggests that most men followed this pattern and this is borne out by marriage records from local churches. The record of marriages at the Manchester Street Wesleyan Chapel, Morpeth, indicate for instance that, at this church, all girls from fisher families in the three decades covered by the records (1901 to 1935) married fishermen. The only exceptions were when the fathers of the girls were deceased.[50] We can surmise that in other cases fathers put pressure on daughters to marry within the fisher community. This pattern parallels what Andrew Blaikie has found in northeastern Scottish fishing communities.[51] Yet, this was not always the case. Some young women had had enough of fishing work and 'married out'.[52] The records of St Ebba, Church of England, Beadnell, reveal this pattern. Of the eighteen fisher marriages in the period 1856 to 1902, four were between fisher women and non-fishermen. We also find one example of a non-fisher woman marrying a fisherman.[53] The same pattern emerges in the marriage records of St Mary's Church, Woodhorn, which lay between the mining town of Ashington and Newbiggin-by-the-Sea. In the period stretching from 1880 to 1921, roughly 25 percent of fisher girls 'married out'.[54]

This pattern of endogamous marriage, which was most prevalent when inshore fishing was at its height, led to a considerable amount of inbreeding. It had been noted in respect to miners in earlier decades but had died out with the in-migration of large numbers of other workers, most notably agricultural labourers, into the pits at the end of the nineteenth century and early twentieth century.[55] As had been the case in mining, at times first cousins married and two brothers frequently married two sisters. One fishing couple that was interested in genealogy traced their family back twelve generations, creating a family tree, and found four points at which the branches overlapped. This pattern of intermarriage is obvious from census data. Among the fishing community of Newbiggin-by-the Sea, eight names predominated: Armstrong, Robinson, Dawson, Oliver, Lisle, Twizell, Dent and Jefferson. This pattern held true for all the inshore fishing communities up and down the coast of Northumberland and, indeed, in other parts of the country and the world.

---

49 Interview by author, Mrs A. 6 December 1998.
50 Manchester Street Wesleyan Chapel, Morpeth, NRO M11/54/56/59.
51 Andrew Blaikie, 'Coastal communities in Victorian Scotland: What makes north-east fisher families distinctive', *Local Population Studies* 69 (Autumn, 2002), pp. 15–31.
52 Interview by author, Mr and Mrs J.L.R. 6 August 1998. This is reflected in the marriage records.
53 Beadnell Marriages, St Ebba, Church of England, 1856–1902, NRO M10 77.
54 Marriage Registers of St Mary's Woodhorn Church, NRO EP 22/12 and 22/15.
55 Royal Commission on the Employment of Women and Children in the Mines, PP 1842 XVI, p. 443.

In the small community of Cresswell, a few miles north of Newbiggin-by-the-Sea, men named Brown made up nine of the ten fisher families (and the lifeboat crew was composed entirely of men of that name), while in Beadnell the names of Fawcus, Dixon and Douglas predominated.[56]

Reinforcing this pattern, community members regarded daughters who married outside unfavourably because the community felt it had lost a skilled worker. Nadel-Klein notes that in Scottish fishing communities fishermen would chase away outsiders who came to court their women.[57] Marriages to miners who had come from fishing families or had been fishermen themselves were the least unpopular of the 'outside marriages'. According to my respondents, and verified by the marriage records of local churches, this was the most common kind of 'outside marriage', miners being usually the geographically closest group. As we have seen, many men moved from fishing into the local mining industry, especially in Newbiggin-by-the-Sea, North Seaton and Ashington. Such men maintained their connections to the fisher community, remaining often in fisher housing instead of moving to colliery housing, and even manning the lifeboat when needed. Family demands however continued to play a large part in the lives of these brides who were expected to come to the family home each morning to help with baiting the lines, indicating again how all consuming was the fishing work.[58] We can surmise that only husbands who were of fishing stock would tolerate such behaviour. Marriages to non-fishing men were another matter. They appear to have happened when girls took the unusual step of entering into domestic service, virtually the only non-fishing employment option open to them.[59] Then, as was the case with the mother of one of my respondents, she might marry a farm labourer. Women from outside who married into the fishing community were never fully accepted and were regarded as foreigners, a pattern found in most fishing communities around the globe.[60]

Pre-nuptial pregnancy and illegitimacy were common in fishing communities as they were in many communities – though much less than in rural communities, as we shall see. The findings of Blaikie suggest that one-sixth of first births in northeastern Scotland occurred within six months of marriage.[61] Evidence from Seafield, a fishing community in Banffshire, Scotland, reveals the same pattern.[62] Though we cannot use aggregate statistics to calculate the rate of illegitimacy in inshore fishing communities as we can in coal

---

[56] Information taken from Census Returns, 1871, 1881, 1891, 1901. Also Land Evaluations, 1910, NRO 2006/3.

[57] Jane Nadel-Klein, 'Granny baited the lines: Perpetual crisis and the changing role of women in Scottish fishing communities', *Women's Studies International Studies* 3, Vol. 23 (2000), pp. 363–72.

[58] Interview by author, Mr J.L.R. 6 July 1998.

[59] Michael W. Marshall, *Fishing: The Coastal Tradition* (London, 1987), p. 70.

[60] Collection of oral interviews made by Paul Thompson and housed at the British Library, QD8/FISH/52 C773.

[61] Blaikie, 'Coastal communities in Victorian Scotland'.

[62] W. Cramond, 'Illegitimacy in Banffshire', *Poor Law Magazine* 2 (1992), p. 578.

mining and rural districts, the fishing population being mixed up with other groups, we can ascertain roughly the frequency of illegitimacy by looking at individual households. In some fishing communities, around 7 percent of fisher households included illegitimate children.[63] In villages such as Cullercoats, near Newcastle upon Tyne, which provided ample opportunity for girls to become full-time hawkers, the illegitimacy rate could be as low as 3 percent, indicating that the independence offered by full-time work made such girls more careful.[64] The calculation of illegitimacy is based upon the number of households which incorporated a single grown-up daughter or daughters and a child or children of the same name, described in the censuses as grandchildren. Barry Reay has noted the tendency in rural communities he has studied to designate illegitimate children in this way.[65] While this method of calculation may overestimate somewhat the degree of illegitimacy, it still provides a rough measure. Such numbers are reflected in the bastardy cases which regularly appeared before the Morpeth Petty Sessions and other courts.[66] One such case involved a claim for maintenance made by Tamar Dent against John Dent, perhaps a cousin, in January 1896.[67] Even if they were awarded maintenance, the women would have had little choice but to stay in the family home and participate in the fishing work.[68]

It was common also for unmarried daughters of twenty-seven years and older to continue living in the family home. In Newbiggin-by-the-Sea in 1881 and 1901, for instance, 13.6 percent and 14.6 percent of fishing households included such women. Half of these did not have illegitimate children. In each of these cases the household usually included three fishermen, all requiring lines to be baited. While, according to Selina Todd, it was not uncommon for girls to stay in the family home well after leaving school, it seems possible that these young women faced pressure to stay in the family home to help bait the lines.[69] One woman who had wanted to continue her education recounted how that had been impossible because 'my family needed me for the fishing work'.[70] These young women, even the ones with the illegitimate children, may of course have married later. Still, these findings contrast with Blaikie's conclusions about a high rate of nuptuality and early age of marriage. Marriage records suggest an average age of marriage. Significantly, in communities such as Seahouses, North Shields and Berwick-upon-Tweed, which continued to have landings of herrings well into the twentieth century, and in which women designated themselves fish

---

63 See Census Returns for Newbiggin-by-the-Sea, 1881, RG/11/5119; 1901, RG13/4836.
64 Census Returns for Cullercoats, 1881, RG11/5119.
65 Barry Reay, 'Sexuality in nineteenth-century England: the social context of illegitimacy in rural Kent', *Rural History* I (November, 1990), pp. 219–48.
66 Morpeth Petty Sessions, Minutes of Evidence, NRO PS 5/12.
67 Register of Court of Summary Justice, Morpeth, NRO PS 5/12, 15 January 1896.
68 Blaikie, 'Coastal Communities in Victorian Scotland'.
69 Selina Todd, *Young Women, Work, and Family in England 1918–1955* (Oxford, 2005).
70 Interview by author, Mrs A. 6 August 1997.

hawkers or herring workers, there was no indication of illegitimate children living in the family home.

The difficulties encountered by men who married outside the fishing community shows the importance of trained women workers. The popular concept was that a woman who had not been brought up to fishing work would not have the skill, resilience and acceptance to do the work, and that a man who married 'outside' would have to leave the fishing if he did not have another female relative to help with the baiting. Reportedly, some men did leave fishing for this reason. Yet, the statement that only girls who had been brought up to baiting could perform this task was a slight exaggeration. Some young women in this position, including one of my respondents, did learn to bait, though never as quickly or as well as those who had been brought up to it, and she required the assistance of her sister-in-law. In another family the retired father did the baiting and, in yet another, the father and mother baited. Rarely did the fisher community fully accept the wife from outside. One fisher woman respondent remembered the fishing community's reaction to a fisherman who married 'outside'. 'Oh! What's our John going to do now that he has married her?'[71] As this comment suggests, and as the respondent remembers, the incomer got no sympathy, the reason being the popular notion that fishermen should marry one of their 'ane kind'. One respondent suggested that, because of the need for skilled wives, marriages were rarely for love but rather for practicality.[72] While this may have been an exaggeration, we know that in pre-industrial production, which inshore fishing resembled, skill was an important factor in the choice of a marriage partner.

Not surprisingly the issue of gender relations in fishing families is nuanced. The comments of observers and scholars are contradictory regarding the balance of power between man and wife. Bertram, writing about Scottish fishing communities in the nineteenth century, described the fisher women as 'head of the household',[73] maintaining that women dominated because of their control of their marketing of most of the fish. Peter Anson, making the same point about the fisher folk of Footdee in Scotland in the 1950s, claimed that they had established a 'petticoat government' there and kept control of the money which they gained from hawking fish.[74] We can assume that the same was true of those women in Northumberland who designated themselves as hawkers or fish workers in the census. It is probable that those who sold on a more part-time basis and combined it with the family fishing work added their earnings to the family funds. If less than the fish hawkers, this did give them authority in the household. But there were other elements to their authority. One of the most important was baiting the lines, which

---

[71] Interview by author, Mr and Mrs B. 6 September 1999.
[72] Interview by author, Mrs A. 6th August 1997.
[73] James G. Bertram, *The Unappreciated Fisherfolk: Their Round of Life and Labour* (London, 1883), p. 3.
[74] Peter F. Anson, 'Scots Fisherfolk', Saltine Society, *Banffshire Journal* (1954), p. 24.

some writers believed brought women considerable respect from men.[75] Respondents said that men regarded the women as experts.[76] The following anecdote, recounted by a respondent, indicates the husband's dependence on his wife. She noted how, when her husband blamed his poor catch upon the supposed inadequate quality of her baiting, she responded by refusing to bait his line that day and went to the cinema instead. As a result, her husband was unable to fish for a whole day.[77] Also, it was generally accepted that wives managed the finances. One respondent, talking about her powerful mother-in-law whose sons fished with their father, noted how the matriarch continued to handle her sons' money even after they had married, determining how much they should give their wives. The respondent, herself a strong-minded woman, refused to comply with this arrangement.[78]

Other evidence, including that of modern scholars, also points to wives having substantial authority. Katrina Porteous, a local historian closely in touch with the community, is adamant that

> fisherwomen had much greater authority than other working-class women by virtue of three factors: first, the social and economic independence that some had gained through travelling with the herring crews in their youth; secondly, the fact that most were responsible for keeping the family accounts, and thirdly, and most strikingly, because of the vital importance of their skill in baiting the lines.[79]

Marilyn Porter in her study of North Atlantic fisheries comes to the same conclusion,[80] as does anthropologist Jane Nadel-Klein.[81] The fisher girls who listed themselves as herring workers or hawkers in the censuses clearly had an occupational identity which was bound to affect their position in the household when they married, especially if they carried on with their jobs. One fisherman, who was able to make a living line fishing even after the Second World War, when most had ceased, said, in explaining his success, 'you had to have a wife who was good with money' and that the relationship between him and his wife was a 'partnership'. The wife said she 'felt necessary'.[82] Another fisherman claimed the 'women had a big say in things'.[83] This authority included decisions about the purchase of boats and houses. Also, the division of labour in inshore fishing was not totally strict. Although women were not allowed to fish, men would, if the situation demanded it,

---

[75] Catherine Czerkawska, *The Fisherfolk of Carrick: A History of the Fishing Industry in South Aryshire* (Glasgow, 1975).

[76] Oral evidence of Mr Smailes.

[77] Interview by author, Mrs A. 6 August 1997.

[78] Interview by author, Mrs R. 6 November 1999.

[79] Correspondence with Katrina Porteous, 13 February 2012.

[80] Porter*, Place and Persistence*, p. 53.

[81] Jane Nadel-Klein, 'A fisher laddie needs a fisher lassie. Endogamy and work in a Scottish fishing village' in Jane Nadel-Klein and Donna Lee Davis, eds, *To work and to weep: Women in fishing economies* (St John's, Newfoundland, 1988), pp. 290–310.

[82] Interview by author, Mr and Mrs J.LR. 6 October 1997.

[83] Oral evidence of Bill Smailes.

bait lines and women would fetch mussels, usually a man's job (though in North Northumberland, a woman's job). Yet men would not sell fish from a creel, which was a very public role associated with women.[84]

Yet there is evidence of inequality, though it too is qualified. Nadel-Klein points to the almost hysterical prohibition against women on boats, a fairly universal taboo which lives on today. She suggests that they may have been seen as having a polluting and endangering effect on the endeavour.[85] In some communities, women were not even allowed on the boats to clean them. This prohibition was even more extreme than the usual one regarding women and the use of machines. It was also apparent in 1927 when the women launchers, unable to find a whole crew to man the lifeboat, offered five of their number to make up the deficit. As it happened, this turned out not to be necessary, some of the boats having come in, making extra men available. The local reporter noted, somewhat ironically, that the men 'would not have been able to hold their heads up had the women manned the lifeboat'.[86] Like fishing, manning the lifeboat was clearly a man's job. At the same time, the fishermen usually named their boats after wives. Thus we have the *Margaret Lisle*, the *Mary Twizell*, and *Lily and Margaret,* to mention just a few. A fitting conclusion about gender relations is that fishing women had some degree of autonomy and considerable domestic power – more authority than most women, certainly most mining women – and that a partnership of sorts existed. But, as Nadel-Klein notes, 'fishing communities were not free of societal values about women's inferiority'.[87] The prohibition against women fishing may have had the aim of maintaining men's monopoly of the high-status job of fishing and of drawing clear gender lines. How better than to suggest that bad luck would ensue if women crossed these lines?

Housework and care of children were totally the province of women, being regarded as not 'masculine'. It is impossible to ascertain the fertility of fisher couples because of their inclusion within the much larger group of offshore fishing couples. Yet anecdotal evidence suggests that inshore fishing couples had large families. A local historian likened them to miners in having seven to eight children.[88] The medical officer of health reports made no mention of high infant mortality, such as we heard in the case of miners. Whereas mining women appear to have suffered a deficit of nutritious food, fisher women had the advantage of an ample supply of high quality protein in the form of fish. It is possible however that they suffered from miscarriages as a result of the heavy physical work that they performed, and that they gave birth to a higher percentage of disabled children than usual as a result of inbreeding. It appears that, as in the nation as a whole, their fertility may have declined in the 1930s. Yet oral evidence and the reports of medical officers of health

[84] Interview by author, Mr J.L.R. 6 September 1998.
[85] Nadel-Klein, 'A fisher laddie needs a fisher lassie'.
[86] *The Morpeth Herald*, 20 May 1927.
[87] Nadel-Klein, 'A fisher laddie needs a fisher lassie'.
[88] Interview by author, Mr H. 6 September 1995.

suggests that large families of seven to eight were still common. The really dramatic decline occurred in the 1940s and 50s. Again, we have no specific statistics for inshore fishing couples and have to rely on anecdotal evidence but, significantly, none of my respondents who had borne children in that period had more than two or three children. We can assume that the difficulty of fishermen in gaining a living from line fishing, together with changing fashions regarding family size, led to a curtailment of fertility. The decline in family size improved the lot of women.

Childcare was however secondary to the fishing work, according to respondents. In fact, it was commonly said that the children 'brought themselves up and had to see themselves out to school in the morning' because wives were so busy with the fishing work.[89] One respondent, looking back regretfully on what she described as the neglect of her children, noted how her baby had fallen out of her pram while she was down at the shore pushing her husband's boat out through the waves.[90] Another woman recalled her mother 'rocking the cradle and trying to bait the line, mussels jumping off the plate – and trying to get the different pans on for dinner'.[91] The family saw children as part of the family workforce and put them to work as soon as possible. For boys, this meant gathering mussels and limpets and helping with the never-ending task of baiting the lines. Fishermen considered their sons too young to go out fishing until they were thirteen or, after the school leaving age was raised in 1918, fourteen. Girls however had the most responsibility, having not only to bait lines before and after school[92] but also to look after the younger children in the family. They became 'little mothers' at a young age.[93] Even before puberty, both boys and girls were well versed in the key aspects of the fishing trade, capable of easing the load of their harried mothers. The result was that their childhood was curtailed.

Housework did not loom as large in the life of the fisher woman as it did in that of the mining women who were consumed by it. To begin with, fisher women did not have the time to devote to keeping their brasses polished and their homes up to the incredibly high standards set by mining wives. Fishing wives did not of course have to deal with the coal dust that pervaded the atmosphere of coal mining towns and villages and the filthy pit clothes. Still, speaking of fishing communities, observers in both the nineteenth and twentieth centuries attest to the high standards of cleanliness, the scrubbed front steps and the snow-white laundry.[94] The Medical Officer of Health for Newbiggin-by-the-Sea remarked in 1874 for instance that 'the women keep the homes remarkably clean' despite the great overcrowding, saying, 'I have over and over again admired the whiteness of the bedclothes and wondered

89 Interview by author, Mr and Mrs B. 6 August 1998.
90 Interview by author, Mrs A. 6 August 1998.
91 Porteous, *The Bonny Fisher Lad*, p. 64.
92 Interview by author, Mr and Mrs J.L.R. 6 August 1997.
93 Mitchell, *The Story*, p. 108.
94 Interview by author, Mr H. 6 October 1996.

how a mother of a large family in that single apartment could keep everything so clean'.[95] The hiring of a teenage girl from another family and the habit of keeping teenage daughters at home did help the wife. In contrast to mining families, fisher people lived beside their extended families in rows of houses or in squares and relied on their families, especially for the care of children.[96] Mining women were more likely to have to depend on neighbours, their extended families not often being present. While fisher women, like mining women, 'possed' their clothes, they were unable to keep to the rigid schedule followed by mining women and usually had to wait for bad weather when the boats could not go out to sea to clean and poss. Yet, as one fisher woman said, 'they were sticklers for cleanliness'.[97] Peter Frank recounts how writers testified to these standards in the 1930s.[98] Like mining women, however, they kept their hands busy when they had a moment free. When the men were not line fishing and the women were free of baiting, they knitted the distinctive ganseys (guernseys) – the waterproof sweaters that their men wore while on the boat – and the long sea boot stockings. Each village had a different pattern for their ganseys so that, if a man drowned, he could be identified as coming from a certain community. The fishing women also made mats, like the mining women and, as we shall see, the agricultural women. When they could, therefore, these fishing women fulfilled their domestic duties diligently, but in line fishing season, the fishing work prevailed.

Conclusion

Fisher women were a confident, assertive and brave group, very conscious of their importance to the wellbeing of the fishing trade. While they saw their domestic duties as important, their identities were as much workers in the fishing as mothers and housewives. In this, they differed markedly from mining women, not only the domestic mining women but also the political mining women. They thought of themselves as business partners of their husbands and realised full well that men could not engage in fishing without their help. The pride with which they wore their traditional outfits of pleated skirts, aprons and shawls in selling fish and on ceremonial occasions – such as marches to raise money for the Royal National Lifeboat Institute and visits to London to receive awards for bravery in launching the lifeboat – is testimony to their consciousness of their identity as fisher women.[99] And they were rightly proud of their work ethic. Andrew Rutter, a local historian, noted: 'idleness was to them a cardinal sin … they took work, and all that

---

[95] Report for the Medical Officer of Health for Newbiggin-by-the-Sea, 1874, NRO 8699/1.
[96] Interview by author, Mrs A. 6 August 1998.
[97] Ibid.
[98] Evidence from Leo Wamsley, *Three Fevers* (London, 1947), p. 10, quoted in Peter Frank, 'Women's work in the Yorkshire inshore fishing industry'.
[99] *The Morpeth Herald*, 3 June 1927; see also pp. 90 and 109.

entailed with a gusto that cannot be described'.[100] Clearly physical delicacy was not part of their image any more than it was of mining women and, as we shall see, female agricultural labourers. Like the activist mining women, many were involved in the public sphere but, unlike mining women, they were also engaged in household production along with their husbands.

[100] Rutter, *A Seahouses Saga*, p. 51.

4

The Inshore Fishing Community: 'A Race Apart'?

We have been talking about the identity of fisher women being that of fish worker and secondarily as housewife and mother, but outsiders defined them, their husbands and the community in general in ways which sometimes, though not always, corresponded with how they defined themselves. At times, the focus was upon women specifically, but often it was upon the community as a whole. These more general comments apply to women as much as to men and must be included in our study. Given its small size, the inshore fishing community made a surprisingly deep imprint on the consciousness of the wider society. The explanation for this lies in the drama which surrounded it. The public revelled in the danger, the bravery of both men and women, the picturesque dress of both, the distinctive culture and the isolation of the fishing community. In fact, the fishing community formed a convenient object upon which to foist a variety of different, often contradictory but always extreme, feelings.

The public at times of tragedy represented the fishing population as victims. This characterisation was especially true if the disaster involved several members of the same family or several families. As had long been the case, outpourings of sympathy occurred, made tangible by the donation of sums of money. When in 1851 eight men from Blyth drowned, leaving eight widows and twenty-seven children, the Lord Mayor of Newcastle Fund collected £1,701 and the town of Blyth and the town of Morpeth donated £50 and £21 respectively.[1] This public reaction reminds us of such mining disasters as in Hartley in 1862. While the public was genuinely sympathetic to the fisher people, the tragedies also fulfilled outsiders' need for drama, no more so than in the nineteenth century, an era which fed on sensationalism.

The local newspapers recounted with great pathos and drama the details of all the tragedies which dotted the nineteenth century and beyond. A local historian noted how he had read accounts of 'women picking bodies off the rocks'[2] after some disasters. In recounting the 1904 tragedy (to which we have already referred) of seven men drowning when several cobles went to the rescue of a stranded vessel, the reporter from *The Morpeth Herald* followed that pattern. Having described how the first six had drowned after trying to cling to the capsized boat, he elaborated in great detail the valiant

[1] *The Newcastle Courant*, 21 March 1851.
[2] Unpublished ms., Mr John Lisle Robinson, 'Fishing Disasters', in possession of author.

efforts of the one survivor to hold on, and his shouting , 'I can't hold on much longer' before he went under, not to emerge. Gathered at the water's edge, the whole community watched this prolonged struggle in horror. The writer goes on, 'When the extent of the disaster was known, women ran around as if demented, ringing their hands and crying piteously. Some swooned and had to be carried away.'[3] Writing about the funeral, the reporter again resorts to dramatic rhetoric:

> Never in its long history going back to medieval times has the old sacred edifice of St Bartholemews looked down on such a multitude … as when six (one body was not found) unfortunate fishermen were interred in the churchyard on the rocky promontory. The village from the station to the churchyard presented an extraordinary throng of people who freely expressed their sympathy for the bereaved people.[4]

Artists added to the drama. Such was the case with the colony of artists that congregated in Cullercoats, just north of Newcastle upon Tyne, in the 1880s drawn, like other artists such as those in Staithes, by the picturesque and dramatic aspects of this rediscovered 'peasantry'. The colony at Cullercoats included Robert Jobling, John Charlton and the American Winslow Homer. They inevitably romanticised the fisher women, in whom they were most interested. Whether depicting them attired in their traditional costume, as did Winslow Homer, or engaged in their everyday task of baiting lines, or setting out to sell their fish armed with their full creels and baskets, or in times of danger, the artists represented the women as noble, resilient, strong and brave. The most riveting of the paintings were those dealing with danger. We find, for example, in Robert Jobling's *Anxious Times* three women gazing desperately out to sea waiting for their husbands, battling the waves to make it to shore, and safety (Figure 4.1).[5]

Another source of dramatic representations of the fishing population, fisher women included, were the rescues that they conducted of their own fishing boats and of other boats in danger. The fishermen received particular attention from the Ministry of Agriculture and Fisheries. Speaking of their record of rescues, the Departmental Committee on Inshore Fisheries in 1914 called the inshore fishing community 'most valuable to the nation and worth every effort to preserve'[6] and noted that 'the lifeboat service depends largely on them'.[7] The men's performance in the naval reserves and their saving of many navy vessels during the First World War furthered endeared them to the nation. The Ministry also noted that the inshore fishing industry, despite its

3   *The Morpeth Herald*, 6 December 1904.
4   Ibid., 9 December 1904.
5   An exhibition was held of these paintings at the Laing Gallery, Newcastle upon Tyne. See Laura Newton with Abigail Booth Gerdts, *Cullercoats: A North-East Colony of Artists* (Newcastle upon Tyne, 2003).
6   Report of the Departmental Committee on Inshore Fisheries (London, 1914), p. xii.
7   Ministry of Agriculture and Fisheries White Fish Subsidy Investigation into the Inshore Fisheries, PRO MAF 209, p. 1548.

Figure 4.1. *Anxious Times*, 1889, by Robert Jobling; one of the group of
Cullercoats painters in Laing Gallery, Newcastle upon Tyne. Depicts the anxiety of
families when a storm had blown up and the boats still had not made it into shore.

small contribution to the food supply of the nation, 'was more than an artistic addition to the scenery, and an aesthetic luxury which is of no concern to the state'.[8] There was no doubt that the government romanticised the inshore fishing industry and was determined to preserve it, saying that it 'produced the greatest number of natural seamen'.[9] Thus, after the end of the First World War, it awarded the inshore fishermen grants to put engines in their cobles. These engines, though rudimentary, increased the fishermen's speed in getting to and from the fishing grounds and were particularly valuable if the weather turned bad.

The bravery of the fisher women did not escape the attention of the authorities and indeed was a constant theme throughout the years. For example, on the occasion of a 1922 presentation being made to two Holy Island women, a speaker for the Royal National Lifeboat Institute said:

> It is gratifying to feel that the wives and daughters of the lifeboat men of Holy Island are so eager to assist in the noble task so often and heroically carried out by the crew and they feel that the actions of the women of Holy Island reflect not merely on themselves but on the women of our maritime race.[10]

The two women launchers, decked out in their picturesque, traditional costumes, along with three lifeboat men, travelled to London to be awarded medals for their bravery.[11] In 1927, four more women were invited to London to be honoured by the Royal National Lifeboat Institute, making this the third time in the previous five years that launchers from Northumberland had gone to London to receive awards.[12]

The most fulsome praise of their bravery came from local sources and was often used to underscore the deep sense of regional pride. The local paper, for instance, was particularly effusive in 1928, noting that the Northumberland launchers were 'second to none in the country' and that for 'a long period of over 104 years … the women of Northumberland have stood out preeminent in their heroism and splendid devotion to that great cause'.[13] Not surprisingly, the local press depicted the rescues in melodramatic terms and the women as valiant, noble heroines. More than once, the papers reported that the women launchers had to push the lifeboat on its wheels over the sand and moorland for a mile or more to launch it at a nearby cove which was nearer to the boat or boats in difficulty. We read further of two women running several miles over the cliffs to alert the Cresswell lifeboat crew that a boat from a neigh-

---

8   Ministry of Agriculture and Fisheries, *Report on Sea Fisheries* for the years 1919, 1920, 1921, 1922 and 1923 (London, 1925).
9   Ministry of Agriculture and Fisheries: 14th Report of Development Committee for year ending 31 March 1924, PRO MAF VIII, p. 429.
10 Quoted in *The Berwick Advertiser*, 7 April 1922.
11 Ibid.
12 *The Morpeth Herald*, 3 June 1927.
13 Ibid., 10 February 1928.

Figure 4.2. *The Women*, 1910, by John Charlton; another of the Cullercoats group of painters in Laing Gallery, Newcastle upon Tyne. Depicts the lifeboat women pulling the lifeboat *Percy* to aid the *Lovely Nellie*. While seemingly overly dramatic, newspaper accounts indicate that this scene was quite common.

bouring village was in danger.[14] Sometimes the local papers reported how the lifeboat women, the waves washing over their heads, formed human chains guiding shipwrecked people to shore.[15] As we have seen, on one occasion, the newspaper wrote in glowing terms about how, when a storm unexpectedly blew up and the men – including the lifeboat crew – were out to sea, the women launchers rose to the occasion by getting together part of a scratch crew made up of retired fishermen and miners who had been fishers. There still being a deficit of crew members, the women bravely offered the services of five of their own to make up the correct number. For the women to join the lifeboat crew would have been to break an important taboo. The situation was saved by several fishermen, having made it back to shore, filling up the empty places. The reporter continued the description of the women's bravery in admiring terms, telling how they launched the lifeboat up to their waists in heavy seas and then waited for three hours in soaking clothes to haul it in.[16] In another crisis, in 1931, we read of how 'it would have been impossible to get the lifeboat into the water but for the help and courage of the women'.[17]

Not surprisingly, these brave actions did not escape the notice of the group of artists resident in Cullercoats in the 1880s. The events provided fodder for

[14] Jill Mitchell, *The Story of the Cresswell Lifeboat* (Cresswell, 1956), pp. 5–6.
[15] *The Morpeth Herald*, 10 February 1928.
[16] *The Morpeth Herald*, 2 May 1927.
[17] The *Shields Daily News*, 28 May 1931.

the artists' perceptions of the fisher women as valiant and noble. The most famous of the resulting pictures is *The Women*, painted by John Charlton in 1910 and reproduced many times. While it might appear melodramatic to the modern eye, the newspaper accounts of the actions of the women launchers reveal it to be true to life. In this Charlton painting, the lifeboat women are struggling to pull the lifeboat, the *Percy,* in through the churning waves (Figure 4.2).

Arthur J. Munby, essayist and barrister, famous in the late nineteenth century for his descriptions of working women involved in hard, dirty, taxing work requiring physical strength, was inevitably drawn to the fisher women. Although he did not visit the Northumberland fisher women, his descriptions of Yorkshire fisher women in his diary, housed at Trinity College, Cambridge, are applicable to those in Northumberland. He described fisher girls gathering limpets from the cliffs, running up and down, oblivious to the danger, stalwart and capable.[18]

At times, the public image of the fishing community was less complimentary. Bertram, describing the fisher folk of Scotland, saw them as a 'race apart' which seldom got an infusion of new blood from outside. As we have seen, these same charges had been directed at miners in the mid nineteenth century.[19] Bertram noted further how fisher people passed down their 'names and curious manners ... from generation to generation'.[20] Even the officials of the Ministry of Agriculture and Fisheries, who looked kindly upon them, described them as 'practically a different race ... and it is only very rarely that intermarriage occurs with the outside'.[21] The unspoken conclusion was that they were inbred. The theme of difference and strangeness is also inherent in the following account of a social event in Cullercoats at which the fisher folk were in attendance. The reporter from the local newspaper described how the master of ceremonies had induced them to sing their traditional sea songs and had been able to reproduce the Cullercoats vernacular.[22] The impression is that one is reading the comments of an anthropologist about a strange tribe of people. We gain the same impression from the commentary of a local newspaper reporter in 1922. In recounting the honourary visit of the three lifeboat men and the two women launchers to London, he included in the dangers which they avoided the electric light, recounting how they had been frightened to turn it on.[23] The undertone is one of derision. Following this account, a rumour spread that the wives and daughters of men drowned in an accident drove from that particular village the only man who had survived the tragedy,

[18] Taken from Munby diary entry, 16 October 1867. Information in Michael Hiley, *Victorian Working Women: Portraits from Life* (London, 1979), Ch. 4.
[19] Royal Commission on the Employment of Women and Children in the Mines, PP 1842 XVI, p. 443.
[20] James G. Bertram, *The Unappreciated Fisherfolk: Their Round of Life and Labour* (London, 1883), pp. 2–3.
[21] *Ministry of Agriculture and Fisheries Report of the Departmental Committee on Inshore Fisheries Vol. 1* (London, 1914), p. 653.
[22] *The Whitley Bay Chronicle and Visitor Gazette*, 22 January 1910.
[23] *The Morpeth Herald*, 7 April 1922.

because he could swim. Again the message is of backwardness.[24] While this rumour is unlikely to be true, we cannot doubt the remarks of the Medical Officer of Health for Newbiggin-by-the-Sea. After praising the fisher women for keeping spotlessly clean houses in difficult circumstances, he went on to describe the fishing community as 'primitive'.[25] Granted that society in the late nineteenth century regarded the word 'primitive' as more acceptable than people today, it still denoted a low place on the evolutionary scale. Another negative remark came from one of my respondents, the daughter of a police chief in Newbiggin-by-the-Sea in the inter-war period. She recounted with some surprise how her father had been quite friendly with the fisher people, as if such a relationship was quite odd.[26] The notion of a 'race apart' was alive and well in the 1990s.

The sense of 'otherness' associated with the fisher people often took on a darker hue. People frequently represented fisher people as being at the bottom of the social pole – 'strange and backward', and, as Nadel-Klein notes, shunned them.[27] Paul Thompson in *Living the Fishing* also stresses the low status of fisher people.[28] A fisher woman spoke of being 'looked down upon if one lived at the fisher end of the town'.[29] One supposed proof of their backwardness and lack of intelligence was their superstitions, characteristic of all fisher people. Most superstitions were tied to the fear of incurring bad luck, whether involving drowning, loss of boats or fishing gear, or poor catches of fish. As in the case of miners, one of the main objects around which such superstitions centred was women. Bad luck seemingly would ensue if a women entered a boat, if she combed her hair before the boat set off or if she had red hair, all rather odd ideas given the women's involvement in the fishing. The same fear of bad luck was associated with mentioning ministers before going to sea, again strange because fisher people were very religious. Another set of superstitions focused on animals such as pigs and rabbits. Merely to mention the name of these animals was to incur bad luck. Although we have no such evidence from Northumberland, in Frazerburgh, Scotland, non-fisher people used to tease fisher people by putting rabbits in their boats. This action caused the fishermen to stay onshore for several days to allow the bad spell to wear off.[30] These superstitions remained until quite recent times.

---

[24] *The Shields Daily News*, 10 November 1885.

[25] Report of the Medical Officer of Health for Newbiggin-by-the-Sea, 1874, NRO 8699/1.

[26] Interview by author, Mrs E. 6 July 1996.

[27] Jane Nadel-Klein, 'Granny baited the lines: Perpetual crisis and the changing role of women in Scottish fishing communities', *Women's Studies International Studies* 3, Vol. 23 (2000), pp. 363–72.

[28] Paul Thompson with Tony Wailey and Trevor Lummis, *Living the Fishing* (London, 1983), p. 222.

[29] Interview by author, Mrs A. 6 August 1997.

[30] David W. Summer, *Fishing off the Knuckle: the Fishing Villages of Buchan* (Aberdeen, 1980), p. 56.

To outsiders, another indication of the lack of intelligence of fisher people was the habit of intermarriage. A common saying was that fisher people were inbred, a charge made against miners in the mid nineteenth century. In the twentieth century, doctors began to express concern about this fact and the possibility of the impairment of mental and physical health.[31] In Scotland, it was quite usual for non-fisher people to talk of fisher cottages as 'dafties row' ('daftie' meaning learning-disabled). Although there is no indication that this name was used in England, the same idea prevailed. Respondents in neighbouring communities referred to some children in fishing communities as being 'not right' because of intermarriage.[32] And David Clark, in his study of Staithes, a fishing community in Yorkshire, found that people from the communities around Staithes made reference to madness in the village with such remarks: 'You've heard of the village idiot? Well Staithes has got six'.[33] Fisher people themselves said that some children were 'not right' and that people married 'too close'. An important incentive to intermarriage was the necessity of finding a wife skilled in the fishing work, as well as the general preference for their 'ane folk'.

Another supposed proof of their lack of intelligence was their poor performance at school. This can be explained by the scant regard that fisher parents paid to the education of their children. Long after other working-class parents had accepted mandatory schooling, fisher families continued to keep their children off school. Girls were needed to 'skein' the mussels and to look after young children. Boys were expected to gather bait or to help with the fishing if a big catch of fish had been brought in. One master wrote: 'The attendance is very irregular this week, the reason is that when there is a quantity of herring brought in by the boats, the children will not come to school.'[34] The next year the teacher reported that the children were not being allowed to come to school until after they had gathered the bait. On another occasion a mother wrote a letter to a teacher telling her that her daughter could not come to school in the morning until she had finished 'skeining' the mussels.[35] According to one respondent teachers were complicit in these absences, requiring only that children come to school to 'keep the registers in good order ... and go home and help with the family business'.[36] This laxness applied particularly to Friday afternoons when children went to the cliffs to gather limpets. Clearly, teachers had bowed to the demands of the fishing industry. But parents did not set much store by school, assuming that fishing would be the future for both boys and girls. Frederick C. Moffatt

---

[31] A. Mitchell, 'On Consanguineous Marriages in Scotland', *Edinburgh Medical Journal* 10 (1965), pp. 1074–85.

[32] Interview by author, 'Over Sixties Club' of the Holy Sepulchre Church, Ashington, 5 April 1996.

[33] David Clark, *Between pulpit and pew: Folk religion in a North Yorkshire fishing village* (Cambridge, 1982), p. 33.

[34] Records of Beadnell Church of England School, 1877–1984, 1 August 1890, NRO CES 26/2.

[35] Ibid., 3 April 1891.

[36] Interview by author, Mr R. 6 October 1998.

quotes a respondent: 'Me father was waitin' for me to leave school so that I could get on the boat.'[37] This pattern of absence from school continued into the inter-war period and beyond, when the authorities were trying harder to clamp down on absenteeism. One man of fisher origin noted how the 'School Board officer was a frequent visitor to fishing family homes'.[38] An entry in the minute books of the town council of Newbiggin-by-the Sea reveals the pervasiveness of the idea of the lack of intelligence and the general inferiority of the fisher people. On receiving a complaint in 1889 from several people at the fisher end of the village, the chairman of the council described the letter as 'unintelligible' and passed over the issue.[39]

The fisher people were also considered essentially alien. As Nadel-Klein notes, 'the aura of cultural foreignness that hangs ominously around the folk is enhanced by the hint of physical danger'.[40] The inhabitants of fisher villages not only live together but also share a hazardous occupation that marks them off as especially tough and insular. She points to two novelists who emphasise the strangeness of fisher people. Alan Hunter in *Gently in the Sun* suggests, for example, that the fisher folk form a true secret society.[41] He describes those of the North East of England thus: 'They aren't ordinary people like you and me.'[42] Another novelist, Henry Wade, in *Mist on the Saltings*, echoes this theme: 'The sea board folk are intensely secretive about themselves and their doings, even in the most trivial matters.'[43] The conclusion of these writings is of strangeness, perhaps verging on deviance. My acquaintance with many fisher people suggests that these authors take a measure of literary licence. The important point however was that this bias existed.

People were particularly apt to make negative comments about fisher women, especially those who appeared in public. Their working in the public sphere and their resulting independence contradicted the prevailing views of women which emphasised dependence, restriction to the domestic sphere and a non-economic role. The greatest fears however concerned the fisher girls who, up until the First World War, travelled north and then down the coast gutting and packing the herring. Though most came from Scotland, Northumberland girls often joined them up north and came down with them, following the herring as far south as Lowestoft. Middle-class women from various religious denominations took it upon themselves to care for the girls, in particular to bandage their hands to protect them against cuts from the

[37] Evidence of Stan Douglas, quoted in Frederick C. Moffatt, '*Two penn'orth of herrin'*: The Story of the Northumberland Fishermen in Words and Pictures (Newbiggin-by-the-Sea, 1982), p. 23.
[38] John Robinson, *Newbiggin-by-the-Sea: a fishing community* (Morpeth, 1991), p. 9.
[39] Urban Sanitary Authority Minute Books, Newbiggin-by-the-Sea, 1891, NRO 1988/2.
[40] Jane Nadel-Klein, 'Occidentalism as a Cottage Industry: Representing the Autochthonous "Other" in British and Irish Rural Studies' in James G. Carrier, ed., *Occidentalism: Images of the West* (Oxford, 1995), pp. 109–32.
[41] Alan Hunter, *Gently in the Sun* (New York, 1959).
[42] Quoted in Nadel-Klein, 'Occidentalism as a Cottage Industry', p. 117.
[43] Henry Wade, *Mist on the Saltings* (New York, 1985; first published 1933), quoted in Nadel-Klein, 'Occidentalism as a Cottage Industry', p. 117.

sharp knives they used and from the resulting pain caused by contact with the salt used to pack the herrings. In 1913 *The Fishing News* made clear that the concern for their physical wellbeing was not the only reason for such solicitude. It noted that 'no expense should be counted too great to keep them strong among the temptations to which their life subjected them and to win them for goodness and purity and blessing'.[44] Others were less sanguine. We hear of horror being expressed at the sight of fisher girls lying on the quay in Newcastle upon Tyne, sleeping between their shifts.[45] The critics gave no thought to the fact that they worked as many as twelve hours per day. The issue was fear of sexual depravity.

Society also scorned fish hawkers despite the fact that they were romanticised by painters and patronised by many housewives who liked their fresh fish. Indeed one supposed characterisation of them has long been part of the pejorative descriptions of working women. Until well into the twentieth century, people described women who talked loudly as 'talking like a fishwife', the implication being that fishwives sounded coarse, raucous and unfeminine when shouting their wares. Even a sympathetic observer described them as having a 'direct manner'.[46] Munby, who found them 'nobler and more interesting than any other', was well aware of the negative view of them. In recounting a meeting at a railway station with fish hawkers whom he knew, he described the reaction of well-dressed passers-by 'who looked astounded at the strange dress and stalwart forms of the fisher girls'.[47] Correspondents who sold fish in the 1930s told of people whom they met on public transportation, while carrying their creels, looking askance at them and moving away to another part of the bus or train. That the fisher women were often married opened them up to the charge not only of crossing gender lines by earning money, but also of neglecting their homes and children.

Fisher folk reacted to such negative representations. As Nadel-Klein has found in her research on Scottish fisher people, and as I have observed in my work in Northumberland, fisher people developed a defensive and almost aggressive sense of self-pride in response to the negative attitudes of outsiders. This attitude almost amounted to a feeling of superiority. Nadel-Klein explained this feeling as a 'weapon against denigration' and the fishing population as a 'defended community which came to cherish their identity as a form of communal property'.[48] The following anecdote reveals this sense of pride. One respondent, a woman of fishing stock, recounted how she had felt she had 'come down in the world' by marrying a miner.[49] Another, comparing fisher people to miners (their usual point of reference), noted that miners never left bequests the size of those of fisher people and seldom owned their

44 *The Fishing News*, 12 December 1913.
45 *The Newcastle Courant*, 18 August 1881.
46 Louise Hamer, *A Brief History of Cullercoats* (Newcastle upon Tyne, 1986).
47 Munby diary entry, 30 December 1869 in Hiley, *Victorian Working Women*, Ch. 4.
48 Nadel-Klein, 'Granny Baited the Lines'.
49 Oral evidence of Mrs W. 20 December 1996.

own houses. Against the charge, made especially by miners, of hoarding money, fishers cited the necessity of saving for damages to their fishing gear and denigrated the 'spendthrift miners'. They also took pride in their own independence, seeing themselves as owing nothing to anyone and being their own masters.[50]

They looked upon their community as being superior. This pride, Nadel-Klein asserts, has become part of their cultural fabric.[51] Instead of being embarrassed by their inbreeding, the fisher people took pride in it, routinely describing their community as one big family and everyone as second cousins, and laughingly saying that, in their degree of intermarriage, they resembled the royal family. The naming habits, which were common in fishing communities throughout the nation, reveal a desire to strengthen the ties within the community. Not content with having overlapping surnames, they used the same Christian names repeatedly. In Newbiggin-by-the-Sea, for instance, we find eight Jack Robinsons and eight Jack Armstrongs out of a population of thirty-eight fishermen. This pattern necessitated in Northumberland, as elsewhere in the nation, the use of nicknames. Thus we have 'Betty's Jack', 'Ned's Jack', 'Grandad's Jack', 'Jack the Whaler', 'Sparrows Jack' and 'Lame Jack'.[52] The fisher people revelled in their closeness, even exaggerating it, and drew distinct boundaries around their communities. Though never a 'race apart', they were as close to being isolated as any group in the nation. They regarded people who came in as foreigners, and tended to mix only with fisher people and to mistrust other people.[53] Their lives were intertwined, one fisher woman said.[54] David Clark found that if fisher families took vacations, a rare event, they visited fisher communities.[55] One of my respondent families illustrates this pattern. The only vacation they took was to a fishing community in Aberdeen, Scotland, called Torry, where they lodged with a fisher family. They clearly felt a real bond with this Scottish fishing family and talked fondly of the experience years later.[56] The sense of community is apparent in times of tragedy when the whole community – not only the affected fishing village, but also all the villages up and down the coast – would rally round to attend the funeral. By the inter-war years, buses would be laid on to facilitate the occasion and hundreds would follow the funeral cortège to the cemetery. Such an event was referred to by the fisher people as a 'fisher funeral' – a reflection of their sense of being a unique community. When one of my fisher respondents, by this time elderly and disabled, heard of an equally elderly fisher friend who had died she was

[50] Ministery of Agriculture and Fisheries Report of Departmental Committee on Inshore Fisheries Vol. I, 1914 (London, 1914), App., p. 2654.
[51] Nadel-Klein, 'Granny Baited the Lines'.
[52] Oral evidence of Mr and Mrs J.L.R. 6 July 1997.
[53] Collection of oral interviews made by Paul Thompson and housed at the British Library, QD8/ FISH/52 C773; see also Hamer, *A Brief History of Cullercoats*, p. 36.
[54] Interview by author, Mrs A. 6 November 1998.
[55] Clark, *Between pulpit and pew*, p. 163.
[56] Interview by author, Mr and Mrs J.L.R. 6 July 1997.

anxious to know if her friend had had a 'proper fisher funeral'.[57] By that date (2010) fishing had barely been practised in the community for fifty years and most of the original fisher people had died.

As the number of fisher people decreased with the decline in the industry in the inter-war years, they sought to perpetuate the close community. They described anyone of fishing blood as 'fisher', giving this distinction to people who had moved into other occupations but who had fisher parents or grand-parents. Some of my own respondents continued to identify themselves as 'fisher', though their connection to the community was through their grand-parents.[58] This pattern was true in other fishing areas. One of Paul Thompson's respondents from Portsoy, Scotland, made the following comment, which could well have come from the mouths of Northumberland fisher people: 'We were fisher then and we're fisher now'.[59] Nadel-Klein has found the same phenomenon in Ferryden and other fisher communities in Scotland. Though Ferryden was no longer a fishing community by the 1960s, the people there continued to see themselves as fisher and

> to talk about the old days when they endured poverty and danger, hunger and widowhood.... Their stories mythologized and made sacred the shared virtues and common hardships that derived from the 'heroic' period of fishing.[60]

In turn, the neighbouring communities still referred to them as inbred and superstitious.

The close sense of community did not preclude jealousy or feuds. Indeed relationships between fisher families were akin to those between siblings, with all the attendant jealousies. Some families had feuds and did not speak to each other for long periods of time.[61] A particularly serious family feud occurred on 1st March 1929, when Charles Armstrong assaulted Tamar Armstrong, injuring her severely. The issue did not end there, for William Armstrong assaulted William Brown and Sarah Jane Armstrong.[62] Local historian Katrina Porteous, who knows the fishing community intimately, claims that these feuds – family or otherwise – often centred on finance, which was so often the provenance of women. Another source of conflict was often over who had the biggest catch of fish.[63] But women could also be competitive. We find periodic cases in the petty sessions of fisher women physically fighting. In 1868, for example, one Margaret Brown fought with

---

57 Interview by author, Mrs J.L.R. 6 July 2010.
58 Interview by author, Mrs R. 6 July 1998.
59 Collection of oral interviews, QD8/FISH/52 C773.
60 Jane Nadel-Klein, 'Reweaving the fringe: localism, tradition, and representation in British ethnography', *American Ethnologist* 3, Vol. 18 (August 1991), pp. 500–15
61 Clark, *Between pulpit and pew*, p. 32.
62 *The Morpeth Herald*, 1 March 1929.
63 Interview by author, Ms Katrina Porteous 6 July 1998.

Jane Brown.[64] That same year, Jane Dent knocked Margaret Renner's head against a wall and tore her hat. Jane Dent was fined £2 with costs of £1. We read also of two fisher women brawling at Cullercoats in 1881.[65] Yet, as one fisherman said and others verified, 'bad feelings were only skin deep; when anyone was in trouble, everyone went round'.[66] All the respondents were unanimous about the fact that doors were never locked, despite the fact that fishermen kept large sums of money in the house.

Women's aggressiveness was not limited to their own community. Like miners' wives, they were ferocious in helping their husbands defend their rights, as was clear in the famous case of fishing in the River Tweed beside Berwick-upon-Tweed in the 1850s. The issue was the restrictions put upon fishermen by the Tweed Fisheries Acts of 1857 and 1859 against fishing for salmon at the mouth of the River Tweed. The aim of these acts was to allow more salmon to swim upstream where they could be caught by the upper class which had the fishing rights. When the fishermen persisted in fishing for salmon at the mouth of the river, the authorities moved in to prevent them from doing so. The entire fishing population then turned out to fish, supported by the non-fisher population. The Tweed Fisheries Acts were widely regarded as class legislation. When policemen tried to stop the fishermen from fishing, they were driven off by women throwing rocks. The fishermen and their wives then attacked the water bailiffs and the police. The women next took to braying and banging tin kettles, a traditional expression of disapproval. Men dressed up in women's nightgowns to avoid being arrested. The authorities, unable to control events, actually called in a gunboat. Several indictments against men and women resulted, but the poaching continued and, on several occasions, women attacked water bailiffs who were attempting to stop it.[67] The authorities and the elite were appalled at the actions of the fisher people, not least the violence of the women. As the calling out of the gunboat suggests, they feared for the social order. For their part, the fishing population and much of the lower class of Berwick on Tweed and Spital felt that the traditional rights of the fishers were being encroached upon by the upper classes, and they were determined not to obey unfair laws. The fisher women's actions have echoes of the mining women's responses to worsening working conditions for their husbands.

Conclusion

The inshore fishing community as a whole, and the women in particular, generally faced an ambivalent response from the outside world. At times of tragedy observers viewed them sympathetically and donated relief money,

[64] Morpeth Petty Sessions, Minutes of Evidence, NRO PS5/11.
[65] *The Shields Daily News*, 21 January 1881.
[66] Oral evidence of Mr Smailes, NRO 8/7.
[67] David Kent, 'Power, protest, poaching, and the Tweed Fisheries Acts of 1857 and 1859: "Send a gunboat!"', *Northern History* LXII 2 (2005), pp. 293–315.

but the rest of the time saw them as a 'race apart', inbred, unintelligent and even deviant. Indeed the inshore fishing community, though not deviant or a 'race apart', was a fairly isolated, inward-looking group and, to a large extent, inbred. Partly as a response to these attitudes but also due to a belief in the value of their work, the community developed a deep sense of pride and a suspicion of outsiders. Regardless of how they were represented by the outside world, the frame of reference of inshore fishermen's wives was their own community.

PART III

FEMALE AGRICULTURAL LABOURERS

5

'Muscular Femininity'

To find the female agricultural labourers of Northumberland we must move inland from the windswept coastal fishing villages and the grimy coal mining towns and villages, to where the Cheviot Hills slope down to the fertile valleys of the River Till and its tributaries. There, in Glendale and further east in Belford – the rural districts studied in most depth – we find women labourers in abundance. These labourers formed an essential part of farming in Northumberland, as they did in the East and West Lothians, Roxburgh and Berwickshire in southeastern Scotland and in Westmoreland, long after women had ceased to be an important part of the farming labour force in the southeast of England – though not, as once thought, in the west of England.[1] They had experiences and self- images very different from those of fishing and mining women. These experiences can be linked to the economic, geographic and demographic structures of the area. We have found a similar congruence between the experience of women in mining and inshore fishing communities and the structural characteristics of their communities.

The key factor in the lives and work of agricultural women was the development in the late eighteenth century of advanced farming, an important part of which was the addition of turnips, sown grasses and potatoes to the cultivation of oats and barley. Turnips were particularly important for feeding the sheep. As Devine has noted – speaking of the same system in southern Scotland – the development of these new crops

> stretched the farmers' busy time, backwards and forwards in the year making it necessary to recruit labour for the new cycle of weeding, sowing, thinning and gathering which endured from spring to early winter.[2]

The problem was however an insufficiency of men to fulfil the needs of this labour-intensive farming in Northumberland, Westmoreland and the Scottish border counties. Farms were frequently isolated in areas that lacked the villages and towns that dotted the countryside in the southeast of the country and could supply labour for farming needs. Furthermore, unmarried

---

[1] For the revised notion that women labourers were still employed in the west of England at least until the end of the Victorian period after they had disappeared from the southeast, see Edward Higgs, 'Occupational Censuses and the Agricultural Workforce in Victorian England', *Economic History Review* LXVIII, 4 (1995), pp. 700–16.

[2] T.M. Devine, 'Women Workers, 1850–1914' in T.M. Devine, ed., *Farm Servants and Labour in Lowland Scotland, 1770–1914* (Edinburgh, 1990), pp. 98–123.

men tended to be drawn away by the relatively high wages in the mines and quarries, and to work on the railways and in and around the city of Newcastle upon Tyne. A system grew up whereby farmers housed married agricultural labourers, called hinds, in cottages on the farms, such cottages being given rent free as part of the yearly contract. Yet even with access to the labour of many of the hinds' sons, the farmers' needs could not be met. What the farmers desired, in addition to these hinds, was a body of labour which was flexible, low cost and reliable, turnip cultivation being very labour intensive.

To fulfil this need they, like those in the border counties of Scotland and Westmoreland, devised a unique system of female labour. Women working in the fields was not limited to these regions. Female family members in small farms, then as later, in Britain and other countries regularly worked in the fields. In England, women had long been employed as labourers all over the country and, until the late 1860s, in the southeastern counties had worked in the notorious gang system which had developed in the 1820s and involved a gang master hiring women and children and taking them from farm to farm to work, often far from their homes. Such was the middle-class panic by the 1860s about the supposed moral depravity caused by this system that the Agricultural Gangs Act was passed in 1867, mitigating the worst of the system.[3] In Northumberland however, as in the borders of Scotland and in Westmoreland, where no such system existed, farmers were able to create and maintain a system of reliable female labour that was extensive and lasted through the inter-war period and beyond. They did this by insisting that their male agricultural labourers provide women workers, a requirement made possible by the lack of a developed industrial system in the region which could have provided alternative female employment. The few textile mills that did exist were situated in market towns such as Wooler, Alnwick and Berwick-upon-Tweed and, according to Norman McCord, the economic and social historian of the North East, were small and short lived.[4] The predominance of aristocratic, large landowners, who were committed to farming through the renting of land to tenant farmers, may have contributed to the lack of growth of substantial industry.

The first hiring arrangement for the female labour system that prevailed from the late eighteenth century until the late 1860s operated as follows: the hinds in Northumberland, as part of their yearly labour contract, were required to provide one or two women to work what was called the bond for the farmer, and to house and feed such workers. If the hinds failed to provide a woman worker, the farmers would not hire them and they would have to

[3]   Nicola Verdon, *Rural Women Workers in Nineteenth-Century England: Gender, Work and Wages* (Woodbridge, 2002), pp. 107–14; Karen Sayer, *Women of the Fields: Representations of Rural Women in the Nineteenth Century* (Manchester, 1995), Ch. 6; Ivy Pinchbeck, *Women Workers and the Industrial Revolution 1750–1850* (London, 1981; first published 1930), pp. 86–90.

[4]   Norman McCord, *North East England: An economic and social history* (London, 1979), p. 57.

find work in another industry or pay a fine of 1p per day.[5] While about one-fourth to one-fifth of hinds were forced to hire an outsider, the bondage could be, and often was, performed by their wives or daughters. In the north of the county, mothers of young children did not perform the bond and thus hired outsiders while, in the south of the county, the tendency was for mothers to continue to work outside and to depend on baby minders or older children for childcare. Wives who worked enjoyed special arrangements: they were allowed to begin work later and to leave work earlier to allow time to do their housework and to prepare meals. Not surprisingly, hinds preferred to hire their own wives or daughters whose wages could be subsumed within the family wage.

These women, up until the 1860s – and even after, when the system which gave them their name had been ended – were called bondagers. This peculiar name did not imply servitude; bondagers were, in every sense of the word, free labour. They bound themselves for a year to work for a hind but were then free to move to another hind. As distinctive as their name was their appearance. Indeed, their picturesque outfit led one early nineteenth century observer to describe them as a 'fit subject for the sketcher's pencil'.[6] As late as 1939, another observer noted that 'the visitor to the farms of Glendale and Tweedside may yet see the "bondager" busy in the field, clad in what may be described as the last remaining peasant costume in England'.[7] The main feature of this picturesque outfit was a large straw hat which was lined with cotton material with a wimple underneath, the aim being to protect the face and neck from the wind and the sun. In the summer, an 'ugly' (a cotton bonnet, held stiff by bones, designed again to protect the face from sunshine) replaced the straw hat. The bondagers took pride in decorating the crowns of the hats with rucking. As Dinah Iredale notes, 'sometimes the rucking was worked into rosettes and these rosettes were decorated with beads, flowers and feathers'.[8] It was a 'work of art', one former bondager noted.[9] A long-sleeved blouse of printed cotton covered the upper body and, over this, was worn a woollen shawl or tweed waistcoat. A short skirt made of drugget – a tough, waterproof material – provided protection for the lower part of the body and was covered by an apron while black stockings and heavy boots, which Cuthbert Bede called 'clod-hopping boots',[10] and leggings made of straw completed the attire (Figure 5.1).[11] At turnip hoeing and at harvest

5   Dinah Iredale, *Bondagers: The History of Women Farmworkers in Northumberland and Southeast Scotland* (Wooler, Northumberland, 2008), p. 27.
6   Cuthbert Bede, *The Adventures of Mr. Verdant Green* (Oxford, 1982; first published 1857), p. 4.
7   Quoted in Dinah Iredale, *Bondagers*, p. 2, from Donald Scott, Agriculture Chapter of *The Three Counties of England*, ed., Sir Cuthbert Hedalam (Newcastle upon Tyne, 1939).
8   Iredale, *Bondagers*, p. 156.
9   Comment of Mona Thompson, quoted in Iredale, *Bondagers*, p. 157.
10 Bede, *The Adventures*, p. 6.
11 L. Taylor, 'To be a farmer's girl: bondagers of border counties', *Country Life* (12 October, 1978), pp. 1110–1112; A.M. Scott, 'Women's working dress on the farms of the east borders', *Costume* X (1977), pp. 41–8.

Figure 5.1. Bondagers, in traditional dress with decorated hats and drugget skirts, taking a break from sorting and weighing potatoes. Illustrates the distinctive costume worn by bondagers until the Second World War. Note how the peculiar hats are decorated, a fact that argues against the charge that these women were 'masculine'.
Ladykirk Farm, near Berwick upon Tweed, c.1900

times white skirts and aprons would replace the rough aprons and drugget skirts, probably because both tasks were cleaner than the labourers' other work. Also, the harvest, being the culmination of many months of work, was a cause for celebration.

Another group of women workers who worked alongside the bondagers, and continued to work long after the bondage system had been abolished, was the cottars. These women were single or widowed female agricultural labourers, sometimes with farm labouring sons and daughters. Some were unmarried women with illegitimate children. These cottars made independent contracts with the farmers and, like the hinds, received rent-free cottages and some perquisites – usually a certain amount of potatoes and, in the nineteenth century, grain. They also had their coal transported. The census returns for 1871 for Glendale indicate that they amounted to 5.3 percent of the agricultural labouring workforce that year.[12] By 1901, their numbers had increased considerably. Idleton in the Rural District of Glendale, for instance, registered 17.9 percent of households headed by cottars.[13] Jane Long, who otherwise writes insightfully of the female farm workers, fails to take note

---

[12] Census Returns for Glendale, 1871, RG11/5189–5194.
[13] Census Returns for Idleton, 1901, RG13/4849.

of their increase.[14] While some sources suggest they were paid the same as other female workers, others suggest they earned slightly more. Frequently, the children of such cottars were also farm labourers but it might be the case that the children were too young to be employed. Oftentimes single sisters lived together, occasionally with a brother, the oldest sister being the house-holder.[15] Observers speak of quite elderly spinsters living in cot houses and working as farm labourers.[16] The census returns, which register cottars as old as sixty-seven and even seventy-two still employed, bear out this finding. Farmers often allowed retired cottars who had given good service, but were no longer able to work, to continue living in their cot houses on condition that they look after a young bondager.

The occupational identity and experience of these women and the wives and daughters who also laboured were unique. In both dress and activity, Northumberland farm women violated middle-class norms of femininity, which emphasised delicacy. With sturdy forearms, shoulders and legs neces-sary to perform work that was heavy, often back-breaking, conducted out-of-doors, in all weathers, and alongside men, they represented a form of 'muscular femininity'.[17] They were widely regarded as having great stamina. Advertisements for women workers stipulated that they be 'strong and suffi-cient'. As we have noted, both mining and fisher women also had to possess physical strength. Yet farming women differed from both mining and fisher women. Theirs is yet another variation in womanhood. Being a woman in agricultural communities in Northumberland meant being skilled in outdoor farming work, knowing how to make butter and cheese and take care of a cow, a pig and perhaps chickens, as well as being well versed in all the usual skills associated with motherhood and household management. But, as in fishing communities, it meant being part of a family economy and thus being central to the survival of the family. Women agricultural labourers had largely disappeared from the fields in southeastern England by the third quarter of the nineteenth century, except at potato picking and harvest times and in the hop growing areas. While Snell assumes that they had disappeared from other areas in England and labels Tess in *Tess of the D'Urbervilles*, who was depicted by Hardy pulling turnips in Dorset in freezing weather, an anachronism, these conclusions are incorrect.[18] Based on his examination of the 1906 Census of Occupation, Higgs has illustrated that women in fact worked seasonally in harvest and turnip harvesting times in Dorset in the 1880s – the era in which Hardy set his novel – and the South West gener-

---

[14] Jane Long, *Conversations in Cold Rooms: Women, Work and Poverty in Nineteenth-Century Northumberland* (Woodbridge, 1999), p. 83.
[15] Census Returns for Lowick, 1871–1901: 1871, RG10/5188; 1881, RG11/5134; 1891, RG12/4270; 1901, RG13/4848.
[16] See for instance recording of Hetha Butler, 11 May 1972 NRO T/20.
[17] Phrase employed by Long, *Conversations in Cold Rooms*, p. 90.
[18] See discussion of Thomas Hardy, K.D.M. Snell, *Annals of the Labouring Poor: Social Change and Agrarian England* (Cambridge, 1985), p. 378.

ally at least through the Victorian period.[19] Certainly, in Northumberland, Westmoreland and southeastern Scotland, they continued to be an essential part of the farming economy throughout our period, working on a year-long basis, though in smaller numbers by the end. In 1871, they represented 35 percent of the agricultural labour force, a total of 5,269; in 1881, 40 percent; in 1911, around 36 percent.[20] By 1931 however their migration to towns had reduced their numbers to 16.7 percent of the agricultural labouring force in Northumberland, 3,323 in actual numbers.[21] In some districts, the percentage was considerably higher. Glendale for instance registered 22.6 percent of its agricultural labouring force female and Belford 18 percent. We can assume that their numbers declined further in the 1930s but, without another census, we must depend on anecdotal evidence.

In 1860, the beginning of our period, the bondage system had already been under attack for a while. Hinds, who had to employ non-family members, were in an unenviable situation. They were required to house and feed the bondagers in their small cottages for a year. They generally received £48 per year from the farmer, out of which they paid the bondagers an average of £12. The sum left over, the hinds claimed, was inadequate to provide for the upkeep of the household. Further, the presence of the bondagers made the living situation of the hinds and their families – already difficult, with as many as six children – unbearable. Many of the houses, which were even worse than those of miners, had only one large room with a small pantry. The unroofed attics were unsuitable for sleeping, being too cold in winter and too hot in summer. The better of the houses had two rooms with an attic.[22] Even with the addition of box beds, which created a division in the one-roomed houses, little real privacy was possible and the young bondagers were forced to sleep with the children, dress in front of them, and to share the hearth with the family. Inevitably, they were privy to the intimate details of family life.

Not surprisingly, some observers were convinced that the system led to sexual depravity, and depicted the bondagers as having loose morals.[23] One writer said that the hinds were unsettled by the presence of 'coarse, blowsy girls'.[24] A Mrs Williams, herself a former bondager, gave a more nuanced picture of the situation. She wrote that

---

[19] Edward Higgs, 'Occupational censuses and the agricultural workforce in Victorian England and Wales', *Economic History Review* LXVIII, 4 (1995), pp. 700–16; C. Miller, 'The Hidden Workforce: female fieldworkers in Gloucestershire, 1870–1901', *Southern History* 6 (1984), pp. 139–61.

[20] *Census of England and Wales, 1871* Vol. III (London, 1873), Tables 11 and 12; *Census of England and Wales, 1881* Vol. III (London, 1883), Table 10; *Census of England and Wales, 1911* Vol. X (London, 1913), p. 122.

[21] *Census of England and Wales, 1931, County of Northumberland* (London, 1934), Table 24. This number may be a little inflated due to the inclusion of women working in gardens and woods.

[22] Annual Report of Sanitary Officer for Glendale, 1874, NRO MH12/9024.

[23] William Fairbanks, *Evils of the Bondage System*, 2nd edn (Kelso, n.d.), p. 11.

[24] Samuel Donkin, *The Agricultural Labourers of Northumberland: their physical and social condition* (Newcastle upon Tyne, 1869), p. 11.

the wife whose face was prematurely robbed of its youthful bloom by the cares and anxieties incident to the wife and mother – was often unnecessarily jealous of the bondager and would take on the bondage herself – leaving her children in the care of one little more than a child herself and this is done with full knowledge of the risk they ran of ill treatment and neglect, for fear of having a bondager.[25]

Women in the south of the county avoided the problem, before the imposition of mandatory education, by using their daughters from an early age as child-minders. Observers therefore represented them as negligent mothers and housekeepers.

The opposition to the bondage system which had begun in the 1830s grew more vociferous in the 1860s, and ultimately was successful in destroying it. In 1837 the hinds had argued that the burdens of housing and feeding the bondager were too great. Without outside support however the campaign failed, and the hinds settled for an increase in wages. The next campaign, which arose in the 1860s, was successful in getting rid of the system largely because of the support of reformers – secular and religious – concerned about the possible immorality to which it led. Curiously, given the ideology of the time, which stressed the delicacy of women, there was no opposition to women doing arduous work in the fields. It was clear that delicacy was a monopoly of middle-class women. Reformers believed that if the wives or daughters of hinds worked with their fathers or brothers, rather than strangers, then there would be no problem, as there would be no chance of immorality.[26] The problem lay in the supposed dangers of unrelated young women living with the hinds' families in crowded houses. The opponents of the bondage system favoured family work in which the daughters worked for their fathers and brothers. This system of work was nothing new. When they could, hinds had always preferred to hire their wives and daughters instead of strangers. The earnings of the daughters were incorporated into the earnings of the family, daughters receiving back a small allowance, if anything at all. Frequently, wives had worked the bondage before children had been born and, when a child was old enough to look after siblings, had gone back into the fields for a somewhat shortened day. The critics, with the support of the hinds, were successful in ending the bondager system, which died out in the late 1860s.

The system of female farm labour however continued even though the bondager system had ended. Family members, usually daughters or sisters, now fulfilled the entire need for female labour. While the hinds were suppos-

---

[25] Mrs Williams, 'The Bondage System' in Anon, *Voices from the Plough* (Hawick, 1869), pp. 34–35.

[26] The same fear of immorality, instead of the arduousness of the work for women, had determined the thinking of the commissioners at the time of the Royal Commission on the Employment of Women and Children in the Mines in 1842. For a discussion of this point, see Jane Humphries, 'Protective Legislation, the Capitalist State and Working Class Men: The Case of the Mines Regulation Act of 1842', *Feminist Review* 7 (1981), pp. 1–34.

edly not obliged to supply woman workers, in actual fact farmers gave preference to those who could. Indeed men without women frequently could not
find work and were forced to leave farm work. Even as late as the 1930s, the
farmers still insisted on seeing the female worker before they would employ
the hind, so important was women's contribution. A sign of continuity was
that the women workers continued to call themselves bondagers and dress
in the traditional costume, though the actual system had ended. This habit
persisted through the inter-war period.[27] As we have seen, though the numbers
of women declined from 35 percent to 16.7 percent from 1871 to 1931, they
remained substantial.

Conditions for women farm workers

As was the case in other industries – and in mining and fishing, as we have
seen – men were the primary workers in the hierarchy of farm work, with
women the secondary workers. Men reserved the most skilled work and the
use of machinery – ploughing and building stacks – for themselves, or determined that their work was defined as the most skilled. The handling of the
all-important horses also fell largely within their purview. The key factor in
the division of tasks was the size of the farm. In small farms, the sexual division of tasks was less rigid and women were sometimes allowed to take on
tasks that were denied them on large farms. Generally, men avoided the most
undesirable tasks on the farm, leaving those to the women. One respondent
said that if a job was 'dirty, awkward or required patience it was likely that
a woman would be expected to do it'.[28] Technological change in the form
of the substitution of the scythe for the sickle for reaping had diminished
the scope of women's work by the third quarter of the nineteenth century.
Women had been as skillful – if not more skillful – with the sickle as men.
Furthermore, for most of the period under study, women were paid much
less than men, though they did at least two-thirds as much work. Their wage
amounted to around 7.5p per day at the beginning of our period compared
to 15p per day for men, and 11p by the end of the century compared to 20p
for men.[29] The exception was harvest work for which they earned double
what they earned at other times – 15p at the start of the period, with food
provided – a result of their efficiency at harvest work and the farmers' need

---

[27] Evidence of Edith Hope in Ian MacDougall, *Bondagers: Personal Recollections of Eight Scottish Farm Workers* (Edinburgh, 2000). See also oral evidence collected for Northumberland by Judy Gielgud, 'Nineteenth Century Farm Women in Northumberland and Cumbria: the Neglected Workforce' (PhD thesis, University of Sussex, 1992).

[28] Gielgud, 'Nineteenth Century Farm Women', p. 110, evidence from oral interviews.

[29] See for instance pay lists of Dancey farm 1899–1903 NRO530/1. These agree with those studied by Gielgud in 'Nineteenth Century Farm Women'.

to get the crops in before it rained.[30] Joyce Burnette's assertion that women did not earn extra wages for harvest work does not hold true for Northumberland.[31] By the 1930s, farmers had raised women's wages to around three-fifths the wages of men year round, the result presumably of a scarcity of women workers.[32]

In spite of the restrictions on their work and their low wage, these farm women were central to the work on farms and performed work that was of great importance. According to the findings of the three government commissions (the 1843 Commission on the Employment of Women and Children in Agriculture, the Commission on the Employment of Children, Young Persons and Women in Agriculture of 1867 and the Royal Commission on Labour in 1890–91), farming in Northumberland could not have been conducted without their contribution. Wilson Fox, commenting in the report to the Royal Commission on Labour of 1893–4 on the agricultural system in Northumberland, remarked, for instance, that, 'If men were substituted it would impose a greater burden on employers than they could bear and the effect of such a change would be to throw the land out of cultivation',[33] because men would have to be paid considerably more than women. Farmers, the farming community, and the women themselves had no doubt of their usefulness and skill and took for granted that their role in farm work was entirely appropriate. While some of the work was considered too heavy for them, generally women were given no allowance for being female. People regarded them as having great stamina. From an early age daughters learned how to hoe in the summer months at their mother's side, beginning work officially at the age of twelve at the beginning of our period in 1860. Later in the period they would begin light work at thirteen or fourteen, at which point they were already adept at wielding tools. To begin with, they worked under the guidance of their mothers or another woman. Later, at the age of seventeen, they were trained and would be expected to be fully capable. Such women, like the men, began work at 6 a.m. After several breaks amounting to two hours – for the purpose of resting the horses – they ended work at 6 p.m. Farm workers, male and female, worked on Saturdays until the 1920s, after which point they had Saturday afternoons off. Depending on the task at hand, the women sometimes worked with hinds, sometimes with a group of women led by a woman leader, often called a woman steward. The latter was a woman of some stature and skill, and earned an extra 5p.

---

[30] It was not uncommon for employers to pay more when tasks had to be performed quickly. Penelope Lane, 'A Customary or market wage? Women and work in the East Midlands, c.1700–1840' in Penelope Lane, Neil Raven and K.D.M. Snell, eds, *Women, Work and Wages in England*, pp. 102–18.

[31] Joyce Burnette, *Gender, Work and Wages in Industrial Revolution Britain* (Cambridge, 2008), p. 157.

[32] Issues of local newspapers in the 1920s and 30s, particularly *The Berwick Advertiser*, give details of wages set at the annual hiring fairs.

[33] Royal Commission on Labour, The Agricultural Labourer Vol. I, PP 1893–4 XXXV, p. 102.

Contrary to a common stereotype that saw women as seasonal workers on farms, the bondagers of Northumberland were involved year round in fundamentally important work, though often in a secondary role to the men. In the springtime, the main tasks for the women workers involved preparing the land for growing the crops. Their first task was clearing the land of stones and thistles and generally weeding prior to ploughing. This latter task was monopolised by men, the argument being that the handles of the plough were too wide for women who were also supposedly unable to lift the share and the coulter clear of the furrow when the plough needed to be turned. As Gielgud has concluded from her interviews of female agricultural labourers, most did find the task difficult.[34] Yet, we have examples of Northumberland women who were strong and big enough to plough. Also this practice was heard of in Westmoreland,[35] as it was in the nation as a whole during the First World War. Elizabeth Roberts and Deborah Simonton suggest that women sometimes did heavy labour on farms, but the old notion of woman as 'the weaker vessel' affected attitudes.[36] On small farms especially, women were allowed to harrow. Such was the case with Annie Guthrie, an interviewee of Ian MacDougall from the inter-war period.[37] This right was significant because it put the women in charge of horses, a role which was jealously guarded by the men. Exclusion from ploughing however left women with the most dirty and onerous of the preparatory work: the fertilising of the fields, a job which men regarded as particularly 'derogatory to their manhood'.[38] Reportedly, they would stand by and watch the women perform it. This task involved first forking the heavy, wet dung out of the byres and middens onto carts, which, because of the heaviness of the wet manure, was one of the women's most onerous tasks. They then drove the carts to the fields and deposited the manure in piles. Hastings Neville described his reactions to this process thus: 'Very painful it is to see them (the women) in the moist alley formed by the steaming walls of stuff (manure) which they fork from side to side.'[39] Next, using rakes, the women spread the manure over the fields in preparation for the planting of corn. We are reminded of the association of women with the body and bodily functions.

In this same season, the women workers planted potatoes and performed other tasks. Violet Clarke, who worked as a farm labourer both before and after her marriage in the 1930s, described her work planting potatoes after the drills had been ploughed by the men.

---

[34] Gielgud, 'Nineteenth Century Farm Women', pp. 108–9.
[35] Commission on the Employment of Women and Children in Agriculture, PP 1843 XII, pp. 109, 112 and 113.
[36] Elizabeth Roberts, *Women's Work, 1840–1940* (Cambridge, 1995; first published 1988) p. 14; Deborah Simonton, *A History of European Women's Work: 1700 to the Present* (London 1998), pp. 131–4.
[37] Evidence of Annie Guthrie in MacDougall, *Bondagers: Recollections.*
[38] John Wilson, *The Newcastle Chronicle*, 21 July 1864.
[39] Hastings M. Neville, *Under a Border Tower* (Newcastle upon Tyne, 1896), pp. 289–90.

I planted potatoes from a pail or bag slung over my shoulder, hanging down my front like a kangaroo pouch, (before this a dratting apron would have been used) which I filled from a cart going in front of us down the drills. If I tipped too many into my pouch I staggered along bent double, dropping a tattie (potato) every twelve inches or so. As soon as my bag was empty I started all over again, toiling all day in that back-breaking position. Behind us planters, came the 'double' or 'drill plough' splitting the drills to cover the tattie.[40]

The women performed other tasks such as burning of hedge trimmings, cleaning out of hen houses, filling in of drains with stones, preparing straw for yelming (thatching) and burning posts to put into the ground before the heavy work of early summer. When the weather was wet, women mended bags inside, sewing them with big needles.

Hay making – the next main task on the farming calendar – once an important area of control for women, had ceased to be so by the mid nineteenth century. Until that point, women had had the central role in reaping this crop, using the sickle with great skill and speed. Indeed it had been well known that 'a maiden ridge of three young women would beat a bull ridge of three young men' in reaping.[41] The scythe however had replaced the sickle and, because of its weight, men had replaced women as reapers.[42] Because of technological change, women thus lost status and were reduced to lower-paid followers whose role was to lift the swathes of hay, shake them and turn them to allow the under-surface to be exposed to the sun and wind to dry. Some of the men also became followers. By the end of the century the mechanical reaper, in turn, replaced the scythe and the rest of the men, except the mechanical reaper drivers, became followers. When the hay was dry, the women and the men would make the hay into cocks or pikes, draw them by sledge and then rake them into bigger cocks, ensuring that the rain would run off. Next, women and men pitched the hay into carts, a very strenuous job. Burnette has asserted that women did not lift the hay but this is not a valid conclusion in the case of Northumberland.[43] The hay was then transported in the carts, the women often driving them, thus again thwarting the rule that women should not control horses. Following that, men made the hay into stacks or, alternatively, put it in the hay barn where women spread it into the corners and pressed it down – an unpopular job, for the barn was 'hot, and airless and full of flying dust and hay seeds and thistles'.[44] As in the case of the spreading of manure, men spurned this unpleasant job.

[40] Violet Clarke, 'Tied to the soil' in Brian P. Martin, ed., *Tales of Old Countrywomen* (Newton Abbot, 1997), pp. 135–45.
[41] Cited by Eve Hostettler in 'Gourlay steel and the sexual division of labour', *History Workshop Journal* IV (1977), pp. 95–100.
[42] Michael Roberts, 'Sickles and scythes: women's work and men's work at harvest time', *History Workshop* VII (1979), pp. 3–28.
[43] Joyce Burnette, *Gender, work and Wages in Industrial Revolution Britain* (Cambridge, 2008), p. 156.
[44] Gielgud, 'Nineteenth Century Farm Women', p. 69.

Figure 5.2. Harvesting corn. Women, like most of the men, have become followers behind the reaping machine, tying the corn into bundles and making stooks. This process post-dated the cutting of corn by sickle and then scythe and predated the reaper binder. Illustrates the deskilling of the women in the harvest but at the same time the sharing of the task with men. Note that the operation of the reaping machine is monopolised by a man.
Craigsfield, Roxburgh, c.1900

August brought the all-important corn harvest in which, as in the case of hay making, women's role had diminished. Again, women had previously been the reapers, wielding their sickles to great effect. The introduction of scythes in place of the sickles reduced them to followers who bound the corn into sheaves and built them into stooks, each stook being made up of eight sheaves of corn standing up in the shape of a teepee, in order to dry. Joyce Burnett has suggested that the women did not construct stooks but in Northumberland they did.[45] The men, except for those who wielded the scythes, also were followers. Violet Clarke recounts how the women had to take account of the lie of the land in order to place the stooks so that the wind could blow through them: 'They faced east to west in straight rows to get the most of the sun and wind ... and great pride was taken in making the best row'.[46] The general opinion was that the women gave better service in gathering behind the scythe than the men, being manually more dexterous and

[45]   Burnette, *Gender, Work and Wages*, p. 155.
[46]   Clarke, 'Tied to the soil'.

Figure 5.3. Women forking hay up to man who is building the stack (considered a skilled male task). Illustrates the fact that women, in stack building, were given the less skilled task.
Way-to-Wooler Farm, Wooler, c.1920s

'though not as strong ... more alert' and being particularly adept at binding the sheaves.[47] By the end of the nineteenth century mechanical reapers had taken over from the scythes, women and men again working as followers, making the sheaves and forming them into stooks (Figure 5.2). In the inter-war period, machines called reaper-binders took over the binding of the corn into sheaves, leaving the followers, both women and men, with only the task of building the stooks.

Throughout the period, the next step after the stooks had dried was to take the sheaves to the yard to be made into stacks, a task in which the women were mostly relegated to a subsidiary role. They, along with the men, performed the heavy task of forking the sheaves onto the cart to the waiting men. Sometimes the women drove the carts to the yard, a job that they reported enjoying and competed for the privilege to do. The next task was to build the stack. The role of women was to fork the sheaves onto the stack where they were caught by the female stack-header, or 'striddler', who then passed them to the male stacker, whose responsibility was to build the stack (Figure 5.3).[48] Stacking was considered an art and jealously guarded

---

[47] MS Schools, NRO 1706.
[48] Oral Evidence of Mr Patton, NRO T139B 28 June 1978.

Figure 5.4. Women hoeing turnips, considered to be their special skill. Note that the women are leading the men. The man at the back is not a supervisor. Illustrates that, in this one case, the women took precedence over the men – an unusual situation.
Kirknewton, c .1900

by the men. The task was so important that if a man failed to build his stacks well and they fell down, he would have difficulty finding employment the next year. One woman reported having built a stack but this was an anomaly caused by the illness of her father, the stacker.[49] Unlike ploughing, women could easily have built the stacks, there being no requirement of strength. But women accepted that this was a male task.

If stacking and ploughing were the quintessential male jobs, then the singling or thinning of turnips was the quintessential female task which, given the importance of turnips as fodder for sheep, gained women considerable status, though never as much as male jobs such as ploughing and stacking. As early as the 1840s, we read of their particular agility with the hoe. Bailey and Cully, agricultural experts in the North East, who were responsible for many of the agricultural improvements in the late eighteenth century, said they had never seen 'turnips so well hoed and completely cleaned or kept in such garden like culture as on the borders'.[50] Farmers noted that women excelled 'in hoeing turnips, such was their speed and deftness',[51] and attributed this

[49] Evidence of Annie Guthrie in MacDougall, *Bondagers: Recollections.*
[50] Quoted in Iredale, *Bondagers*, p. 109.
[51] MS Schools, NRO 1706.

skill to their smaller stature and to their being trained by their mothers from a young age.[52] In this job, the men who also participated would not consider moving ahead of the women leaders who set the pace (Figure 5.4).[53]

The months between late summer and autumn and winter were taken up with potato picking, turnip pulling, and stock feeding, laborious tasks which men eschewed, but all very important. Women described potato picking as back-breaking work. A digger, operated by a man and pulled by a pair of horses, exposed the potatoes. Each picker had a measured out stent (length) from which she picked the potatoes which she placed into pails, emptied into pokes (bags) or swills (wire baskets) and then carried to pits where they were covered by thick bunches of straw topped by soil. Violet Clarke described being absolutely tired out after each day of tattie picking; 'no thought to getting up to mischief in those days', she commented.[54] Turnip pulling was no more pleasant because it was often carried out when frost was on the ground. Women spoke of their fingers being 'numb and raw with the cold and wet' in the winter mornings.[55] 'Another back-breaking job', one interviewee called it.[56] The women pulled up the turnip by the roots, cut off the shaws and the root tips with a shawing hook and loaded the turnips into one cart, the roots into another. A cutter cart, which had a wooden-handled iron wheel on the side and a drum with sharp spikes in the middle, cut the turnips into thick strips which would be carted out to the sheep and cattle in the fields and hemmels (structures located in the fields to house cattle in the winter) twice a day. This task of feeding the sheep and cattle was both demanding and important. Even more onerous was the task of cleaning out the hemmels, removing manure, another unsavoury task spurned by men. Potato sorting was another winter job, entailing dividing the potatoes in the pits into those for planting and sale, and those for eating. This task resulted in the usual frozen hands. Mending bags with large needles, cutting and leading chaff, dressing meadows, filling stones at the kiln and dressing corn were additional winter jobs

The threshing of the corn, performed by a steam threshing machine which travelled from farm to farm at the beginning of the year, was next on the farming calendar. Women's role in this task subsidiary. Their main job was to stand by the men who fed the sheaves into the drum of the threshing machine, untying the rope around the sheaves and handing them to the men (Figure 5.5). Though the task was simple, it left the women and the feeder choking with thick smoke from the machine and the dust or chaff blowing around. Another dusty job was raking the chaff from under the threshing mill into a sheet and carrying it to the hemmel for feed or bedding for the animals. Depending on how soft it was, hinds' wives used it for mattresses. Women

52 Devine, 'Women Workers, 1815–1914'.
53 Evidence of Mona Thompson, Iredale, *Bondagers*, p. 133.
54 Clarke, 'Tied to the soil'.
55 Evidence of Annie Guthrie in MacDougall, *Bondagers: Recollections*.
56 Evidence of Edith Hope in MacDougall, *Bondagers: Recollections*.

Figure 5.5. Women assisting at the threshing machine. Note the woman on top helping feed the machine with corn and being subjected to a lot of dust. In this task, the women are in their customary helping role, men monopolising the use of machinery as usual.
South Linton Farm, Morpeth, c. 1915

also helped the men at the 'moth end' (mouth) of the mill where the milled corn dropped into bags weighing 101.8 kilograms (224 pounds) which had to be tied and carried up the stairs of the granary. Though men almost always did this job, which was hard and dangerous because of the lack of rails on the stairs, unusually strong women were known to perform this task. Reportedly, women were able to carry 76.3 kilograms (168 pounds) compared with the 101.8 kilograms (224 pounds) carried by men. Though threshing was dusty work, many women reported liking it because of the camaraderie.

Thus farming work for women agricultural labourers fitted into the general pattern of women's work in late nineteenth and early twentieth century England. The common pattern in industry as a whole was for new machinery to be monopolised by men. Though there was very little technological change in farming in the period, indeed not until after the Second World War, what little there was led to the deskilling of women. The displacement of the sickle by the scythe was one such example. Though the scythe was indeed too heavy for most women to yield, the next innovation, the mechanical reaper, was not beyond their reach. If they could drive carts with horses to perform the task of harrowing there was no reason why they could not operate a reaper which was drawn by horses. Again however, we see machinery being monopolised by men. Much of the women's work – such as helping with stacking and with the threshing mill – fell into the usual pattern of being regarded as unskilled, and the really disagreeable task of dealing with dung, spurned by men, was left to them. As many authors have pointed out, it was common to deem women's work, regardless of what it was, unskilled and men's work as skilled.[57] The exception to this in our farming communities was the hoeing of turnips. So important were turnips to the economy of the farm, and so expert the women, with their typical female nimble fingers, that this largely female task was widely regarded as skilled. This indicates that a specific set of circumstances could result in an outcome outside the norm. Otherwise, the sexual division of labour followed the usual pattern of men occupying the high status jobs.

The women farm workers were therefore central to every operation in the farming calendar. That the farmers considered them vital is evident at every annual hiring fair right up through the end of our period, long after the official ending of the bondager system in the late 1860s. By the turn of the twentieth century, as tensions between daughters and fathers began to appear and young women became less willing to stay on the farm and work with their fathers and, in some cases, moved to cities, the farmers appear to have become more ready to offer the contract for the rent-free house to single women. Thus, there was an increase in the numbers of cottars who, as we saw, had reached 17.9 percent of households in Idleton by 1901. It is tempting to think that the explanation for this increase lies in the low wages paid to female workers. Undoubtedly, this was a factor. Men cost more. Also, the landlord saved himself the expense of building more cottages. But economics is not the whole explanation. These women fitted into the usual characterisation of female employees: dexterous, careful and conscientious workers who left their workplaces completely neat. More than that, many were excellent and valuable workers. It was generally accepted that 'at many branches of farm work, a good girl will do more than an average man'.[58] Later in 1893, reporting to the Royal Commission on Labour, Wilson Fox remarked that 'women will do as much work as men'.[59] Twentieth-century observations attest to their value. One farmer noted that they 'they were a terrible handy thing to have on a farm,[60] while a former hind remarked that 'they could turn their hand to anything on a farm'.[61] Their skill in working with turnips, the all-important crop for feeding the sheep, was of particular value.

[57] There is a substantial literature on gender and technology. See Cynthia Cockburn, *Machinery of Dominance: Women, Men and Technical Know-how* (London, 1985); Judith A. McCaw, 'Women and the history of American technology', *Signs* 4 (Summer, 1982), pp. 798–828; Eleanor Gordon, *Women and the Labour Movement in Scotland 1850–1914* (Oxford, 1991), Ch. 1 is particularly useful, as is Carol E. Morgan's *Women Workers and Gender Identities 1835–1913: The Cotton and Metal Industries in England* (London, 2001), Ch. 1.

[58] Royal Commission on the Employment of Children, Young Persons and Women in Agriculture Second Report, PP 1868–9 XIII, p. 136.

[59] Royal Commission on Labour, The Agricultural Labourer Vol. I, PP 1893–4 XXXV, p. 117.

[60] Oral evidence of Wat Thompson, School of Scottish Studies Archives, 1974, quoted in Iredale, *Bondagers*, p. 109.

[61] Interview by author, Mr W. 20 June 2009.

It appears that, at times, the farmers preferred to hire women workers rather than men, given that women worked for less and were more proficient than men at singling turnips. We read the rather odd comments of the bishop of the Anglican Church in Glendale who cited the unusual case of a farmer offering employment to the wife of a hind instead of the hind, leading to the roles of the husband and wife being reversed. The husband was forced to care for the house and the children, a situation that caused the bishop much consternation. He claimed that 'women have ousted the men'.[62] Some women reported that, even after they were married and had retired from full-time work, the farmers would come and beg them to return to work at busy times in the farming calendar. This pattern continued after World War Two.

While women workers had a lower status than the men and men monopolised the highly skilled jobs of ploughing and building stacks, we see some mitigating factors. Not all jobs were gender specific. Both men and women worked as followers in harvest time, women, as we saw, being recognised as doing better work than men. Men on occasion worked with women singling the turnips and, in this task, ceded authority to them. The women themselves reported that the men respected them as workers. One former Scottish bondager, commenting about her work in the inter-war period, said: 'Ah. The men respected the bondagers.... Ah never had any man say oh you were only a woman, ye cannae dae (cannot do) the job. Oh ah never heard that.'[63] The companionability that many respondents report attests to an atmosphere of respect. Male respondents, in talking about the women workers, reflected this sentiment. The woman leader or steward had a position of some authority on the farm, having gained her position through experience and skill. The farmers' willingness to make individual contracts with women, which allowed them rent-free houses, is further testament to their value.

Also, while women generally accepted their lower status and wages, this did not preclude assertiveness. They demanded the right to drive carts and won, thus thwarting the rule that men alone dealt with horses and overcoming the opposition of the men who said that the women were too 'soft' on the horses.[64] They also competed with men in building the best stooks. Some of the strongest women boasted about being able to do as much work as men and about being able to lift heavy sacks of corn. Nor did they always accept their low wages. On at least one occasion, they threatened the farmers that they would strike if their requests for better conditions were not met. They demanded:

> eighteen pence a day and in haytime eighteen pence and our tea and in corn harvest three shillings and our tea and if you think it two (too)much

---

[62] *Glendale Parish Magazine*, NRO EP 33/88 (May, 1896).
[63] Evidence of Annie Guthrie in MacDougall, *Bondagers: Recollections*.
[64] Interview by author, Mr W. 7 August 2007.

you must take it into consideration the price of your beef and mutton eggs butter and chease (cheese) and consider that we have them to bye (buy).[65]

In 1873, they went on strike for two days. The strike arose out of attempts by the National Agricultural Labourers Union to unionise the hinds of Northumberland and to end the practice of employing women as agricultural labourers in Northumberland, whom it believed were depressing the wages of the hinds. The women farm workers, wishing to retain their jobs, asked to form a union of their own. Their response to the lack of support from the union was to go on strike.[66] On another occasion, the women of Haydon Bridge went on strike for an increase of 30p per year. The farmer conceded and the other farmers followed suit, being forced to go along.[67] These were but a few of the examples of resistance that occurred in a workforce that was usually cooperative, but never overly compliant.

Female farm workers' identity

As such assertiveness suggests, the women workers, like fisher women, were proud of their work and regarded it with a degree of professionalism. As Eleanor Gordon has found, such pride in work, even if much of it was unskilled, was not unusual.[68] In her study *Women and the Labour Movement in Scotland* Gordon quotes one Edinburgh compositor who, though enduring low pay and status, insisted: 'I loved my work...we all did.'[69] This sentiment is echoed by Diana Gittens, who on the basis of oral history maintains that women who worked full-time had more pride in work than in family and leisure[70] and by Jayne D. Stephenson and Callum G. Brown in their study of women's work in Sterling.[71] Interviewees who invariably answered positively to questions about their experiences working on farms indicate such pride in work. A typical response from the many women who were interviewed was that they would go back and do it again. Even allowing for the role nostalgia played in these comments, it is clear that the experiences of these women were positive and that they felt that they played a valuable role in the farming economy. Their attachment to the bondager outfit – which many continued to wear into the 1930s, as they did in Westmoreland and south-eastern Scotland – is another indication of a positive self-image and that it, like the fisher woman's dress, was an important badge of their identity. Jane

65 Maureen Brook, *Herring Girls and Hiring Fairs: memories of the Northumberland coast and countryside* (Newcastle upon Tyne, 2005), p. 53. She gives no indication of time or place but we can assume that it occurred during the labour troubles of 1873 and 1874.
66 August 1873 issues of *The Labourers Union Chronicle*.
67 *The Hexham Courant*, 4 July 1874.
68 Eleanor Gordon and Esther Breitenbach, eds, *The World is Ill Divided: Women's Work in Scotland in the Nineteenth and Early Twentieth Centuries* (Edinburgh, 1990), Intro.
69 Quoted in Gordon, *Women and the Labour Movement*, p. 36.
70 Diana Gittens, *Fair Sex: Family Size and Structure 1900–1939* (London, 1982), p. 182.
71 Jayne D. Stephenson and Callum G. Brown, 'The view from the workplace: women's memories of work in Sterling' in Gordon and Breitenbach, eds, *The World is Ill Divided*, pp. 5–28.

Long has suggested that they were abandoning their outfit by the end of the nineteenth century, but there is no indication that this was the case.[72] The standards of appearance set by the women stewards is a further indication of pride. On Monday mornings, the women stewards would inspect the appearance of their woman workers. If anyone was not sufficiently tidy, the steward would send that person home to get up to standard, even though much of the work in which she was about to engage was rough and dirty.[73]

The identity of these farming women differed considerably from the norm both in the nineteenth and the twentieth centuries, and differed also from that of mining and fisher women. The bondagers' work certainly did not fit notions of 'work fit for women', and their 'muscular femininity' was a contradiction in terms given the rigid division of feminine and masculine characteristics of the late nineteenth and early twentieth centuries. They developed strong muscles on their arms, legs and shoulders and their arms became suntanned – not the fashion of the day. Further, their working garb was rough. Their identity therefore was different from that of most other women. Observers throughout the nineteenth century differed on the question of the suitability of farm work for them. Some represented them as masculine. The Canon of Durham, W.S. Gilly, writing in 1842, was scathing about the employment of women in Northumberland, stating:

> The greatest evil in our agricultural districts, is the degradation of the female sex, by their employment in labour adapted for men ... like heavily laded beasts of burthen ... their skin is wrinkled, their faces burnt, their features masculine, and they sink into a premature decrepitude more hideous than that of old age.[74]

John Wilson, writing in *The Newcastle Chronicle,* was equally concerned. Their 'toil ... weakens the frame and blunts all finer feelings'. He was particularly worried that they spent 'their days up to their ankles in reeking filth', and worried that 'constant labour and exposure by day in the field and the absence at night must tend materially to unsex them, both morally and physically'.[75] In similar vein, Godolphes of Osham stated that outdoor work 'tarnishes the purity of their minds and feelings and makes them manly'.[76] Others worried about the process of their being hired and farmers looking 'them up and down as if they were horses'.[77] Even Doyle, in the

---

[72] Long, *Conversations in Cold Rooms,* p. 110. The problem may be that she did not extend her study into the twentieth century.
[73] Evidence of Mona Thompson, interviewed by Iredale, *Bondagers,* p. 133.
[74] W.S. Gilly, *The Peasantry of the Border: An Appeal on their Behalf* (Edinburgh, 2002; first edition 1841), p. 20.
[75] *The Newcastle Chronicle,* 21 July 1864.
[76] Royal Commission on the Employment of Children, Young Persons and Women in Agriculture First Report, PP 1867–8, XVII, p. 88.
[77] Quoted in Iredale, *Bondagers,* p. 83.

1843 Commission Report, though approving of their work, thought them somewhat 'masculine'.[78]

Other observers saw their physical strength as an asset however. In his 1854 novel, Cuthbert Bede's hero meets 'great strapping damsels of three or four woman-power' engaged in rough agricultural duties.[79] Arthur Munby, ever the admirer of strong working-class women, was also bound to be attracted to them. Although never actually able to interview them, having heard about them, he commented favourably upon them as 'hardy and lusty' lasses.[80] Others too supported the employment of women in the fields, challenging the dominant definition of what it meant to be a woman. Henley, the Commissioner for Northumberland for the 1867 Royal Commission on the Employment of Children, Young Persons and Women in Agriculture noted:

> The Northumbrian women who do these kinds of labour are physically a splendid race; their strength is such that they can vie with the men in carrying sacks of corn, and there seems to be no work in the fields which affects them injuriously however hard it may appear.[81]

Medical men who gave evidence to Henley were unanimous that the work did not harm the women. Henley further noted that some carried sacks as heavy as 57.3 kilograms (126 pounds) upstairs. He saw them as fine specimens of women and believed there was nothing incongruous about women being strong. In fact he saw them as 'producing and rearing a fine race'.[82] This opinion fitted in with the eugenic debates of the time which resonated with worry about the deterioration of the race. Later, experts such as Wilson Fox, who reported for the Royal Commission on Labour in 1892–4, and then again in 1905, echoed this praise. In 1893, he commented:

> Those who have seen them in their useful and becoming attire looking the picture of health and working actively and cheerfully must be impressed with the fact that their employment is considered no hardship, and that it has made them physically a race of which Northumberland can be proud.[83]

The only criticism which Henley himself raised was of the cottars, whose independent situation as widows or single women, he thought, might lead to immorality. Again the fear of the sexuality of lower-class women, uncontrolled by men, raised its head, even in the case of one so supportive of the bondagers.

---

[78] Commission on the Employment of Women and Children in Agriculture, PP 1843 XII, p. 316.
[79] Bede, *The Adventures*, p. 4.
[80] Karen Sayer's conclusions from the A.J. Munby Diary, 1862, Trinity College Library, Cambridge in *Women of the Fields*, p. 114.
[81] Royal Commission on the Employment of Children, Young Persons and Women in Agriculture First Report, PP 1867–8 XVII, p. 53.
[82] Ibid., p. 54.
[83] Royal Commission on Labour, The Agricultural Labourer Vol. I, PP 1893–4 XXXV, p. 304.

The farming community, the women included, appear to have been immune to this debate over their womanliness or lack of it. They obviously took for granted their work in the fields and probably would have been astonished to know that such a debate was going on. They clearly regarded physical strength as an asset, which it surely was, and boasted of the weights they could carry. To them, there was no contradiction between womanliness and strength. One bondager noted her embarrassment at being slight in build and being passed over at the hiring fairs, at which physical strength was an advantage.[84] Reportedly, farmers would examine the girth of the arms of the young women and would enquire as to their physical health before offering them employment.

Physical strength did not preclude an interest on the part of the farm women in feminine matters. While their working garb was rough, as befitted their dirty, outdoor job, they took care to line their distinctive straw hats with attractive material and to decorate them quite elaborately. Further, they were assiduous in wearing these hats to keep their complexions from being spoiled by the sun. They were as anxious as other women to preserve their pale complexions, the fashion of the day. This concern was an issue of gender, not of class. As we have seen, they were careful to turn themselves out for work looking smart, even though the work was dirty. What was reported as 'a love of dress', seen in the amount of money the independent bondagers spent at the tailor's, is a further indication of their interest in their appearance. While we can assume some exaggeration in the criticism levelled at them for what was regarded as their spendthrift ways, it is clear that they liked to put on a show when they went to church and attended dances.[85] Henry Tremenheere commented thus on their appearance at the kirn suppers, the festivities at the end of the harvest. It is 'difficult to distinguish a farm servant from the daughter of a statesman or a substantial farmer … she will appear at the dance in a white muslin dress, white kid boots and gloves'.[86]

Conclusion

These farm women had a unique identity. They were not masculine, despite their rough work, their equally rough garb and their fundamentally important role in what was erroneously thought of as a male industry. The false description of masculinity and femininity grew out of the nineteenth-century rigid definition of feminine and masculine characteristics which, along with other traits, saw women as delicate and men as strong. Thus, if a woman was strong she was inherently masculine. We might well ask however why Henley, and Fox (who followed him in giving evidence to the government

---

[84]   Taylor, 'To be a farmer's girl'.

[85]   Gielgud, 'Nineteenth Century Farm Women', p. 153.

[86]   Royal Commission on the Employment of Children, Young Persons and Women in Agriculture Second Report, PP 1868–9 XIII, p. 139.

in 1893 and 1905), were so admiring of them and anxious to show that their work was acceptable. In this same period, people were beginning to question women working in what was regarded as masculine tasks. The women who worked at the pit head in Lancashire were a case in point. They were the object of a vigorous campaign to get rid of them, as Angela John describes in *By the Sweat of their Brow: Women Workers at Victorian Coal Mines*.[87] The women white-lead workers described by Jane Long,[88] and the Bal Maidens – female tin workers in Cornwall[89] – both did physically hard and dirty work. The concern about women working in what were regarded as male tasks was centred on sexuality, reformers being unconcerned about the onerous nature of the work, as long as it did not involve the possibility of sexual impropriety. This same attitude had underlain the reports of the commissioners of the Royal Commission on the Employment of Women and Children in the Mines in 1842 when researching the work of women in the mining districts outside the North East.[90]

Once the true bondager system had been ended in the late 1860s, the women farm servants were the daughters and sisters of the hinds and therefore, in the minds of observers, 'protected' from sexual abuse. It was no accident that Henley was worried about the independence of the cottars. One cannot help thinking that the farmers, who were adamant that the women were necessary for farming to be productive in Northumberland and benefitted greatly from their work, influenced men such as Henley and Fox. The anomaly of women working full-time in the fields at tasks that in other places were regarded as belonging to males was based on the importance of turnip farming, which was so important in Northumberland, as in southeastern Scotland and in Westmoreland. The southeast of England had a different farming economy.

As the examination of their outdoor work has suggested, agricultural labouring women played a very important role in the farming economy in Northumberland, as well as in the border counties of Scotland. At the same time wives and daughters, like their fisher counterparts, made a substantial contribution to the family economy. But the role of these women was multifaceted, as was their identity. At one and the same time, they were robust farming women dressed in their distinctive outfit which proclaimed their pride in their outdoor work and they also had a domestic role which was fundamental to the survival of their families.

[87]   Angela John, *By the Sweat of their Brow: Women Workers at Victorian Coal Mines* (London, 1980).
[88]   Long, *Conversations in Cold Rooms*, Ch. 3.
[89]   Sharron P. Schwartz, '"No place for a woman": Gender at work in Cornwall's metalliferous mining industry', *Cornish Studies* 8 (2000), pp. 69–96.
[90]   Jane Humphries, 'Protective Legislation, the Capitalist State and Working Class Men: The Case of the 1842 Mines Regulation Act', *Feminist Review* 7 (1981), pp. 1–34.

6

'Clever Hands' – Household, Demographics and Autonomy

As we have suggested, the role of labouring farm women in Northumberland, Westmoreland and in southeastern Scotland was multifaceted. In addition to playing a very important role in the farming economy, wives and daughters of hinds made a substantial contribution to the family economy. Like inshore fishing, a household economy, reminiscent of pre-industrial times, prevailed in these agricultural farming families. Given the low wages of the hind, the wives' farming and domestic skills and ability to manage a meagre budget were vital to the survival of the family. Their important role inevitably brings up the question of the degree of the authority they enjoyed. The previous groups of women we have studied had varying degrees of authority in the household: fisher women most of all, though mining women – particularly those who were involved in political activities – had a considerable say in their households, and even the more typical domestic woman had more power than is immediately obvious. The degree of authority enjoyed by farming women varied depending on the group to which they belonged: wives, bondagers, cottars or daughters. The picture is, in fact, curiously mixed.

One aspect of their domestic role was onerous maternal duties. The *Census of Fertility* of 1913 indicates that agricultural workers in the nation as a whole had higher fertility than all other groups in the nation, except coal miners. In the years 1881–86, they averaged 7.72 births compared to 8.88 for miners working at the face.[1] When infant and child mortality is taken into account, agricultural labourers ended up with more live children than did miners.[2] Official fertility reports dealing with the 1930s suggest that, by then, the fertility of agricultural labourers exceeded that of miners by around 3–3.5 percent.[3] The completed family size of agricultural labourers (that is accounting for the deaths of children) was approximately 3.1–3.2 compared with 3 for miners, both figures a significant decrease from earlier. But the situation of wives of agricultural labourers was considerably more favourable than that of the mining women in that their infants and children enjoyed

---

[1]   *Census of England and Wales, 1911, Vol XIII. Fertility of Marriage* (London, 1917), Table 31.
[2]   Ibid., Table 30.
[3]   *The Registrar-General's Decennial Supplement, England and Wales, 1931, Part IIB Occupational Fertility 1931 and 1939* (London, 1952), Tables 3, 4, 11 and 13; *Census 1951, England and Wales Fertility Report* (London, 1959), Table 3.9.

better health. Both national and regional statistics bear this conclusion out. *The War Cabinet Committee on Women in Industry* in 1919 found that the only classes with lower infant mortality rates than hinds were the middle and upper-middle classes.[4] The *Census of England and Wales* of 1931 produced similar findings and, in addition, found that mortality rates of one to two year olds were lower than average.[5] Glendale fell into this pattern, having infant mortality rates half those of other districts in Northumberland in 1910.[6] These rates were not an anomaly. Ten years later, in 1920, the Medical Officer of Health for the Rural District of Glendale confirmed that Glendale registered much lower infant mortality than England and Wales as a whole.[7] The completed family size of agricultural labourers continued to be higher than that of miners.

Also, farming mothers, despite a heavy workload, had other advantages over many working-class women. They do not seem to have suffered from the high rate of miscarriages that mining women did. It is possible that the unpolluted air in rural districts, together with good food, led to better health on the part of women, infants and children. Furthermore, farming wives lacked the burden of preparing miners' baths which involved mining women lifting heavy tubs of water several times daily. Though it is difficult to find proof of this, it is possible that they may have had fewer pregnancies. What is clear is that they were spared much of the grief of infant mortality suffered by their counterparts in mining. Also farming, being a safe occupation – unlike fishing and mining – prevented them from having to face the losses of sons and husbands in accidents; a more favourable situation that was to change somewhat with the introduction of tractors following World War Two.

Agricultural wives and daughters played a vital economic role in the family well into the twentieth century.[8] In this respect, they were like fisher women. Hinds were one of the lowest paid groups in the nation. Even though hinds in Northumberland earned more than those in the south of the country, their wages amounted to around only 90p per week in the late nineteenth century, compared with £1.50 or more earned by miners. In the 1920s, they averaged £1.20 compared with £2.10 earned by miners. The money earned by women was thus crucial to the survival of families. Wives usually continued to work in the fields after marriage, those in the north of the county stopping work when they had given birth, with those in the south continuing. Before the late 1860s this pattern necessitated, as we have seen, hinds with working wives employing a bondager until a daughter was old enough to look after the

[4]   *Report on War Cabinet Committee on Women in Industry* (London, 1919), p. 233.
[5]   *Census of England and Wales, 1931, Occupational Tables, Agricultural Labour* (London, 1934), Table 16.
[6]   *The Berwick Advertiser*, 18th March 1910.
[7]   Annual Report of the Medical Officer of Health for the Rural District of Glendale, 1920, Wansbeck Environmental Health Office.
[8]   For a discussion of the household economy, see Jane Humphries, '"Lurking in the wings": Women in the historiography of the industrial revolution', *Business and Economic History* Second Series, 20 (1991), pp. 32–46.

younger children. After the introduction of education legislation in the 1870s, daughters could look after younger siblings only when they had reached the age of twelve, subsequently thirteen, and then fourteen. If there were no younger children by that point, girls entered the fields to work with their mothers. Wives who worked full-time were given a different schedule of work: they were allowed to begin work later than usual to see to their families' needs in the morning and to return home earlier in the afternoon to make meals and do their housework. Even if they did not go back to work full-time after their children had reached an appropriate age, wives invariably worked on the farm at busy times: turnip-thinning, harvest, threshing, and potato-picking. Frequently, the farmers called on them to work.[9] Daughters were also central to the family economy. After the end of the bondage system, daughters took on the full responsibility for providing the female labour though, often, the wife might also work outdoors.

Wives adopted a variety of other subsidiary activities which were essential to keeping the family going, thus following the pattern of many other working-class women including, as we have seen, mining and fisher women. Some tasks were unique to farming women however and sometimes earned them as much as fisher women's work. In the early decades of our period, one form their financial contribution took involved the family ownership of a cow. In such cases wives took care of the cow, producing milk, butter and cheese for the family and for sale, earning at times £10 per year. Some earned considerable sums selling butter alone, while others kept chickens and sold the eggs.[10] We hear of one family in which the money earned from the wife's keeping of chickens paid for all the food for the family for one year. Some wives worked part time for the tenant farmers who employed their husbands, milking the farmers' cows or cleaning the farmhouse, while others took in laundry. One former bondager remembered her mother washing blankets for the big house. As in mining and fishing districts, some women took in lodgers. Others, expert in sewing, earned some money by making clothes for neighbours on their treadle sewing machines, staying up late at night after their children had gone to bed.[11] Wives also made and sold quilts.[12]

Another essential skill of the wife was the management of scarce resources. As in the case of mining and fisher women, hinds' wives were responsible for managing the family budget, a task of great responsibility which demanded a clever balancing act and much ingenuity. If the wife of a hind did not have such skills, the family would quickly fall into poverty. It was important to produce nourishing meals for little cost. The vegetables grown by the hinds in their generous gardens, the availability of potatoes which were one of the

---

9   Judy Gielgud, 'Nineteenth Century Farm Women in Northumberland and Cumbria: the Neglected Workforce' (PhD thesis, University of Sussex, 1992), p. 98.
10   Evidence of the selling of butter and eggs, 'News Clippings' c.1871, NRO 315/2.
11   Evidence of Agnes Todd in Ian MacDougall, *'Hard Work, Ye Ken': Midlothian Women Farm Workers* (East Linton, 1996).
12   Oral evidence of Archie Thompson, NRO T-034.

perquisites of the hinds' job and the produce of the pig, which most hinds' families reared, made this task easier. Hinds' wives were skilled at caring for the pig – an all-important source of food – feeding it with kitchen scraps through the year and then, when it came to pig-killing time, collecting the blood, scraping the bristles off the skin, cleaning out the intestines for use as sausages, preparing the sausages, making black puddings out of the blood, curing the bacon and generally using every bit of the animal. Wives produced hearty meals of broth, meat, potatoes, vegetables and puddings and made butter and cheese, the production of which was skilled work requiring careful preparation in the form of the scalding of instruments. It also required large amounts of water to be carried.

Another essential skill the women possessed was the production of clothing, bedding and matting. Most wives were able to make clothes for their children, usually out of larger clothes. One woman recounts how her mother made clothes out of dresses given her by people who worked in big houses, the material being better than the cotton which they could purchase. This woman was full of praise for her mother's 'clever hands'.[13] Hinds' wives frequently made underwear out of flour bags which reportedly produced very soft and comfortable material when washed and, in addition, turned the pieces of men's shirts that were not worn out into girls' dresses. Mothers also made the outfits of drugget cloth which the bondagers wore, knitted sweaters and socks, and darned and mended endlessly, as did mining and fishing women. Further, they made mattresses and pillows out of the chaff left over from the threshing. All this work ensured great savings in money. The only real expense for children was footwear, which was generally bought with the money wives earned by harvest work. In wintertime, women made quilts from scraps of clothing and also, like the miners' wives, made 'hooky' and 'proggy' mats to cover the crude floors of the cottages, bringing a necessary element of comfort.

Such activities and housekeeping in general took a great deal of time and were difficult, given the challenging circumstances which wives faced. As we have noted, most of the hinds' houses were very small in the late nineteenth century, no more than one large room or two rooms into which a couple and six children might be crowded and often, until the late 1860s, a bondager.[14] Many houses even lacked a privy and were damp and ill ventilated.[15] While there was an improvement in housing by the turn of the twentieth century, homes remained relatively small. As in mining communities, the rate of improvement speeded up in the inter-war period, three and four-roomed

---

13 Evidence of Agnes Todd in MacDougall, *'Hard Work, Ye Ken'*.
14 Hastings M. Neville, *Under a Border Tower* (Newcastle upon Tyne, 1896), p. 290. He notes the existence of many one-roomed houses as late as the 1890s.
15 Annual Report of Medical Officer of Health for Rural District of Glendale, 1874, NRO MH 12/9024.

houses becoming more common.[16] To add to the wives' burdens, the lack of piped-in water until the inter-war period and, in some places, not even then, made housekeeping difficult. Wives had to carry water from standpipes outdoors and shared between several families, and sometimes even from nearby streams or wells. They cooked and baked over open fires which had to be kept constantly lit. Laundry was an even more onerous task involving, as it did for mining and fisher women, the heating of water either in set pots beside the fire or in pots on the fire, 'possing' the wash, rinsing and mangling it and drying it in weather that was often damp. Frequently, women ran in and out all day with laundry as showers of rain came and went. Often, like mining and fisher women, they hung clothes to dry inside on pulleys or on racks around the fire in the kitchen/living room/bedroom, making the already crowded room even more uncomfortable.

The skills needed to run a house well did not stop some middle-class observers railing against the supposed 'masculinity' of female labourers and offering a very critical assessment of the wives' domestic abilities. It is true that the most extreme criticism of the farm workers' wives, appearing in the evidence to the Royal Commission on the Employment of Children, Young Persons and Women in Agriculture in 1867, was directed not at the Northumberland women but at those in the southeastern counties and reflected nothing short of moral panic.[17] The middle-class concern, which Kathleen Canning has found about the bodies of German textile workers, is very apparent in the attitudes to these workers.[18] Middle-class observers were convinced that the rural population in the south had degenerated into 'a savage race' and that the women ran 'slovenly and slatternly households', the discomfort of which caused 'the alienation of their husbands'.[19] Though never as dramatic as this, the criticism of the bondagers of the North East was still striking. John Wilson, writing in *The Newcastle Chronicle* on July 21, 1864, represented them as poor housewives and mothers, stating that their work rendered them 'unfit for their future spheres as wives and mothers'. This comment echoes earlier criticism. William Howitt in *The Rural Life of England*, 1844, states, for instance:

> They can hoe turnips and potatoes to a miracle, but they know little of the approved method of cooking them. They rake hay better than comb children's hair; drive a cart or a barrow with a better grace than rock a cradle, and help more nimbly in the barn than in the ingle.[20]

---

[16] The Annual Reports of the Medical Officer of Health for Rural District of Glendale (Wansbeck Environmental Health Office) through the 1920s and 30s show the bit-by-bit improvement in housing.

[17] Karen Sayer, *Women of the Fields: Representations of Rural women in the Nineteenth Century* (Manchester, 1995), p. 13; Nicola Verdon, *Rural Women Workers in Nineteenth-Century England: Gender, Work and Wages* (Woodbridge, 2002), p. 109.

[18] Kathleen Canning, *Gender History in Practice: Historical Perspectives on Bodies, Class and Citizenship* (Ithaca, 2005).

[19] Sixth Report of the Children's Employment Commission, 1862, PP 1867, XVI, p. 1017.

[20] William Howitt, *The Rural Life of England* (London, 1971; first published 1844), p. 236.

Henley, responsible for reporting on Northumberland for the 1867–8 Commission on the Employment of Children, Young Persons and Women in Agriculture, gave a more accurate if somewhat fulsome assessment. As anxious to defend the farm women of Northumberland against the charge of poor housekeeping as he had been to prove their womanliness, he declared that anyone who doubted they were anything but fine housekeepers should do the following:

> That they just visit the women once they become wives and mothers. They would be received with a natural courtesy and good manners that would astonish them.... He will soon be offered a chair in front of the large fire with the never absent pot and oven, the mistress meanwhile continuing duties baking, cooking and cleaning. Not one word of complaint will be heard, but he will be told that though "working people" they are not poor and a glance at the sturdy furniture, the ample supply of bacon over his head, the variety of cakes and bread on the board, the store of butter, cheese and meal in the house will convince him of that fact. He will leave that cottage with the conviction that the field has had no degrading effect and that he has been in the presence of a thoughtful, contented and unselfish woman.[21]

To Henley and some later observers, these women were nothing short of paragons of virtue. The contrast between his representation and the negative representations is startling. It parallels the difference between some middle-class assessments of the women farm workers' womanliness, or lack of it, and his. Henley, as we have seen, saw no contradiction between physical strength and femininity while others, adopting the ideology of the time, found these traits incompatible. We can assume that much of the criticism of the women of the southeastern counties arose from the belief that such 'unfeminine women' could not possibly fulfil womanly tasks. While Henley's praise was somewhat lavish, other contemporary reports suggest that most hinds' wives fell into the category of 'good wives'. W.S. Gilly, a contemporary of Howitt, observed in 1841 that, in spite of the deficiencies in the construction of the houses, the women 'give them a decent and comfortable appearance'.[22] Others described pretty crockery, handsome clocks, carved chests and calico covering up the rafters while rud stone, used to polish the windowsills and steps, made them more attractive.[23] The conclusion of the official observers, such as Henley and Fox, was that, of all the female farm workers in the country, only those in Northumberland carried out their domestic duties properly. The oral evidence that Gielgud collected attests that good housekeeping was a long tradition which continued into the twentieth century.

---

[21] Royal Commission on the Employment of Children, Young Persons and Women in Agriculture First Report, PP 1867–8 XVII, p. 54.

[22] Rev. W.S. Gilly, *The Peasantry of the Border: An Appeal on their Behalf* (Berwick-upon-Tweed, 1841), p. 11.

[23] William Howitt, *The Rural Life of England*, pp. 133–5.

The domestic skills of the wife had great significance. Together with their money-making endeavours, they determined the survival of the family almost as much as did those of the male. They passed these skills down to daughters, and the fact that these daughters might become farm workers did not impede such passage. They helped in the survival of their families in other ways. As Gielgud notes of the inter-war years, wives oiled the social wheels in the community and created the bonds that bound together networks of aid.[24] Throughout our period, when new families came onto the farm, women made them welcome with ready-cooked meals and practical help in setting up their houses, and children were kept off school to welcome them.[25] Like mining wives, hinds' wives helped each other out in times of need – during illness, pregnancy, delivery and bereavement. Wives did laundry for each other, and helped out with care of children and the sick and in laying out the dead, thus ensuring that their family would gain help when it was in need. As in mining communities, mutual helpfulness was of paramount importance in these rural communities, where extended families tended not to live in close proximity to each other, as was the case in fisher communities.[26] Common to mining communities and many other working class-communities, wives set the tone of the family. For all that the environment was rural and settlements spread out, hinds' houses were grouped together in rows or arranged in squares, and life was fairly public. There was thus plenty of opportunity for neighbours to see each other and to judge whether children were well turned out and whether laundry was sufficiently clean. The group pressure, while not as strong as in mining communities, was still in evidence in these settlements. The wives' domestic role was thus of paramount importance, socially as well as economically.

It is not surprising therefore that wives should wield some authority in hinds' households and should have a say in decision making. To begin with, a substantial proportion of women headed households, either as widows looking after working sons and daughters, or as single women with small or working children. Even in traditional households, the wives' financial contribution to the family was substantial, perhaps as much as that provided by fisher women. Respondents attest to the fact that mothers were the centre of their families. As in most working-class houses, women had the banker's role. While adult sons continued to live at home, mothers took charge of their wages and gave them pocket money, just as the fisher women did. As they got older, sons paid board and controlled the rest of their pay. At times, wives were the ones who decided that the family should move from one farm to another. Such removals (or 'flittings', as they were called in the North East and in Scotland) were frequent, often yearly, events, occasioned by a variety

[24] Gielgud, 'Nineteenth Century Farm Women', p. 46
[25] Chatton School Log Book, 1884–96, NRO EP 62/33, 13 May 1887.
[26] This was the conclusion of Gielgud from her oral interviews, 'Nineteenth Century Farm Women', p. 65.

of factors: the promise of a slightly higher wage; the opportunity for sons or daughters to be employed at the new farm; a dispute between the hind and the farmer; but often the cause was disagreements between the wives of hinds.[27] While probably lacking the authority of fisher wives, hinds' wives were more powerful than the average mining woman who lacked the ability to add as much to the family income.

The degree of authority and/or autonomy of the other women involved in farming work depended on the group to which they belonged. The bondagers, prior to 1866, were relatively independent. They were free agents who went to the hiring fairs where they made yearly or six-monthly contracts with the hinds. Further, they had the freedom to move from one employer to another once every six months or a year and some exercised such freedom of choice, opting for a hind's household with few small children. While they worked long hours, they were freer than young women in domestic service, their only other employment option. Domestic servants were exceptionally tied to their position, allowed only one afternoon off per week and subject to the often tyrannical control of their mistresses. The bondagers' employers, coming from the same class as they did, were unable to exert the same kind of authority over them. One observer noted that there were 'no controls' over the bondager.[28] Others observed that bondagers did not see themselves as servants.[29] It was no accident that these young women regarded farm work as 'freer' than domestic service and more remunerative. Though some vague expectation existed that these young women were to help the hinds' wives with housework, few appeared to have done so. They also lacked the usual control of parents, which in that period would have been quite strict. In the 1860s, critics made much of their relative financial well-being. It was said that they regularly spent much money at the tailors and turned up at church well-clad. Such comments probably reflected some exaggeration because they were uttered at a time when the system of bondage was under attack, and a certain amount of antipathy prevailed towards the bondagers. In fact, though they did have disposable income, they would almost certainly have sent most of their wage back to their families. Yet there was no disputing the fact that they had a freedom denied to most young women their age, and that this situation contrasted with the ideas of the time.[30] It fed into the fears of the untrammeled sexuality of the lower classes.

Cottars, of all the groups of women field workers, exercised the most independence and, as we have suggested, their numbers had increased considerably over the period as farmers were increasingly anxious to recruit female workers. While Glendale registered 5.3 percent of its agricultural households

27 Interview by author, Mr W. 6 July 2009.
28 William Fairbanks, *Evils of the Bondage System*, 2nd edn (Kelso, n.d.), p. 20.
29 'Social conditions of our agricultural labourers', *Journal of Agriculture* (July 1853–March 1855), pp. 143–53.
30 Jane Long, *Conversations in Cold Rooms: Women, Work and Poverty in Nineteenth-Century Northumberland* (Woodbridge, 1999), p. 98.

headed by cottars in 1871,[31] Idleton, in the rural district of Glendale, registered as many as 18.2 percent in 1901[32] and, in the same year, Belford and Chatton registered 10 percent.[33] As we have seen, they made contracts with the farmers on a yearly basis, received rent-free houses and the perquisites of potatoes and, in addition, had coals transported for them. They were thus able to live as independent householders, a rare privilege for women in this period. A measure of their independence is the criticism levelled at them by Henley, the reporter for Northumberland for the Commission of 1867–70 who, as we saw, railed against cottars living on their own in cottages, insisting that this practice led to immorality.[34] Unfortunately, he gave no explanation of this assessment, and we are left wondering if the very fact of their independence led him to assume their immorality. Yet, people in Northumberland appear to have accepted the cottar system as completely normal.

The situation of these cottars varied. Sisters living together, a fairly common arrangement which often went on until old age, were assured a degree of security as were other groups of two, called 'double cots'. Cottars with working children were obviously very comfortable. In Kyloe in 1901, for instance, we find Jane Forster, a widow and farm worker of fifty-six, living with her three daughters, all farm workers.[35] That same year Isabella Smith, widow and farm worker, was living in Bamburgh with her two farm-servant daughters and one son, who was a hind.[36] Others lived marginal existences. The widows without working children or unwed cottars with underage children were in an unenviable position. Elizabeth Dickson, with three children aged twelve, ten and nine, and Grace Robson, with three children aged ten down to three, both widows living in Lowick in 1881, would have been hard pressed to make ends meet and would have had to pay for child minders.[37] They might have required aid from the parish. Retired cottars, who were allowed to stay on in their cot houses in return for looking after a bondager, probably also had little to spare. One such person was Jane Kennedy of Lowick.[38] Yet, they were all still householders in their own right. Anecdotal evidence suggests that, in the twentieth century, a considerable number of women continued to live independent lives as a result of farmers' need for female workers.

Another group of women who enjoyed a considerable degree of autonomy were widows who kept house for sons and daughters who were farm workers, but who were not listed as farm workers themselves. We can assume that

---

[31] Census Returns for Glendale, 1871, RG10/5189–5194.
[32] Census Returns for Idleton, 1901, RG13/4849. Long takes no account of the increase in cottars because her study stops before this point. Long, *Conversations in Cold Rooms*, p. 83.
[33] Census Returns for Belford and Chatton, 1901, RG 13/4843.
[34] Royal Commission on the Employment of Children, Young Persons and Women in Agriculture First Report, PP 1867–8 XVII, p. 140.
[35] Census Returns for Kyloe, 1901, RG13/4847.
[36] Census Returns for Bamburgh, 1901, RG13/4843.
[37] Census Returns for Lowick, 1881, RG11/5134.
[38] Census Returns for Lowick, 1901, RG13/4848.

they had been married to hinds and themselves worked on the farms in busy times. We find them a significant but not very large group in the beginning of the period. In Glendale in 1871, for instance, they represented 10 percent of agricultural labouring families.[39] By the end of the century however they had increased greatly in some districts. In 1901, Belford and Chatton registered 43 percent, while Idleton registered 42 percent.[40] This curious situation requires some explanation. It is unlikely that so many hinds in these districts had died. Assuming that the calculations of the census enumerators were correct, the most likely explanation was that farmers were deliberating attracting widows with grown children with the offer of rent-free houses. A further possibility is the out-migration of males. Such women were in a fairly secure position. Thus in 1901 in Chatton, in the rural district of Glendale, we find Mary Ann Gibson, widow, living with five children aged thirteen to twenty-nine, all working on the farm.[41] This situation was unusual for the number of employed children, but it was not uncommon for a widow to be looking after up to three working adult children. At any rate, in terms of the autonomy of women, the results were significant.

The situation of daughters, certainly when they were young, was entirely different. They lacked both independence and autonomy. Even when the bondage system had prevailed, fathers had always expected daughters to work with them or their brothers in the fields. Families had hated hiring bondagers because of the loss of money involved and the inconvenience of having strangers in the already overcrowded homes, and had done so only if wives or daughters had been unavailable. After the abolition of the bondager system in the mid 1860s, daughters, or wives, became the sole source of female workers. Technically, farmers did not insist in the contract that hinds produce female workers but, in reality, hinds without female workers were often unable to find employment, and daughters had to fulfil that role.[42] In these situations, fathers would earn a family wage out of which daughters would receive a small amount of pocket money from their mothers.[43] The concept of a family wage rather than an individual wage was not unusual in the nineteenth century and indeed well into the twentieth century, the family

---

39 Census Returns for Glendale, 1871, RG10/5189–5194.
40 Census Returns for Belford and Chatton, 1901, RG13/4843.
41 Census Returns for Chatton, 1901, RG13/4849.
42 This was clear in accounts of the Hirings (hiring fairs) in the local newspapers, for example *The Hexham Courant* and *The Berwick Advertiser*.
43 T.M. Devine, 'Women Workers, 1850–1914' in T.M. Devine, ed., *Farm Servants and Labour in Lowland Scotland, 1779–1914* (Edinburgh, 1990), pp. 98–123. It was common for wages of young people to be 'tipped up'. This practice has been commented on often in regard to other industries. See for instance, Joanna Bornat, '"What about that lass of yours being in the union?": Textile workers and their union in Yorkshire, 1888–1992' in Leonore Davidoff and Belinda Westover, eds, *Our Work, Our Lives, Our Words: Women's History and Women's Work* (London, 1986), pp. 55–75.

being seen as an economic unit.[44] In the agricultural family, obligations to family, whether fathers or brothers, took precedence over almost all the daughters' desires. It is true that it was common for family obligation to play an important role in the lives of young people up to the Second World War – for women in particular – but the degree to which it did in Northumberland, in Westmoreland and in the southeastern border counties of Scotland, where the same employment system prevailed, was unprecedented.[45] Only the prospect of marriage freed a young woman from such obligations and, even then, often the marriage had to be delayed and the couple had to take a parent to live with them.[46] Fathers used daughters to bargain for higher wages, to retire early and to gain promotions for sons.[47] There is no doubt that these young women were sacrificed to the family. A man with several daughters working could expect to be 'very snug' and could hope to earn in excess of £100 per year, a substantial sum.[48] As Wilson Fox noted in his 1893 report to the Royal Commission on Labour, a household composed of father and as many as five sons and daughters, all of them working on the same farm, was not uncommon.[49] One such family was that of John Cairns, living in Idleton in 1901, with three daughters and two sons working on the farm.[50] Such a family might earn as much as £200 per year.

Several Scottish respondents in Ian MacDougall's study related how they were bonded. 'Ah was never consulted. Ah would just be telt (told). Ye're gaen (going) to work oot (out). And that was that,' related Mary King.[51] Another reported having to give up her aspirations to remain at school because 'I was needed at home as my sister who worked out was getting married and faither (father) had to have a bondager or else move to another ferm (farm).... Looking back, ye wonder ... but at the time it just seemed ye had to do it.'[52] The claims of their brothers might also determine their future. Margaret Moffat recalls: 'Oh, ah wisnae (wasn't) consulted.... But, oh, ah didnae (didn't) bother because we were just a joined wi yin another (with one another) ee see.'[53] When her two brothers moved to another farm,

[44] For a general statement on the lack of an individual wage see Jane Humphries, '"Lurking in the wings": Women in the historiography of the industrial revolution', *Business and Economic History* 29 (1991) pp. 32–46; Leonore Davidoff and Catherine Hall, '"The hidden investment": women and the enterprise' in Pamela Sharpe, ed., *Women's Work: The English Experience 1650–1914* (London, 1998), pp. 239–93.

[45] Eleanor Gordon and Esther Breitenbach, eds, *The World is Ill Divided: Women's Work in Scotland in the Nineteenth and Early Twentieth Centuries* (Edinburgh, 1990), Intro. Family obligations were paramount right up through the inter-war period.

[46] Gielgud, 'Nineteenth Century Farm Women', pp. 214–216.

[47] Royal Commission on Labour, The Agricultural Labourer Vol. I, PP 1893–4 XXXV, p. 298; J.D. Dunbabin, *Rural Discontent in Nineteenth Century Britain* (London, 1964), p. 164.

[48] *The Kelso Chronicle*, 19 January 1866.

[49] Royal Commission on Labour, The Agricultural Labourer Vol. I, PP 1893–4 XXXV, p. 102.

[50] Census returns for Idleton, 1901, RG13/ 4849.

[51] Evidence of Mary King in Ian MacDougall, *Bondagers: Recollections of Eight Scottish Farm Workers* (Edinburgh, 2000).

[52] Evidence of Jean Leid in MacDougall, *Bondagers: Recollections*.

[53] Evidence of Margaret Moffat in MacDougall, *Bondagers: Recollections*.

she had no option but to accompany them. Again, they did not consult her. Yet another girl had to give up her work as a domestic servant, which she liked, to come home and work with her brother in order that he retain his job. Several others recalled how they had wanted to be nurses but there was really no alternative option to farm work, other than domestic service, which many spurned. Although many appeared to have resigned themselves to farm work, most, as we have seen, recalled enjoying it and finding it a 'satisfying kind of life',[54] stressing its companionability. One recalled her working life as being 'happy days'.[55]

Yet later, as the daughters became slightly older, the power dynamic became more complicated. Often, the young women became responsible for providing a home for their parents. Sometimes daughters continued working, or came back from domestic service, in order to retain the rent-free house for the sake of their parents and perhaps siblings after their fathers had retired or died. They then became the head of the household, designated thus in the census returns. One respondent of MacDougall's, a young women named Margaret Paxton, whose father had died, told of working on a farm in order to gain the rent-free cottage for her mother, herself and her siblings.[56] We find another young woman who gained the rent-free house for her retired mother and father, who had been the steward on the farm. A few women in this situation, such as Annie Guthrie, were as young as their early twenties.[57] This situation was not unusual. The reality was that the family had become dependent on the daughter. While being the head of the household entailed some status, the comment of Annie Guthrie, interviewed by MacDougall, suggests that some felt trapped by family obligation. She remarked: 'But ah knew ah had to help ma parents and ah just carried on.'[58] Yet by the inter-war period an increasing number refused to sacrifice themselves to their families, and left for the towns. The 1930s saw the numbers of bondagers reduced to 16.7 percent of the agricultural labouring force in Northumberland, women accounting for four-fifths of the migration out of farm work.[59]

Complicating the family situation further was the factor of illegitimacy. Young women in these rural areas exhibited high rates of illegitimacy. In this respect, middle-class observers were right to be concerned. Every year in our period, from 1860 to 1939, rates of illegitimacy in the rural areas we have been studying were very high, as they were in many rural districts in the country. If we take the aggregate statistics of the Registrar General for

---

[54] Evidence of Annie Guthrie in MacDougall, *Bondagers: Recollections.* Gielgud's interviewees confirmed this point, 'Nineteenth Century Farm Workers', p. 95.
[55] Evidence of Jean Leid in MacDougall, *Bondagers: Recollections.*
[56] Evidence of Margaret Paxton in MacDougall, *Bondagers: Recollections.*
[57] Evidence of Annie Guthrie in MacDougall, *Bondagers: Recollections.*
[58] Evidence of Annie Guthrie in MacDougall, *Bondagers: Recollections.*
[59] R. Henderson, 'Some sociological aspects of farm labour in North Northumberland', *Agricultural Economics Society Proceedings* IV (April 1937), pp. 299–321.

several rural districts and compare them to the rates for England and Wales for random years we get the following results.

Table 6.1. Percentages of illegitimate births in three Northumberland rural districts compared to percentages for England and Wales, 1879–1938

Year	England and Wales	Belford	Wooler	Ford
1879	4.14	8.7	10.9	10
1882	5.1	9.6	5.4	8.6
1892	3.2	11	3.6	9.8
1896	4.4	9.8	10.5	5.8
1899	4.2	12.6	8.1	9.9
1902	3.8	11	3.6	9.8
1904	4	4.3	7	3.8
1906	4	10.9	8.4	4.9
1909	4.3	10.3	11.3	2.2

Year	England and Wales	Belford	Glendale*
1911	4.4	9	4.9
1914	4.4	6.6	8.2
1922	4.6	12.2	13.7
1924	4.3	5.8	6.7
1927	4.6	7.9	11
1928	4.7	10	6.8
1930	4.8	5.3	9.7
1933	4.6	1.8	7.2
1935	4.4	8.6	4.2
1938	4.4	5	6.8

* Glendale = Wooler and Ford Combined

Source: *Registrar-General's Annual Reports of Births, Marriages and Deaths in England, 1871–1914*. After 1920, *Registrar-General's Statistical Review* (London, appropriate years).

It is obvious that rates of illegitimacy were highest in the early decades and that there was a slight decrease after 1910 and in the inter-war years, probably because many young women had migrated off the land. Still, there were spikes in certain years – such as 1922 and 1927 – and, in most of the other years, the rates were still substantially higher than the national average. But these are aggregate statistics which include groups other than agricultural labourers. When we look at the individual census returns and isolate the agricultural labouring families, the result is quite startling. In Glendale in 1871 19.2 percent of hinds' households included illegitimate children.[60] Chatton, in the rural district of Glendale, that same year registered 23 percent

---

[60] Census Returns for Glendale, 1871, RG10/5189–5194.

of agricultural labouring households housing illegitimate children. Some had more than one illegitimate child.[61] In Tughall, one Isabella Neelon, cottar aged forty-one, was supporting five illegitimate children.[62] The situation had changed a little by the end of the century. In 1901 Idleton, in Glendale, registered 15 percent of agricultural labouring households with illegitimate children.[63] In that same parish, we come across the startling example of one Annie Hartley, retired steward (leader of women workers) with one illegitimate daughter of forty-four who had two illegitimate daughters of twenty-six and twenty-two, who, in turn, had four illegitimate children between them. This reminds us of Peter Laslett's theory of a 'bastardy prone sub society' in which illegitimacy was inherited.[64] The determination of illegitimacy is the same as that used for fishing communities. Again, it may produce some overestimation of the phenomenon. Significantly, this household pattern is virtually non-existent in the non-farm labouring families in the various parishes of Glendale. Unfortunately, the lack of census returns in usable form after 1901 makes it impossible to make detailed calculations for the twentieth century.

Church records reveal a steady number of baptisms of babies born out of wedlock.[65] Such baptisms even occurred in the Presbyterian Church, the most strict of the churches in the area.[66] It is true that illegitimacy amongst the membership caused much hand wringing. Each time a mother with a child born out of wedlock applied to have it baptised, the moderator of the church made a visit, then carefully recorded how he had remonstrated with the offending woman. After she had admitted to the sin of fornication and had persuaded him she was truly penitent, the elders readmitted her to the fellowship of the church and had the baby baptised.

Premarital sex and pregnancy before marriage was not unusual, especially in rural districts. Indeed, an association between women working in the fields and bastardy had long been recognised.[67] Further, if Reay's evidence from rural Kent and J. Robson's from Colyton can be generalised, much of the rural population as a whole appears to have had sexual relationships before marriage.[68] In Reay's study of rural Kent in the nineteenth century, 60 percent of women were pregnant before marriage and 10 percent of babies were

---

[61] Census returns for Chatton, 1871, RG10/5189.

[62] Census Returns for Beadnell, 1881, RG11/5127.

[63] Census Returns for Idleton, 1901, RG13/4849.

[64] See Peter Laslett, Karen Oosterveen and Richard M. Smith, eds, *Bastardy and its Comparative History* (London, 1980), pp. 217, 219 and 339.

[65] For instance Lowick Parish Church, NRO AT97; Bellingham United Reform Church Baptisms, 1803–1900, NRO PT 7 and 8.

[66] Embleton Prebyterian Chapel Baptisms, 1833–1905, NRO PT 15; Protestant Records GSU2193522, Beaumont Church, NRO M2026.

[67] Commission on the Employment of Women and Children in Agriculture, PP 1843 XII, xv.

[68] Barry Reay, 'Sexuality in nineteenth-century England: the social context of illegitimacy in rural Kent', *Rural History* 1 (November 1990), pp. 219–48; J. Robson, 'Prenuptial pregnancy in rural areas of Devonshire in the nineteenth century: Colyton, 1851–1881', *Continuity and Change* 1 (1986), pp. 113–34.

illegitimate. These findings correlate with those from Colyton, and indeed mining communities in Northumberland. Such rates also correspond with the aggregate statistics for Northumberland rural areas. Premarital sex was part of normal courtship patterns, Reay maintains, not an example of deviancy or a matter of shame. We can assume that the same attitudes prevailed in rural districts in Northumberland. It is more than likely that some of the pregnant Northumberland women married their partners, but the census records suggest that many did not.

We find curious variations in contemporary attitudes to and explanations of these sexual habits. Henley, the reporter for the 1867–70 Commission for Northumberland, always a supporter of the female farm workers, and a great influence on later government reports, refused to believe that there were any lapses of morality among the farm workers. As we saw, the only fear he voiced was of cottars living in houses by themselves, a practice which he said, 'was not conducive to morality'.[69] He blamed what illegitimacy there was upon the migration of girls.[70] Fox later, in the Royal Commission on Labour in 1893, obviously depending for his conclusions upon Henley, praised the generally high level of morality.[71] People who looked more closely however were much less sanguine about the sexual habits of female farm workers, generally calling their morals 'loose in the extreme'.[72] Before the mid 1860s, critics put the blame upon the notorious bondager system, which had girls living in the crowded houses of the hinds, and upon hinds being tempted by 'lusty' girls. The independence of such young women disturbed many at a time when female independence was anathema. But, in fact, the pattern of illegitimacy continued long after the bondager system had been abolished. Many who gave evidence to the 1867–70 commission blamed the sexual immorality on women working alongside men in the fields, and the vulgar conversations that prevailed.

Others blamed the occasional social gatherings which farm workers attended and the associated revelry. The half-yearly and yearly hiring fairs, held at all the local market towns, became the object of criticism and efforts were made to replace them by a registry system of hiring. The problem for the critics was that, once the business of the day was over, the population – many from outlying districts – made the most of the opportunity for leisure and for meeting friends. The events took on all the trappings of carnivals with booths, merry-go-rounds, strolling players and stalls but also 'drinking and other boisterous merriment'.[73] One very critical observer called them

---

[69] Royal Commission on the Employment of Children, Young Persons and Women in Agriculture First Report, PP 1867–68 XVII, p. 53.
[70] Ibid., p. 140.
[71] Royal Commission on Labour, The Agricultural Labourer Vol. I, PP 1893–4 XXXV, p. 304.
[72] Royal Commission on the Employment of Children, Young Persons and Women in Agriculture Third Report, PP 1870 XIII, p. 122.
[73] Gielgud, 'Nineteenth-Century Farm Women', p. 188.

'drunken debauches of rustic barbarism'.[74] The yearly kirn suppers held by the farmers after the harvest had some of the same characteristics and were also suspect. Much anticipated events, centuries old, they took place in the barns which had been cleaned and decorated by the hinds' wives. The farmers, grateful for their crops having been successfully harvested, provided the food and drink. After they and their wives had retired from the festivities at a relatively early hour, the dancing and drinking went on until five and six in the morning, and, not content with one night's revelry, the merrymakers resumed the next night to finish the food and drink.[75] Whether such conviviality led to illicit affairs is unknown, but those who were concerned about immorality saw the situation as rife with opportunities.

People puzzled over the issue of illegitimacy. It was common to note that, in other respects, the women farm workers and the population generally were very respectable and law abiding, with larceny, prostitution and marital infidelity being largely unheard of.[76] Further, there were no cases of infanticide in the district such as were seen in the town, and very few cases of concealment of birth – a common occurrence in cities.[77] A conviction on this charge usually led to women being 'bound over under their own recognizance in ten pounds to be of good behavior and to come up for judgment if called upon',[78] the courts being somewhat lenient in such cases. The local newspaper goes into detail about one case of what appears to be, if not infanticide, then concealment of birth, but for which the young woman was found innocent. The case involved a girl hiding the body of a baby beneath straw at the bottom of an outhouse. The finding was that the baby was dead at birth and that the straw had blown over the body – an unlikely occurrence.[79] This situation was however unusual and probably explained by the fact that the young woman lived with her aunt and uncle. Had she lived with her parents she would probably have revealed her pregnancy because, as observers noted, 'illegitimacy was not looked upon with sufficient horror'.[80] Writing of the borders of Scotland, Barbara Robertson noted that extra-marital pregnancy was considered merely as a 'misfortune'.[81] Indeed, families seemed to accept

---

[74] *The Morpeth Herald*, 27 February 1880.

[75] Descriptions in local newspapers.

[76] Royal Commission on the Employment of Children, Young Persons and Women in Agriculture First Report, PP 1867–8 XVII, pp. 58–60; Royal Commission on the Employment of Children, Young Persons and Women in Agriculture Third Report, PP 1870 XIII, pp. 438–9.

[77] There were several comments on the lack of infanticide and concealment of birth. See for example, Royal Commission on the Employment of Children, Young Persons and Women in Agriculture Third Report, PP 1870 XIII, p. 249.

[78] Calendar of Prisoners tried at the Assizes and Quarterly Sessions 1903–13, 29th September 1909 NC 6/2; Another trial, NC 6/13 on 29 October 1901.

[79] *The Berwick Advertiser*, 16 May 1898.

[80] Royal Commission on the Employment of Children, Young Persons and Women in Agriculture Second Report, PP 1868–9 XIII, p. 139.

[81] Barbara W. Robertson, 'In bondage: the female farm worker in south east Scotland' in Gordon and Breitenbach, eds, *The World is Ill Divided*, pp. 117–36.

the fact of illegitimate children. And as daughters were needed for work, parents had in fact no choice but to do so.

Several factors lay behind this pattern of illegitimacy. Certainly premarital sexual relations played a role but pregnancy in many lower-class communities did not preclude marriage; indeed it usually led to marriage, as we have seen in fisher and mining communities. Mitigating against that outcome in rural districts of Northumberland was a skewed sex ratio which favoured men and often prevented young women from getting married when they got pregnant or getting married at all. The following table indicates how skewed the sex ratio was.

Table 6.2. Numbers of men for every 100 women in two agricultural districts compared to two Northumberland mining districts and the County of Northumberland as a whole, 1911, 1921, 1931

Year	Glendale	Belford	Ashington	Bedlingtonshire	Northumberland
1911	90	80	109	110	99
1921	89	82	107	107	96
1931	89	87	109	108	102

Source: *Census of England and Wales, 1911, Conditions as to Marriage in Administrative Counties in Urban and Rural Districts*, Vol. VII (London, 1914), Table 10. *Census of England and Wales, 1931, Preliminary Report* (London, 1935), Table III.

As we have seen, the illegitimacy rate was relatively low in these mining communities though, according to medical officers of health, the rate of premarital pregnancy was high, couples in these circumstances usually marrying. The marriage rates in Glendale attest to the fact that many pregnant women did not have that option. In the age group twenty to forty-five, in 1871, 52.6 percent of women in Glendale were unmarried. This figure compared to 34 percent for England and Wales.[82] The marriage rate of men was also much lower than the national average.[83] The same pattern is apparent in 1911, although the numbers are higher because of the different age group used by the census. Using the age group fifteen to forty-five, we find that Ashington and Bedlingtonshire registered 70 and 75 percent married compared to 55 and 57 percent respectively for Glendale and Belford.[84] We must assume that many men sired children by a number of different women. Criminal abortion was an option, but does not seem to have been resorted to as often as in urban areas. We can deduce this from the paucity of cases of abortion from rural areas appearing in the court records. Cases in the cities are numerous however. One man, who gave evidence to the Commission on

[82] *Census of England and Wales, 1871 Vol. X, Northern Counties* (London, 1873), pp. 507 and 509.
[83] Long, *Conversations in Cold Rooms*, p. 87.
[84] *Census of England and Wales, 1911, County of Northumberland* (London, 1912), Table 18.

the Employment of Children, Young Persons and Women in Agriculture in 1868, suggested that illegitimacy rates were high because girls who had gone into domestic service in town came back home to have their babies.[85] This argument may have been valid in some cases. Certainly, domestic servants could not stay in their positions if they had become pregnant. But this factor probably accounts for only a small minority of the illegitimacy cases.

Other factors played a role in illegitimacy. One was the reluctance of men to marry because of the lack of housing and the necessity of providing a women worker.[86] Permissive attitudes to illegitimacy also played a role. It was clear indeed that illegitimacy was not regarded 'with sufficient horror'. Such attitudes may have been linked to the labour intensity of the kind of farming practised in Northumberland, and the substantial family income which resulted from numerous workers in the household. The census returns indicate that parents accepted the illegitimate children of their daughters as their grandchildren, and listed them thus. Further, they suggest that the mothers of the young women looked after these children while the daughters worked as farm workers, thus fulfilling the needs of the farmers. We find, for instance, the household of George Thompson, fifty-two year old hind and his wife, with two daughters – farm labourers of twenty-three and twenty – and a grandson of five months.[87] We can assume that the wife cared for the child. It was of course to the advantage of parents to keep their daughters at home. As we have seen, throughout the period, men who could offer female workers were favoured by the farmers and young women were often tied to the parents' household because of this necessity and because of the need for childcare for their child. The existence of illegitimate children made for a mutual dependency. It appears that the culture of rural districts accepted this pattern. We have to remember that some of the farming areas were fairly isolated from urban areas and therefore slow to adopt modern points of view. Besides, the young women with illegitimate children may have married later. Others may have achieved some independence later as cottars, especially if their children became farm workers too, as some clearly did.

Conclusion

A product of a particular economic, geographic and demographic situation, women farm labourers played a very significant role in making farming in Northumberland profitable. But, as we saw, by the 1930s fewer and fewer young women were prepared to work on the land. As education improved, along with knowledge of the outside world, girls became aware that jobs in the city could offer better remuneration, and many migrated. Anecdotal

---

[85] Evidence of Mr. Richard Huntly King, Royal Commission on the Employment of Children, Young Persons and Women in Agriculture First Report, PP 1867–8 XVII, Appendix c, p. 249.

[86] Royal Commission on the Employment of Children, Young Persons and Women in Agriculture First Report, PP 1867–8 XVII, p. 418.

[87] Census Returns for Chatton, 1881, RG11/5136.

contemporary comments suggest that the bulk of migrants were female. The isolation of the farms was another factor. Women were also less willing to put the demands of their fathers above their own, and fathers were less able to assert their authority. As they left the land, men had to take over the women's jobs on the farm. But many of them left too, drawn in increasing numbers by higher wages in other industries. Thus, farmers were forced to abandon some of their turnip farming and turn the land over to grass. Wives of hinds who were left continued to work on the farm in busy times such as singling, threshing, potato picking and of course harvesting, supplementing the family income as before. But the heyday of the bondager was over. The few who were left became less distinctive after the Second World War as, influenced by the war-time land girls, they began to wear trousers, abandoning the picturesque bondager outfit, with its large, decorative hat.

Their experience had been as distinctive as the outfit that they had worn, and different from that of mining and fisher women. Being an agricultural labourer meant contributing to a household economy, as a young woman and wife would have done in pre-industrial times and as fisher women did. That contribution was both vital and required, as we have seen, not only because of the remuneration but also because it enabled the hind to be employed. Theirs was a 'muscular femininity', far removed from the ideals of the late nineteenth and early twentieth century. It meant that they should be strong, resilient and capable of performing arduous, dirty and skilled work – work that was performed by men in other districts. But, regardless of what the critics said, they also had domestic skills. When they married, they had to add to the family income, manage a meagre budget, rear and process a pig, keep a cow, make butter and cheese, in addition to all the normal cooking, laundry and childcare. Like mining women, they were judged by their neighbours on how well their house and children were cared for. Despite these burdens, many women, especially the widows and the single women, had a degree of autonomy denied to many other women.

CONCLUSION

The preceding pages indicate that the experiences of mining, fisher and farming women differed significantly. Indeed, they varied as much as the environments in which the women lived: grimy pit villages with pit heaps looming over them; picturesque, wind-blown fishing villages with boats drawn up on the white sand; isolated farms on the slopes of the Cheviot Hills or in the valleys, sheep scattered over them. It is true that in places such as Newbiggin-by-the Sea mining was conducted alongside fishing and, in some others, farming existed alongside fishing. Further south in the county, it co-existed with heavy industry. Yet for many communities the contrast did exist. This divergence in the experiences of these women indicates that we cannot assume that to be a woman meant the same thing, even within the working class, within the same region. A 'good wife' in a mining household got up at all times of the night to prepare food, to wash the grime off her husband's back, to prepare endless baths if there was more than one worker in the household, to keep a spotless house in a grimy, dust-filled atmosphere and, when possible, to earn some extra money. In the case of some, to be a mining woman meant to play an important role in politics. Fisher women's role was quite different. They needed to be skilled in the day-long preparatory work necessary for line fishing, in packing herring, in managing the finances and in hawking fish from the creel. The experience of farming women diverged from that of both mining and fisher women. Their lot involved rough, arduous and often filthy work in the fields in the frequently harsh Northumberland weather, looking after cows and pigs and making butter and cheese, an important source of added income.

A further divergence between the experiences of the women grew out of the difference in the economic structure of their families. While mining women in Northumberland had originally assisted their husbands in the pit, they had been removed from employment in the late eighteenth century and a male-breadwinner pattern had replaced a family economy.[1] Consequently mining women, with the exception of small entrepreneurial efforts, lost the chance to be economically productive and therefore lost most of their

---

[1] Sara Horrell and Jane Humphries, 'Women's Labour Force Participation and the Transition to the Male-Breadwinner Family, 1790–1865', *Economic History Review* 48 (1995), pp. 89–117; Wally Seccombe, 'Patriarchy Stablized: The Construction of the Male Breadwinner Norm in Nineteenth-Century Britain,' *Social History* 11 (1986), pp. 53–76.

authority, though they retained some by control of their homes. A minority in the twentieth century gained significant status through political action. Fisher women, as participants in household production – assisting their husbands in the craft of inshore fishing – had a much greater role in all decision making. Furthermore, their selling of fish and their work packing herring gave them disposable income which, though undoubtedly contributing to the family coffers, added to their status. Agricultural labouring women too, though not assisting their husbands like fisher women, were part of a family economy and contributed significantly to the household income. They also therefore enjoyed an authority denied most mining women.

There were other clear differences between the three groups of women. The degree to which they breached the public/private divide also diverged. While the activist mining women spent their lives in the public sphere after entering the male world of politics, most mining women stayed closeted in the domestic sphere, venturing out only to work in the harvest on neigh-bouring farms, and episodically when protesting particular grievances. Thus we have the unusual example of an extreme public/private divide within the same group. Fisher women selling fish and agricultural women selling their home-made butter and cheese also strayed out of the private world of the home. Fisher women in particular often travelled far. Both of these groups also differed greatly from mining women in their degree of political involve-ment. Though both took political action sporadically in reaction to particular grievances, they did not match the mining women activists, who made poli-tics the centre of their lives.

All three groups shared some characteristics. They all diverged completely from the bourgeois ideal of womanhood. While delicacy was prized among the middle class, these women were all physically strong, muscular and resilient, and thought weakness and delicacy abnormal. Their rough dress and lack of corsets also set them apart, as did their work outside, in the case of fisher and farming women and the political mining women. Yet, they were not mascu-line, as they were often represented. Nor did their sexual behaviour conform to bourgeois standards. Although none of these groups was guilty of untram-melled sexuality, as many middle-class observers feared, their sexual morals were more relaxed than those of the middle class, which stressed modesty and chastity. Further, they were prone to riotous behaviour in defence of the interests of their communities and sometimes violence towards each other. Such behaviour was the antithesis of middle-class notions of femininity but they did not, as feared, form a threat to the social order. Also, fisher and farming women and, to a lesser extent, mining women, contributed to the earnings of their family at a time when the prevailing ideology stressed that men should be the sole providers for the household. In the case of agricultural work and fishing work, widows and single women could earn a livelihood on their own, a fact that did not accord with the dominant ideology of the separation of spheres. Their situation reveals how economic factors could take precedence over ideology.

Yet that particular ideology was never as rigid in the middle class as the rhetoric would have it. A number of historians, for instance, have pointed to the active role played by middle-class women in business and that the idea of the division of public and private does not always hold up. Most recently Nicola Phillips, in her exhaustive study of women in business, has concluded that, despite 'the huge body of didactic literature prescribing domestic felicity as the pinnacle of female ambition ... significant numbers of women at every stage of their lifecycle were in business in a wide variety of different trades'.[2] Maltby and Rutterford also point out that 'women were an important class of stock market investors'.[3] Earlier research by Leonora Davidoff and Catherine Hall found many instances of women being involved in the family business. They give the example of Catherine March, the daughter of Reverend March, helping her father with his ministerial duties by writing letters and receiving callers, and the daughter of an Essex estate agent copying all his large corre-spondence.[4] Regardless of these examples, the ideology of separate spheres still prevailed and, not surprisingly, fisher and farming women attracted criti-cism from other classes.

One cannot ignore the similarities between mining, fisher and agricultural women. It must be remembered that all three groups of women fulfilled a double role. While fishing and farming dominated the whole of the fisher-men's and hinds' existence, the women combined work in these industries with maintaining a household and raising children. This factor was true not only of wives but also of widows and of many single women, some of whom were heads of households, bringing up illegitimate children. And their work in their respective industries, though regarded as less skilful than that of men, was invaluable. A fisher woman took pride in her expertly baited lines, in the amount of fish she was able to sell from her creel and the financial decisions that she helped make, while a farm worker like Violet Clarke could look with pleasure at the perfect line of stooks that she had raised. That the women farm workers and fisher wives wore their work-specific outfits is indicative of this feeling. Such pride is not surprising. Eleanor Gordon has stated that women did not regard their work negatively, even when it was at the lower end of the 'skills and status hierarchy'.[5] Although the mining women were limited to small entrepreneurial endeavours and the taking-in of lodgers, the laborious task of caring for miners on shift work while keeping a spotless

---

[2] Nicola Phillips, *Women in Business, 1700–1850* (Woodbridge, 2006), p. 175.

[3] Josephine Maltby and Janette Rutterford, '"She Possessed her Own Fortune": Women Investors from the Late Nineteenth Century to the Early Twentieth Century', *Business History* 2 (2006), pp. 220–53.

[4] Leonora Davidoff and Catherine Hall, '"The hidden investment": women and the enterprise' in Pamela Sharpe, ed., *Women's Work: The English Experience, 1650–1914* (London, 1998), pp. 239–93.

[5] Eleanor Gordon and Esther Breitenbach, eds, *The World is Ill Divided: Women's Work in Scotland in the Nineteenth and Early Twentieth Centuries* (Edinburgh, 1990), Intro.

house was a source of considerable pride, as Williamson, in describing his grandmother, has shown us, and those who became involved in politics took enormous satisfaction in being the backbone of the Labour Party.

Adding to this work was their onerous domestic responsibilities: the ingenious management of their households, regardless of the industry. This task was an extremely skillful one, especially if resources were scarce. As we have seen, women made clothes out of larger items of clothing or any suitable piece of material, even flour bags. Furthermore, they made most of the food for their families from scratch. In addition, all three groups found ingenious ways of piecing together extra money for the family, such as taking in sewing, hanging wallpaper, doing baking or even, in the case of mining and fisher women, participating in the corn harvest. Their strategies to provide for their families reminds us of the findings of Elizabeth Roberts, though the environments and some of the means they used were different.[6] The lot of these women was made more difficult by frequent pregnancies and the almost continuous burden of nursing babies. Looking back at the inter-war period, men whom I interviewed expressed admiration for the womenfolk, saying that they worked harder than they themselves. One fisherman voiced this view in the words, 'women did not have a fair crack of the whip',[7] while a miner said that 'women had the rough end of the stick'.[8] Even allowing for the effect of modern thinking about the role of women, it is hard to dismiss such remarks, so pervasive were they.

Thus, the images presented in the Introduction of the three groups of women as tragic victims – miners' wives waiting anxiously at the pit head when an accident had occurred; fishermen's wives staring out to sea in a storm, praying that the boats would make it to shore; Tess scratching at the frozen soil, pulling turnips – while all valid, do not tell the whole story. All these women clearly had agency in that they were not the passive creatures of middle-class ideology, but active participants in their own destiny and in the destiny of their families. And it is hard to think of their husbands being able to dominate them. Power relationships were, and are, ambiguous and complex. Certainly patriarchy prevailed, with the possible exception of the fisher community. Men expected the bulk of the food and certain male privileges such as money for tobacco. They also felt that they were the breadwinners. But it is doubtful that women felt inferior to the men, given the variety of skills they possessed. Also, as Joanna Bourke has noted, such was the control that women, especially mining women, exercised over the household, that it became a power base for them.[9] Moreover, their meticulous care of

---

[6]   Elizabeth Roberts, 'Women's strategies, 1890–1914' in Jane Lewis, ed., *Labour and Love: Women's Experience of Home and Family, 1850–1940* (Oxford, 1886), pp. 243–48.

[7]   Oral interview by author, Mr J.L.R. 7 June 1998.

[8]   Oral interview by author, Mr R.A. 8 July 1979.

[9]   Joanna Bourke, 'Housewifery in working-class England 1860–1914' in Pamela Sharpe, ed., *Women's Work: The English Experience*, pp. 332–58.

their children created an inter-generational loyalty, an important factor given the insecurities of mining life.[10]

We have been describing the lives of these women and ascribing meaning to them. But, what meaning did they ascribe to their lives? The few auto-biographical authors we have – Mary Wade,[11] Adeline Hodges[12] and Violet Clarke[13] – are concerned with describing the lives and work of mining women and farming women respectively and do not address the self-concepts of these women. The oral interviews however go some distance in filling that gap. They suggest that women had a strong sense of self-worth and, further, that they took their arduous lives for granted. The exception to this was some of the young people: farm girls who had aspired to become nurses but had to settle for farm work, though quite soon adjusting to it;[14] those who, by the turn of the twentieth century, had left the countryside for work in the town. Also, it is clear that all three groups of women saw themselves as hard working and conscientious, in whatever field they were involved, and diligent in maintaining the standards of respectability: a clean house, well-cared-for children and a well-stocked table. Their standard was the needs of their families. That ethos, and the experience of their mothers, was their frame of reference, not the standards of the bourgeoisie. They believed, for instance, that it was perfectly acceptable to do rough, even masculine, work and did not regard it as demeaning or unwomanly, and all these women exhibited considerable physical strength. Those who were deeply involved in the church or in politics undoubtedly found further meaning in these institu-tions, and a separate identity which they could articulate. The reality however is that few of these women probably took the time or effort to evaluate their place in the world or certainly to articulate it.

Yet the consciousness of these three groups of women was not identical. While all these women saw themselves mothers, wives and housekeepers, their self-representation was more complex. The mining women saw them-selves as providing the special nurture their husbands needed to enable them to work in an extremely difficult and dangerous job, which was fundamental to the economy of the nation. The miners' leaders never missed an opportu-nity to make the latter point.[15] Fisher women, like their husbands, felt part of a long tradition of people bound to the sea, providing its bounty for the public. For their part, agricultural workers felt a similar bond with the land

[10] See Bill Williamson's comment about the mother-centred families in *Class, Culture and Community: A Biographical Study of Social Change in Mining* (London, 1982), p. 119.
[11] Mary Wade, *To the Miner Born* (Stocksfield and London), 1984.
[12] Adeline Hodges, 'Up the Ladder', Tuesday Club. Occasional Paper, No. 2, N.D.
[13] Violet Clarke, 'Tied to the soil' in Brian P. Martin, ed., *Tales of old Countrywomen* (Newton Abbot, 1997), pp. 135–45.
[14] Evidence from the interviews conducted by Ian MacDougall, *Bondagers: Recollections of Eight Scottish Women Farm Workers* (Edinburgh, 2000).
[15] Minutes of National Union of Mineworkers, Ashington Branch, 1900–1914, Ashington, Northumberland.

and a pride in helping make it productive. Also, as we have seen, the experience of being a woman was different for each of these three groups of women.

Often these three communities were fairly isolated from each other, and contact with other groups which might have provided a different point of view was limited. Such was the case with rural communities farthest from the coast. But one must not overestimate the isolation. Miners, fishers and agricultural people had more interactions in less remote areas, where they lived in relatively close proximity to each other. Both mining and fisher women near the coast engaged in harvest work and potato picking. In some villages, such as Beadnell, a few fisher daughters worked as agricultural labourers.[16] We also hear of miners playing football with fishermen in Newbiggin-by-the-Sea, though many of the miners may have originally been fishermen.[17] When the lifeboat put out to sea without a full contingent of its crew, often miners, obviously ex-fishermen, made up for the deficiency.[18] There was also a degree of contact between miners and fishermen in times of need. On one or two occasions, miners and fishermen helped each other out, the miners giving vegetables to the fishermen on one occasion, the fishermen giving fish to the miners on another.[19] The fights outside the pubs and the derogatory name-calling was more common, however, the miners referring to the fishermen as 'hoarders of money'; the fishermen calling the miners 'spendthrifts'. Some fishermen left fishing for mining and other trades when fish was scarce, but many continued to live in fisher housing instead of moving to colliery housing and becoming part of the mining culture. While many of these men remained in the trades to which they had moved, others came back to fishing when fish became plentiful again, liking the independence that the trade offered them.[20] Fisher daughters in some areas married miners, but most of those appear to have come from fishing stock. But such contact between the three groups, women included, was always tempered by the tendency 'to keep to themselves'.

Although much government attention was paid to all three groups, they appeared oblivious to it and were saved from having to deal with the often critical views of other classes: of the mining population as riotous drinkers, of fisher people as secretive and in some ways deviant and of agricultural workers as ignorant and immoral. These communities had their own ideologies which grew out of their own requirements. As we have seen the women's frame of reference was the needs of their families together with the experience of their mothers, not the standards of the bourgeoisie. Womanliness meant

---

16 Census Returns for Beadnell, 1881, R11/5127.
17 Interview by author, Mr and Mrs J.L.R. 6 July 1997.
18 See for instance Jack Lisle Robinson, 'Fishing Disasters', in possession of author. The lifeboat crew of Newbiggin-by-the-Sea in 1938 included six miners, all ex-fishermen.
19 *The Morpeth Herald*, 15th December 1880; *The Blyth News*, 10 December 1878.
20 Interview by author, Mr J.L.R. 5 July 1997.

a different thing to each of these groups of women and to the middle class. They, for example, regarded it as perfectly acceptable to perform rough, even masculine work and did not see it as demeaning and unwomanly.

This study contributes to themes addressed by other historians. One is the issue of job segregation based on gender. All three groups of women, no matter that they made valuable economic contributions to their families, suffered from job segregation and were denied the use of machinery. The miners and fishermen banned their wives from going near the pit or, in the case of the fisher women, even at times inside the boat. The superstitions surrounding these prohibitions gave a force to them not found in other industries. As in the case of other occupations, men monopolised the most skilled jobs: cutting the coal underground in the case of mining; in fishing, going out to sea and catching the fish. The hierarchy of tasks was most obvious in farming, where men and women worked together. The farmers and hinds prohibited women from ploughing, building stacks, feeding the threshing machine and looking after the horses. Further, the men prevented the women from entering the stables, a male domain. Some scholars, such as Katrina Porteous, argue that the prohibition against women cutting coal and fishing represented a practical division of labour, mining and fishing being dangerous jobs, unfit for women who were responsible for the care of children.[21] While this is undeniable there was no reason, as I have noted, why other male jobs were closed to women. One was the building of stacks of corn, to which great importance was attached and for which the male stacker gained great status. In explaining why women did not stack, one interviewee of Ian MacDougall, Jean Leid, replied that it was a 'skilled job', thus accepting that 'skilled jobs' were the province of men.[22] Underscoring the existence of a hierarchy of tasks, men spurned certain jobs which were deemed fit only for women. Interviewees insisted that any job that was 'dirty, awkward or required patience', such as the pulling of turnips and the handling of dung, was left to women.[23] As we have seen, the men stood by and watched the women performing the extremely onerous and nasty task of forking the dung.[24] And in fishing, men would not be caught dead hawking fish, although there is one example of a male hawker from Beadnell.[25]

But, as Carol E. Morgan and others have suggested, the division of labour was often not as fixed as it appeared, thus indicating that skill was a social construct and, as John Rule has suggested, that 'definitions of skilled and unskilled work were as much rooted in social and gender distinctions as in

---

[21]   Correspondence with Katrina Porteous, 14 February 2012.

[22]   Evidence of Jean Leid in MacDougall, *Bondagers: Recollections.*

[23]   Judy Gielgud, 'Nineteenth Century Farm Women in Northumberland and Cumbria: the Neglected Workforce' (PhD thesis, University of Sussex, 1992), p. 110, evidence from oral interviews.

[24]   We can't help thinking of the association between women and bodies and bodily functions.

[25]   Correspondence with Katrina Porteous, 14 February 2012.

technical aptitude'.[26] As we have seen, an interviewee of Ian MacDougall, Annie Guthrie, recounted how she had to build stacks when her father was ill, thus indicating that the job was not beyond the capacity of women.[27] This task involved placing the sheaves of corn in the proper order so that the stack did not fall down, and skill was definitely involved. And that they drove carts and harrowed on certain farms and in certain areas showed that, contrary to accepted wisdom, women were perfectly capable of dealing with horses. Furthermore, during the First World War, women regularly ploughed using horses. In several tasks in farming, men and women worked alongside each other. Such was the case in harvest time when both men and women acted as 'followers', following the men with the scythes and, later, with the reaping machines, gathering up the corn in bundles and then forming them into stooks. Further, in contrast to the usual pattern of women's work being regarded as unskilled, women in agriculture were lauded for their singling of turnips, the all-important crop. In inshore fishing, we see the same fluidity in the sexual division of labour. Although baiting lines was seen as a woman's job, men frequently, if time was short, took over a line, baiting along with their wives. We also hear of retired fishermen helping their daughters bait lines.

But job segregation based on gender was not limited to outdoor work. It prevailed in the home. Domestic work and childcare were the complete province of the women. Most of the men in all these communities, as elsewhere, regarded involvement in such work as threatening to their masculinity. The miners' wives of the 'Over Sixties Club' told amusing stories about how, in the inter-war period, men feared even being seen drying the dishes and, if this occurred, would be subjected to all kinds of jokes about wearing a 'pinnie' (an apron).[28] But, at the same time, women jealously guarded their dominance of the domestic sphere. Nowhere was this more obvious than among the mining women whose home was their power base, whose domestic accomplishments were admired by the men and who would have resented the intrusion of their husbands in their sphere. There is no indication that the division of labour was any different in fisher homes. In agricultural labouring households the man, as one respondent noted 'was done when he came in from outside work' and took no part in the running of the household, not even taking in the coal.[29]

Another theme which echoes the work of several other historians is the persistence of the system of household production and the family economy into the modern era. As we have seen, a true household economy existed in fishing in which all the family, children included, were involved. The situ-

---

[26] John Rule, 'The property of skill in the period of manufacture' in Patrick Joyce, ed., *The Historical Meanings of Work* (Cambridge, 1987), pp. 108–12.

[27] Evidence of Annie Guthrie in Ian MacDougall, *Bondagers: Personal Recollections*.

[28] Interview by author, 'Over Sixties Club' of the Holy Sepulchre Church, Ashington, 5 April 1996.

[29] Correspondence with Mrs W. 26 February 2012.

ation in farming was somewhat different. While a product was not being produced, a family economy clearly existed and the family, the daughters in particular, took part in the endeavour. A combined wage was paid to the father. The findings of Sonya O. Rose, in her examination of the hosiery industry, echo this situation. She writes:

> In the domestic hosiery industry the husband and father directed the work of the household members. The hosier paid him the wages due for the work done by the whole family working as a unit and held him responsible for the completed garment.[30]

If the degree to which the daughters of hinds were sacrificed to the family in farming was extreme, generally it was common for the claims of the family upon young people to last well into adulthood.[31] This pattern remained until well into the twentieth century. Men seldom earned a wage sufficient to support their families, especially if there were several young children.[32] It was common for daughters to hand their pay packet over to their mothers and receive a small sum back. Only when they reached their mid twenties or had prospects of marriage did they begin to pay board and control the rest of their wage. The claims upon daughters are most obvious in fisher and farming households, but even in mining households daughters were often kept at home to help with the work, especially if there were several pit workers.

A further factor of historical importance is that all these women worked and earned money, even the mining women, though with some exceptions, this money was subsumed in the family income. An analysis of the work of these women underscores the fact that many more women worked than was thought to be the case, and the censuses suggest.[33] Through the use of various sources, written and oral, I have been able to elucidate their roles in some detail. Even though most were not listed in the censuses – the only exceptions being the single agricultural labourers and the married labourers who worked full-time – they were very much part of the workforce. Indeed they were central to it – even the mining women without whom the miner could not have pursued his calling. Their history therefore is as much labour history as it is women's history. This work shows how one cannot easily separate the two fields of study.

[30] Sonya O. Rose, *Limited Livelihoods: Gender and Class in Nineteenth-Century England* (Berkeley, 1992), p. 139.
[31] Gordon and Breitenbach, eds, *The World is Ill Divided*, Intro.
[32] Jane Humphries, '"Lurking in the wings": Women in the historiography of the industrial revolution', *Business and Economic History* Second Series, 20 (1991), pp. 32–46.
[33] For problems with the censuses in ascertaining the number of working women see Edward Higgs, 'Women, Occupations and Work in the Nineteenth Century Censuses', *History Workshop Journal* 23 (1987), pp. 59–80; Nigel Goose, 'Women workers in industrial England' in Nigel Goose, ed., *Women's Work in Industrial England: Regional and Local Perspectives* (Hartford, 2007) pp. 1–28; Bridget Hill, 'Women, Work and the Census: A Problem for Historians of Women', *History Workshop Journal* 35 (1993), pp. 78–94.

Despite some similarities between these mining, fishing and agricultural women, definitions of womanhood differed between them as they no doubt did between other women in the working class, and as they certainly did between them and other classes. To be a woman and a 'good wife' meant something different in each community, so much so that a popular saying in all three communities was that a woman had to be 'brought up to it'.

GLOSSARY OF DIALECT WORDS

Bait pokes – sacks in which miner's snacks were carried down the pit

Bondager – woman hired by hind to perform the bond

Braying – verbally harassing

Byres – structures where cattle were housed

Candymen – men employed by the coal owners to evict the striking miners from their rent-free houses

Clarty – muddy

Cloot – cloth or rag

Coble – small boat used by inshore fishermen which was suited to being pushed out through the waves where there were no harbours

Cottars – women who lived independently and rent free in cottages and worked for the farmers

Dadd – Beat against a wall

Daftie – Scottish word meaning learning-disabled

Deputy – official in the mine, overseen by the overman

Dratting apron – rough apron with a pouch in the front to contain the seed potatoes which were to be planted; used up to early twentieth century

Drugget – heavy, waterproof material not unlike denim with which bondagers' skirts were made

Flittings – removals for houses which often happened yearly

Ganseys – Guernsey sweaters which fisherwomen knitted. They were waterproof and each village had a different pattern so that a drowned man could be identified

Ingle – fireside

Hemmels – structures to house cattle in the winter

Heuk – hook

Hewer – coal cutter who worked at the face and had the highest status in the mine

Hind – agricultural labourer

Hodge – a pejorative term used to describe an agricultural labourer, the implication being that he was uneducated, unintelligent and unsophisticated

Hookie and proggie mats – floor coverings made at home by wives with odd pieces of cloth hooked into a canvas frame in pre-designed patterns

Keepie-back – term used for the money which the man kept back out of his wages for his own use instead of handing his whole pay packet to his wife

Ken – Scottish word meaning 'know'. Thus 'to ken' is 'to know'

Kirn suppers – centuries-old celebrations held at the end of the harvest; farmers and labourers participated, with drink and food provided by the farmers as a sign of gratitude

Midden – term used to describe the pit into which the sewage from the barns would drain

Mucky – dirty and unkempt

Nettie – outhouse (rudimentary lavatory)

Overman – official in the pit who was in charge of the deputy but answered to the manager

Pinnie – a small, dressy apron with which working women replaced the overall-type coverings after they had finished the heavy cleaning for the day

Pit flappers – flannel undershirts worn by miners underground

Possing – agitating laundry in a barrel with a wooden stick to remove dirt

Privy midden – dump into which the sewage from the nettie would drain

Putter – underground haulage worker in the mine

Redding the lines – clearing the odd bits of fish and bait left over after fishing prior to baiting them with fresh bait

Rucking – folds created in material for decoration

Rud stone – coarse limestone with cement texture which, when rubbed on stone, created a pleasing effect

Shaws – leaves at the top of a turnip

Skein – skin

Stent – length

Stook – a collection of sheaves of corn set up on end in a teepee form in order to dry

Striddler – name given to a female agricultural labourer who stood on the stack catching the sheaves which were being forked up

Swill – basket used to hold fishing lines

Tattie – potato

Tipped it up – refers to the practice of husband or sons and daughters handing over their unopened pay packet to their wife/mother and usually receiving back a small amount of pocket money

Ugly – cotton bonnet worn in summer by bondagers. It had a curtain at the back to protect the neck and a shade encircling the front, almost concealing the face, the point being to keep the sun off the face

Yelming – thatching

SELECT BIBLIOGRAPHY

British Parliamentary Papers

Decennial Censuses
Census of England and Wales, 1871 (London, 1872 and 1873).
Census of England and Wales, 1881 (London, 1883).
Census of England and Wales, 1891 (London, 1893).
Census of England and Wales, 1911 (London, 1912 and 1913).
Census of England and Wales, 1911, County of Northumberland (London, 1912, 1913 and 1914).
Census of England and Wales, 1911, Vol. XIII Fertility of Marriage (London, 1917).
Census of England and Wales, 1921, County of Northumberland (London, 1923).
Census of England and Wales, 1931 (London, 1931, 1934 and 1935).
Census of England and Wales, 1931, County of Northumberland (London, 1933, 1934 and 1935).
Census 1951 England and Wales, Fertility Report (London, 1959).
Census of England and Wales 1961, Fertility Tables (London, 1966).

Other Documents and Publications

The Registrar-General's Decennial Supplement England and Wales, 1921, Part II Occupational Mortality, Fertility and Infant Mortality (London, 1923).
The Registrar-General's Decennial Supplement England and Wales, 1931, Part IIa Occupational Mortality (London, 1938).
The Registrar-General's Decennial Supplement England and Wales, 1931 and 1939, Part IIB Occupational Fertility (London, 1953).
The Registrar-General's Supplement to the 65th Annual Report (London, 1904).
The Registrar-General's Decennial Supplementary Report, 1901–10 (London, 1916).
The Registrar-General's Decennial Supplementary Report, 1910–1915 (London, 1923).
The Registrar-General's Annual Reports on Births, Deaths and Marriages

(London 1871–1939), published annually by His Majesty's Stationery Office.

Royal Commission on the Employment of Women and Children in the Mines, PP 1842 XVI.

Commission on the Employment of Women and Children in Agriculture, PP 1843 XII.

Sixth Report of the Children's Employment Commission, 1862, PP 1867 XVI.

Royal Commission on the Employment of Children, Young Persons and Women in Agriculture, PP 1867–68 XVII; PP 1868–9 XIII; PP 1870 XIII.

Royal Commission on Labour The Agricultural Labourer Vol. I PP 1893–4 XXXV.

Annual Reports of Inspectors of Mines, 1875–1914: PP 1875 XVI– PP 1914–16 XXVIII.

Report on War Cabinet Committee on Women in Industry (London, 1919).

Ministry of Agriculture and Fisheries Report of Departmental Committee on Inshore Fisheries Vol. I (London, 1914).

Ministry of Agriculture and Fisheries Report on Sea Fisheries for Years 1919, 1920, 1921, 1922 and 1923 (London, 1924).

Ministry of Agriculture and Fisheries, Statistical Tables (London, 1923–1937).

Documents at Northumberland Archives

Census Material

Census Returns for 1871, 1881, 1891 and 1901 for the following urban districts, rural districts and parishes in Northumberland.

Fishing villages: Cullercoats; Newbiggin-by-the-Sea; Beadnell; Seahouses; Embleton and Craster.

Agricultural districts: Glendale; Idleton; Kyloe; Lowick; Chatton; Belford and Bamburgh.

Court Records

Petty Sessions of Morpeth NRO PS/5–4-12.

Assizes and Quarterly Records NRO NC/2 and NC/13.

Register of Court of Summary Justice Morpeth NRO PS /5/12.

Education Records

School Records for Beadnell Church of England School NRO CES 26/2.

Log Book Chatton School, 1884–96 NRO EP 62/33.

MS Schools NRO 1706.

Northumberland County Council Education Committee Minute Books NRO NCC/CM/ED.

Manuscript Collections
Margaret Gibb Papers, NRO 2973/4.

Farm Records
Dancy Farm Pay Lists, NRO 530/1.

Church and Chapel Records
Ashington Primitive Methodist Circuit Records, NRO M3/3–16.
Manchester Street Wesleyan Chapel, Morpeth, NRO M11/54/56/59.
Sr. Ebba Church of England, Beadnell Marriages Records, 1856–1902, NRO M10/77.
Ashington Primitive Methodist Chapel Marriage Records, NRO M11/59.
Bedlington Primitive Methodist Chapel Marriage Records, NRO M11.
St. Andrews Newbiggin-by-the-Sea Parish Records, NRO 4455.
St. Mary's Church Woodhorn Marriage Records, NRO EP/22.
Embleton Presberterian Chapel Baptisms, 1833–1905, NRO PT 15.
Beaumont Church, NRO M 2026.
Lowick Parish Church, NRO AT97.
Bellingham United Reform Church Baptisms, 1803–1900, NRO PT7 and 8.

Northumberland Local Government Records
Urban Authority Records for Newbiggin-by-the-Sea, NRO 1988/2.
Urban Authority Records for Ashington, NRO 1987/4.
Morpeth Board of Guardians Union Minutes, NRO GMO/1.
Land Evaluations, 1910, NRO 2006/3.

Labour Party Records
Wansbeck Division Labour Party Minute Books, NRO 527/a/1–3.
Wansbeck Division Advisory Council Committee Book, NRO 4015/1/3.
Northumberland Labour Women's Advisory Committee Books, NRO 4415/1/1.
Northumberland Labour Women's Conference Book, NRO 4415/7.
Morpeth Federation of Labour Women's Sections Minute Books, NRO 4415/3/1.

Coal Mining Records
Northumberland Coal Owners Association Minute Books, NRO 00263/3.
National Coal Board Records, NRO 00263/B.
Ashington Coal Company Directors' Records, NRO ZMD 54/4.
Ashington Mining School Records, NRO CES/1.

Health Records
Annual Reports of the Medical Officer of Health for Northumberland, 1895–1939, NRO 3897/1–8.

Records at Other Locations

National Archives, Kew
Ministry of Agriculture and Fisheries Committee of Inquiry into the Fishing Industry. PRO MAF 383/11 1958.
Ministry of Agriculture and Fisheries 14th Report of the Development Commission for Fisheries for the year ending 31 March, 1924. PRO MAF/ VIII, 429.
Ministry of Agriculture and Fisheries White Fish Subsidy Investigation into the Inshore Fisheries. PRO MAF/ 209, 1548.

London School of Economics Archives
Records of Women's Labour League COLL MISC 114.
Records of Women's Co-operative Guild, 1890–1938 COLL MISC 0268.

The Co-operative College, Manchester
Annual Reports of the Women's Co-operative Guild, 1890–1930.

British Library
Oral Interviews of Scottish fishing people conducted by Paul Thompson, QD8/FISH/52 C773.

Miners Hall, Ashington, Northumberland
Minutes of Ashington Branch of Miners Federation of Great Britain, 1900–14.

Institute of Mining Engineers, Newcastle upon Tyne
Report of South Shields Committee on Accidents in Mines Pamphlet XXIVb

Wansbeck Environmental Health Office
Annual Medical Officer of Health Reports for Urban Districts of Ashington, Bedlingtonshire, Newburn, Newbiggin-by-the-Sea and of Rural District of Glendale.

Newspapers and Periodicals

The Alnwick News
The Banffshire Journal
The Berwick Advertiser
The Blyth Weekly News
Costume
Country Life
The Edinburgh Medical Journal
The Glendale Parish Magazine
The Hexham Courant

The Kelso Chronicle
The Labour Woman: A Monthly Paper for Working Women
The Labourers' Union Chronicle
The Lancet
The Morpeth Herald
The Newcastle Chronicle
The Newcastle Courant
The North of England Farmer
The Northern Democrat
The Shields Daily News
The Whitley Advertiser
The Whitley Bay Chronicle and Visitor Gazette

Unpublished Theses

Collins, Claire, 'Women and Labour Politics, 1893–1932' (PhD thesis, London School of Economics, 1991).

Curpreet, Kaur Maine, 'The role of women on the Manchester city council' (MPhil thesis, Manchester University, 1991).

Gielgud, Judy, 'Nineteenth Century Farm Women in Northumberland and Cumbria: the Neglected Workforce' (PhD thesis, University of Sussex, 1992).

Hall, Valerie G. 'Aspects of the political and social history of Ashington, a Northumberland coal mining community, 1870–1914' (PhD thesis, University of London, 1993).

Hall, Valerie G., 'The English coal mining community' (MA thesis, University of North Carolina at Chapel Hill, 1978).

Lambertz, Janet, 'The politics and economics of family violence from the late nineteenth century to 1948' (MPhil thesis, University of Manchester, 1984).

Primary printed sources

Armstrong, Chester, *Pilgrimage from Nanthead* (London, 1938).

Bede, Cuthbert, *The Adventures of Mr. Verdant Green* (Oxford, 1982; first published 1857).

Bertram, James G., *The Unappreciated Fisher Folk: Their Round of Life and Labour* (London, 1883).

Bowley, A.L. and A.R. Burnett-Hurst, *Livelihood and Poverty* (London, 1915).

Cole, G.D.H., *Labour in the Coal Mining Industry* (Oxford, 1923).

Coombes, B.L., *These Poor Hands: the Autobiography of a Miner Working in South Wales* (London, 1939).

Davies, M. Llewelyn, ed., *Maternity: Letters from working-women collected by the Women's Co-operative Guild* (London, 1978; first published 1915), Introduction by Linda Gordon.

Donkin, Samuel, *The agricultural labourers of Northumberland: their physical and social condition* (Newcastle upon Tyne, 1869).

Duckershoff, Ernst, *How the English Workman Lives* (London, 1899).

Elderton, Ethel M., *Report on the English Birth Rate. Part I. England North of the Humber* (London, 1914).

Fairbanks, William, *Evils of the Bondage System*, 2nd edn (Kelso, n.d.).

Fynes, R., *The Miners of Northumberland and Durham: a History of their Social and Political Progress* (Newcastle, 1986; first published 1873).

Galloway, Robert L., *Annals of Coal Mining and the Coal Trade* (London, 1898).

Gilly, Rev. W.S., *The Peasantry of the Border: an Appeal on their Behalf* (Berwick upon Tweed, 1841).

Hardy, Thomas, *Tess of the d'Urbervilles*, 2nd edn (New York, 1979).

Hope, E.W., *Report on the Physical Welfare of Mothers and Children in England and Wales*, for Carnegie Trust of the United Kingdom (Liverpool, 1917).

Howitt, William, *The Rural Life of England* (London, 1971; first published 1844).

Jevons, H. Stanley, *The British Coal Trade*, 2nd edn (London, 1920).

Kelly's Directory of Northumberland and Durham (London, 1897).

Liefchild, John R., *Our Coal and our Coal Pits. The People in them and the Scenes around them* (London, n.d.)

Llewlyn, Richard, *How Green was my Valley* (First published Plymouth, 1939).

Metcalfe, Francis J., *Colliers and I* (Manchester, 1903).

Neville, Hastings M., *Under a Border Tower* (Newcastle upon Tyne, 1896).

Parkinson, George, *True Stories of Durham Pit Life* (London, 1912).

Patterson, William, *Northern Primitive Methodism* (London, 1909).

Phillips, M., ed., *Women and the Miners' Lockout* (London, 1927).

Rowe, J.W.F., *Wages in the Coal Industry* (London, 1923).

Salmon, John, *The Coble: a Few Papers Written During Leisure Hours of the Winter of 1884–5* (South Shields, 1885).

'Social conditions of our agricultural labourers', *Journal of Agriculture*, New Series (July 1853–March 1855), pp. 143–153.

Welbourne, E., *The Miners' Unions of Northumberland and Durham* (London, 1923).

Whitehead, C., *Agricultural Labourers* (London, 1870).

Williams, Mrs, 'The Bondage System' in Anon., *Voices from the Plough* (Hawick, 1869).

Young, Arthur, *Northern Tour* (London 1770–1).

Secondary Sources Printed After 1945

Anson, Peter F., 'Scots fisherfolk', *Banffshire Journal* (1954), p. 24.

Banks, Olive, *Becoming a Feminist, The Social Origins of "First Wave" Feminism* (Athens, Georgia, 1987).

Baylies, Carolyn, *The History of the Yorkshire Miners 1881–1919* (London, 1993).

Benson, John, *The Penny Capitalists: a Study of Nineteenth-century Working-class Entrepreneurs* (London, 1983).

Blaikie, Andrew, 'Coastal communities in Victorian Scotland: what makes North-east fisher families distinctive?', *Local Population Studies* 69 (Autumn, 2002), pp. 15–31.

Bornat, Judith, '"What about that lass of yours being in the union?": Textile workers and their union in Yorkshire, 1888–1922', Leonore Davidoff and Belinda Westover, eds, *Our Work, Our Lives, Our Words. Women's History and Women's Work* (London, 1986), pp. 55–75.

Bourke, Joanna, *Working-Class Cultures in Britain: Gender, Class and Ethnicity* (London, 1994).

Bourke, Joanna, 'Housewifery in working-class England 1860–1914' in Pamela Sharpe, ed., *Women's Work: the English Experience 1650–1914* (London, 1998), pp. 332–58.

Bradley, Harriet, *Men's Work, Women's Work: a Sociological History of the Sexual Division of Labour in Employment* (Minneapolis, 1989).

Brook, Maureen, *Herring Girls and Hiring Fairs: Memories of the Northumberland Coast and Countryside* (Newcastle upon Tyne, 2005).

Brookes, Barbara, *Abortion in England, 1900–1967* (London, 1988).

Buchanan, Ian, 'Infant feeding, sanitation and diarrhea in colliery communities 1880–1911' in Derek J. Oddy and Derek S. Miller, eds, *Diet and Health in Modern Britain* (London, 1985), pp. 148–77.

Bullock, Jim OBE, *Bowers Row: Recollections of a Mining Village* (Wakefield, 1976).

Bulmer, Martin, 'Sociological models of the mining industry', *Sociological Review* 23 (1975), pp. 61–92.

Bulmer, Martin, ed., *Mining and Social Change: Durham County in the Twentieth Century* (London, 1978).

Burnett, J., *Useful Toil: The Autobiographies of Working People from the 1820s to the 1920s* (London, 1974).

Burnette, Joyce, *Gender, Work and Wages in Industrial Revolution Britain* (Cambridge, 2008).

Burnette, Joyce, 'The wages and employment of female day labourers in English agriculture, 1740–1850', *Economic History Review* LVII (2004), pp. 664–90.

Canning, Kathleen, *Gender History in Practice: Historical Perspectives on Bodies, Class and Citizenship* (Ithica, 2006).

Carr, Giselda, *Pit Women: Coal Communities in Northern England in the Early Twentieth Century* (London, 2001).

Challinor, Raymond, *The Lancashire and Cheshire Miners* (Newcastle upon Tyne, 1972).

Chaplin, Sid, 'Durham Mining Villages' in Martin Bulmer, *Mining and Social Change*, pp. 59–82.

Charlton, Cissie, *Cissie* (Northumberland, 1988).

Church, Roy, *The History of the British Coal Industry Volume 3, Victorian Pre-eminence* (Oxford, 1986).

Clark, David, *Between Pulpit and Pew: Folk Religion in a North Yorkshire Fishing Village* (Cambridge, 1982).

Clarke, Violet, 'Tied to the Soil' in Brian P. Martin, ed., *Tales of Old Country-women* (Newton Abbot, 1997), pp. 135–45.

Cockburn, Cynthia, *Machinery of Dominance: Women, Men and Technical Know-how* (London, 1985).

Cole, G.D.H., *The History of the Labour Party from 1914* (London, 1948).

Collette, Christine, *For Labour and for Women: the Women's Labour League, 1906–18* (Manchester, 1989).

Colls, R., *The Colliers' Rant* (London, 1977).

Cramond, W., 'Illegitimacy in Banffshire', *Poor Law Magazine* 2 (1982), p. 578.

Czerkawska, Catherine, *The Fisherfolk of Carrick: a History of the Fishing Industry in South Aryshire* (Glasgow, 1975).

Davidoff, Leonore, *The Family Story: Blood, Contract and Intimacy, 1830–1960* (London, 1999).

Davidoff, Leonore, '"The separation of home and work?" Landladies and lodgers in nineteenth and twentieth century England' in Leonore Davidoff, *Worlds Between: Historical Perspectives on Gender and Class* (Cambridge, 1995), pp. 151–79.

Davidoff, Leonore and Belinda Westover, eds, *Our work, Our Lives, Our words: Women's History and Women's Work* (London, 1986).

Davidoff, Leonore and Catherine Hall, '"The hidden investment": women and the enterprise' in Pamela Sharpe, ed., *Women's Work: the English Experience 1650–1914* (London, 1998), pp. 239–93.

Davison, Jack, *Northumberland Miners' History* (Newcastle upon Tyne, 1973).

Dennis, Norman, Fernando Henriques and Clifford Slaughter, *Coal is our Life* (London, 1956).

Devine, T.M., 'Women workers, 1850–1914' in Devine, ed., *Farm Servants and Labour in Lowland Scotland, 1770–1914* (Edinburgh, 1990), pp. 98–123.

Devine, T.M., ed., *Farm Servants and Labour in Lowland Scotland, 1770–1914* (Edinburgh, 1990).

Fox, John and Peter Goldblat, *Longitudinal Study: Socio-demographic Mortality Differentials* (London, 1982).

Frank, Peter, 'Women's work in the Yorkshire inshore fishing industry', *Oral History* 4, I (Spring, 1976), pp. 57–72.

Gaffin, Jean and David Thomas, *Caring and Sharing: The Centenary History of the Co-operative Women's Guild* (Manchester, 1983).

Garside, W. *The Durham Miners* (London, 1971).

Gittens, Diana, *Fair Sex, Family Size and Structure 1900–1939* (London, 1982).

Glucksmann, Miriam, *Cottons and Casuals: The gendered organisation of labour in time and place* (Durham, 2000).

Goose, Nigel, ed., *Women's Work in Industrial England: Regional and Local Perspectives* (Hatfield, Hertfordshire, 2007).

Gordon, Eleanor and Esther Breitenbach, eds, *The World is Ill Divided: Women's Work in Scotland in the Nineteenth and Early Twentieth Centuries* (Edinburgh, 1990).

Graves, Pamela, *Labour Women: Women in British Working-class Politics 1918–1939* (Cambridge, 1994).

Griffin, A.R., *The Miners of Nottinghamshire Vol. I* (Nottingham, 1956).

Haines, Michael, 'Fertility and Occupation: Coal Mining Populations in the Nineteenth and Early Twentieth Centuries in Europe and America', Papers of the Population Association of America, 1974.

Hall, Valerie G, 'Contrasting female identities: women in coal mining communities in Northumberland, 1900–1939', *Journal of Women's History* 2 (Summer, 2001), pp. 117–31.

Hall, Valerie G., 'Differing gender roles: women in mining and fishing communities in Northumberland, 1880–1914', *Women's Studies International Forum* 27 (2004), pp. 521–30.

Hamer, Louise, *A Brief History of Cullercoats* (Newcastle upon Tyne, 1980).

Hartman, M. and L.W. Banner, eds, *Clio's Consciousness Raised* (New York, 1971)

Henderson, R., 'Some sociological aspects of farm labour in North Northumberland', *Agricultural Economics Society Proceedings* IV (April, 1937), pp. 299–321.

Higgs, Edward, 'Occupational censuses and the agricultural workforce in Victorian England and Wales', *Economic History Review* LXVIII (1995), pp. 700–16.

Higgs, Edward, 'Women, Occupation and Work in the Nineteenth Century Censuses', *History Workshop Journal* 23 (1987), pp. 59–85.

Hiley, Michael, *Victorian Working Women: Portraits from Life* (London, 1979).

Hill, Bridget, 'Women, Work and the Census: A Problem for Historians of Women', *History Workshop Journal* 35 (1993), pp. 78–94.

Hodges, Adeline, 'Up the ladder', Tuesday Club, Occasional Paper No. 2, n.d.

Horn, Pamela, *Labouring Life in the Victorian Countryside* (London, 1976).

Horrell, Sara and Jane Humphries, 'Women's labour force participation and the transition to the male-breadwinner family', *Economic History Review* XLVIII (1995), pp. 89–117.

Hostettler, Eve, 'Gourlay steel and the sexual division of labour', *History Workshop Journal* IV (1977), pp. 3–28.

Hostettler, Eve, 'Women farm workers in eighteenth and nineteenth-century Northumberland', *History Workshop Journal* IV (1977), pp. 40–2.

Howkins, Alan, *Reshaping Rural England, A Social History, 1850–1925* (London, 1991).

Humphries, Jane, *Childhood and Child Labour in the British Industrial Revolution* (Cambridge, 2010).

Humphries, Jane, '"Lurking in the wings": women in the historiography of the industrial revolution', *Business and Economic History* 20 (1991), pp. 32–46.

Humphries, Jane, 'Protective legislation, the capitalist state and working class men: The case of the 1842 Mines Regulation Act', *Feminist Review* 7 (1981), pp. 1–33.

Hunter, Alan, *Gently in the Sun* (New York, 1959).

Iredale, Dinah, *Bondagers: the history of women farmworkers in Northumberland and south-east Scotland* (Berwick-upon-Tweed, 2008).

John, Angela V., *By the Sweat of their Brow: Women Workers at Victorian coalmines* (London, 1980).

John, Angela V., ed., *Our Mothers' Land: Chapters in Welsh Women's History 1830–1930* (Cardiff, 1991).

Jones, Rosemary A.N., 'Women, collective action: the *ceffyl pren* tradition' in Angela V. John, ed., *Our Mothers' Land*, pp. 17–42.

Joyce, Patrick, ed., *The Historical Meanings of Work* (Cambridge, 1987).

Kent, David, 'Power, protest, poaching, and the Tweed Fisheries Acts of 1857 and 1859: "Send a gunboat"', *Northern History* LXII 2 (2005), pp. 293–315.

Kirkup, Mike, ed., *Pitmen Born and Bred: Award Winning Stories from Britain's Coalfields* (Ashington, 1994).

Laing Galleries, *A Brief History of Cullercoats* (Newcastle upon Tyne, 1984).

Lane, Penelope, 'A customary or market wage? Women and work in the East Midlands' in Lane, Raven and Snell, eds, *Women, Work and Wages in England 1600–1850* (Woodbridge, 2004), pp. 102–18.

Lane, Penelope, Neil Raven and K.D.M. Snell, eds, *Women, Work and Wages in England, 1600–1850* (Woodbridge, 2004).

Laslett, Peter, Karen Oosterveen and Richard M. Smith, eds, *Bastardy and its Comparative History* (London, 1980).

Lawson, Jack, *A Man's Life* (London, 1944).

Lewis, Jane, *Women in England, 1870–1950: Sexual Divisions and Social Change* (Sussex, 1984).

Lewis, Jane, ed., *Labour and Love: Women's Experience of Home and Family, 1850–1940* (Oxford, 1986).

Liddington, Jill and Jill Norris, *One Hand Tied Behind Us: The Rise of the Women's Suffrage Movement*, third edition (London, 2000).

Long, Jane, *Conversations in Cold Rooms: Women, Work and Poverty in Nineteenth-century Northumberland* (Woodbridge, 1999).

MacDougall, Ian, *Bondagers: Recollections of Eight Scottish Women Farm Workers* (Edinburgh, 2000).

MacDougall, Ian, *'Hard work, ye ken': Midlothian Women Farm Workers* (East Linton, 1996).

Maltby, Josephine and Janette Rutterford, '"She Possessed Her Own fortune": Women Investors from the Late Nineteenth Century to the Early Twentieth Century', *Business History* 2 (2006), pp. 220–53.

Marshall, Michael W., *Fishing, the Coastal Tradition* (London, 1987).

McCaw, Judith A., 'Women and the history of American technology', *Signs* 4 (Summer, 1982), pp. 798–828.

McCord, Norman, *North East England: an Economic and Social History* (London, 1979).

McCullough-Thew, Linda, *A Tune for Bears to Dance to: a Childhood* (Northumberland, 1992).

Miller, C., 'The Hidden Workforce: female fieldworkers in Gloucestershire, 1870–1901', *Southern History* 6 (1984), pp. 139–61.

Mitchell, A., 'On consanguineous marriages in Scotland', *Edinburgh Medical Journal* 10 (1965), pp. 1074–85.

Mitchell, Jill, *The Story of the Cresswell Lifeboats* (Cresswell, 1956).

Moffatt, Frederick C., *'Two penn'orth of herrin': The Story of the Northumberland Fishermen in Words and Pictures* (Newbiggin, 1982).

Morgan, Carol E., *Women Workers and Gender Identities 1835–1913: The Cotton and Metal Industries in England* (London, 2001).

Murphy, Eileen, 'A Democracy of Working women: The Women's Co-operative Guild', *North West Labour History Journal* 28 (2003), pp. 67–80.

Nadel-Klein, Jane, 'A fisher laddie needs a fisher lassie. Endogamy and work in a Scottish fishing village' in Jane Nadel-Klein and Donna Lee Davies, eds, *To Work and to Weep: Women in Fishing Economies* (St John's, Newfoundland, 1988).

Nadel-Klein, Jane, 'Granny baited the lines: perpetual crisis and the changing role of women in Scottish fishing communities', *Women's Studies International Forum* 3 (2000), pp. 363–72.

Nadel-Klein, Jane, 'Occidentalism as a cottage industry: representing the autochthonous "other" in British and Irish rural studies' in James G. Carrier, ed., *Occidentalism: images of the west* (Oxford, 1995), pp. 109–32.

Nadel-Klein, Jane, 'Reweaving the fringe: localism, tradition, and representation in British ethnography', *American Ethnologist* 3 (August, 1991), pp. 500–15.

Newcastle Central Library, *A Brief History of Cullercoats* (Newcastle upon Tyne, 1984).

Newton, Laura with Abigail Booth Gerdts, *Cullercoats: A North-east Colony of Artists* (Bristol, 2003).

Oddy, Derek J. and Derek S. Miller, eds, *Diet and Health in Modern Britain* (London, 1985).

Oren, Laura, 'The welfare of women in laboring families: England, 1860–1959' in M. Hartmann and L.W. Banner, eds, *Clio's Consciousness Raised*, pp. 226–44.

Phillips, Nicola, *Women in Business, 1700–1850* (Woodbridge, 2006).

Pinchbeck, Ivy, *Women Workers and the Industrial Revolution, 1750–1850* (London, 1981; first published 1930).

Pocock, Douglas, *A Mining World: the Story of Bearpark, County Durham* (Durham, 1985).

Porteous, Katrina, *Beadnell: A History in Photographs* (Gateshead, 1990).

Porteous, Katrina, ed., *The Bonny Fisher Lad: Memoirs of the North Northumberland Fishing Community* (Seaham, 2003).

Porter, Marilyn, *Place and Persistence: The Lives of Newfoundland Women* (Avebury, 1993).

Reay, Barry, 'Sexuality in nineteenth-century England: the social context of illegitimacy in rural Kent', *Rural History* 1 (November 1990), pp. 219–48.

Roberts, Elizabeth, *A Woman's Place: An Oral History of Working-class Women, 1890–1914* (Oxford, 1984).

Roberts, Elizabeth, 'Women's strategies, 1890–1914' in Lewis, ed., *Labour and Love*, pp. 243–48.

Roberts, Elizabeth, *Women's Work, 1840–1940* (Cambridge, 1995; first edition 1988).

Roberts, Michael, 'Sickles and scythes: women's work and men's work at harvest time', *History Workshop Journal* VII (1979), pp. 95–100.

Robertson, Barbara W., 'In bondage: the female farm worker in south east Scotland' in Gordon and Breitenbach, eds, *The World is Ill Divided*, pp. 117–36.

Robinson, John, *Newbiggin-by-the-Sea: A Fishing Community* (Morpeth, 1991).

Robinson, John Lisle, 'Fishing disasters', unpublished ms., in possession of author (Newbiggin-by-the-Sea, 1980).

Robson, J., 'Prenuptial pregnancy in rural areas of Devonshire in the nineteenth century: Colyton, 1851–1881', *Continuity and Change* 1 (1986), pp. 113–34.

Rose, Sonya O., *Limited Livelihoods: Gender and Class in Nineteenth-century England* (Berkeley, 1992).

Ross, Ellen, '"Not the sort that sit on the doorstep": respectability of pre-war London neighbourhoods', *International Labor and Working-Class History* 27 (Spring, 1985), pp. 39–59.

Rule, John, 'The property of skill in the period of manufacture' in Joyce, ed., *The Historical Meanings of Work*, pp. 108–12.

Rutter, Andrew Craig, *A Seahouses Saga* (Stockport, 1998).

Sayer, Karen, *Women of the Fields: Representations of Rural Women in the Nineteenth Century* (Manchester, 1995).

Schwartz, Sharron P., '"No place for a woman": gender at work in Cornwall's metalliferous mining industry', *Cornish Studies* 8 (2000), pp. 69–96.

Scott, A.M., *Costume* X (1977), pp. 41–8.

Scott, Gillian, *Feminism and the Politics of Working Women: The Women's Co-operative Guild 1880s to the Second World War* (London, 1998).

Scott, Joan W. and Louise A. Tilly, *Women's Work in Nineteenth Century Europe* (New York, 1987).

Seccombe, Wally, 'Patriarchy Stabilized: The Construction of the Male Breadwinner Norm in Nineteenth-Century Britain', *Social History* II (1986), pp. 53–76.

Sharpe, Pamela, ed., *Women's Work: The English Experience, 1650–1914* (London, 1998).

Simonton, Deborah, *A History of European Women's Work, 1700 to the Present* (London, 1998).

Snell, K.D.M., *Annals of the Labouring Poor: Social Change and Agrarian England, 1660–1900* (Cambridge, 1985).

Stephenson, Jane D. and Callum G. Brown, 'The view from the workplace: women's memories of work in Sterling' in Gordon and Breitenbach, eds, *The world is ill divided*, pp. 5–28.

Summer, David W., *Fishing off the Knuckle: The Fishing Villages of Buchan* (Aberdeen, 1980).

Supple, Barry, *The History of the British Coal Industry, Volume 4: The Political Economy of Decline* (Oxford, 1987).

Szreter, Simon, *Fertility, Class and Gender in Britain, 1860–1940* (Cambridge, 1996).

Szreter, Simon and Kate Fisher, *Sex Before the Sexual Revolution: Intimate life in England 1918–1963* (Cambridge, 2010).

Taylor, James and Liz, *Harvests of Herring* (Frazerburgh, 1992).

Taylor, L., 'To be a farmer's girl: bondagers of border counties', *Country Life* (October 12, 1978), pp. 1110–12.

Thompson, Paul with Tony Wailey and Trevor Lummis, *Living the Fishing* (London, 1983).

Todd, Selina, *Young Women, Work and Family in England 1918–1950* (Oxford, 2005).

Turner, Ian, 'A spot of bother: civil disorder in the North East between the wars', *Bulletin of the North East Labour Society* 18 (1984), pp. 40–7.

Verdon, Nicola, 'A diminishing force? Reassessing the employment of female day labour in English agriculture, c. 1790–1850' in Lane, Raven and Snell, *Women, Work and Wages*, pp. 190–232.

Verdon, Nicola, *Women Rural Workers in Nineteenth-century England: Gender, Work and Wages* (Woodbridge, 2002).

Wade, Henry, *Mist on the Saltings* (New York, 1985; first published 1933).

Wade, Mary, *To the Miner Born* (Stocksfield, 1984).

Webb, Sidney, *The Story of the Durham Miners, 1662–1921* (London, 1921).

Wilkinson, Tom, 'Choppington Pit' in Kirkup, ed., *Pitmen Born and Bred*, pp. 20–2.

Williams, E.W., *The Derbyshire Miners: a Study in Industrial and Social History* (London, 1962).

Williamson, Bill, *Class, Culture and Community: A Biographical Study of Social Change in Mining* (London, 1982).

Zweig, Ferdinand, *Men in the Pits* (London, 1949).

Interviews by Author and Others

Agricultural Labouring Women Chapters

Interviewees Mr and Mrs W. 7 August 2007; 6 July 2009.

Oral evidence of Archie Thompson, NRO T-034.

Oral evidence of Mr Patton, NRO T139B 6.28.78.

Oral interviews of Dinah Iredale in *Bondagers: The history of women farm-workers in Northumberland and Southeast Scotland* (Berwick-upon-Tweed, 2008).

Oral interviews of Ian MacDougall in *'Hard work, ye ken': Midlothian Women Farm Workers* (East Linton, 1996).

Oral interviews of Ian MacDougall in *Bondagers: Recollections of Eight Scottish Women Farm Workers* (Edinburgh, 2000).

Fisher Women Chapters

Interviewee Mrs A. 6 August 1997; 6 August 1998.

Interviewees Mr and Mrs B. 6 September 1999.

Interviewee Mr H. 6 September 1995; 6 October 1996.

Interviewee Mr J.LR. 6 July 1997; 8 July 1997; 6 October 1998.

Interviewees Mr and Mrs J.LR. 6 August 1997; 6 August 1998.

Interviewee Mrs R. 6 July 1998; 6 September 1998; 6 October 1998; 6 November 1999.

Interviewee Mrs W. 6 July 1995.

Interviewee Katrina Porteous, 6 July 1998.

Oral evidence of Bill Smailes, NRO 8.70.

Oral evidence of Scottish fishing people collected by Paul Thompson housed in British Library, QD8/FISH/52 C773.

Mining Women Chapters

Interviewee Mrs C. 8 June 1997.

Interviewee Mrs D. 7 June 1998.

Interviewee Mrs E.T. 23rd June 1998.

Interviewee Mrs F. 5 July 1977; 5 August 1977; 6 August 1977; 6 August 1980.

Interviewee Mrs J. 6 August 1997.

Interviewee Mrs L. 14 July 1993.

Interviewee Mrs L. 15 July 1998.

Interviewee Mr M. 7 May 1977; 22nd September 1980.

Interviewee Mrs M. 6 June 1977; 6 May 1988.

Interviewee Mrs M.T. 7 June 1996; 7 August 1998.

Interviewee Margaret Gibb, 6 August 1980.

Interviewee Mrs N. 6 June 1995.

Interviewee Mrs O. 6 May 1988.

Interview of the 'Over Sixties Club' of the Holy Sepulchre Church, Ashington, 5 April 1996.

Interviewee Mrs Q. 7 June 1998; 30 June 1999.

Interviewee Mrs R. 10 November 1977.

Interviewee Mrs T. 6 April, 1988; 23 June, 1988

Interviewee Mrs T.W. 6 July, 1980

Mining Record Survey, Northumberland Archives, 1977.

Oral evidence of Tom Douglas, NRO T/141, 7 January 1978.

Index

Regions and Regionalism in History

Volumes already published